A Heart for Europe

A HEART FOR EUROPE

The lives of Emperor Charles
and Empress Zita of Austria-Hungary

by

James and Joanna Bogle

First published in 1991
This new edition published in 1993

Gracewing
Fowler Wright Books
Southern Ave, Leominster
Herefordshire HR6 0QF

Gracewing Books are distributed

In New Zealand by
Catholic Supplies Ltd
80 Adelaide Rd
Wellington
New Zealand

In Australia by
Charles Paine Pty
8 Ferris Street
North Parramtta
NSW 2151 Australia

Distributed by:
ANGELUS PRESS
2918 Tracy Avenue
Kansas City, Missouri 64109
(816) 753-3150 o Fax (816) 753-3557

ISBN 0 85244 173 8

Typesetting by Print Origination (NW) Ltd
Printed by The Cromwell Press,
Broughton Gifford, Melksham, Wiltshire SN12 8PH

Foreword

Recent events in Central and Eastern Europe and the collapse of the Soviet empire built in Yalta, under conditions the speed and vigour of which nobody could foresee, have drawn attention once more to the historical events which have led to the present situation. We must go back to their roots, which lie deep down, especially to the affairs of World War I and their consequences. Had different decisions been taken then the tragedies of our continent, whether Hitlerism or Communism, could perhaps have been avoided.

That the tragedies were not inevitable is best shown by the book of a great French political thinker, Jacques Bainville, "Les Consequences de la Paix", written immediately after the treaties of Versailles, St. Germain and Trianon. He predicted the rise of Hitlerism and the Second World War.

In World War I Emperor Charles of Austria, King of Hungary, tried desperately to end the bloodshed with a constructive peace. Many are the reasons why he could not succeed. It staggers the imagination if one considers what would have happened had this man of peace been successful in his endeavours.

The principles for which he stood are still valid in our day. After his death he was considered by many an unlucky ruler, a marginal figure of history. Nowadays, more than half a century after his death, judgement concerning him is changing, particularly in the light of what happened after the First World War and especially of Yalta and its consequences.

In this sense historians have been turning their attention to him and to his spouse, Empress and Queen Zita. Many of the lies which were told concerning them have been proven to be false. This is important, since the present generation has the task to rebuild a European Community, the fulfilment of the ideals for which Emperor King Charles had stood.

The authors of this book, Mr and Mrs Bogle, have joined the widening circle of historians trying to present an objective picture. One can only wish their book a well-deserved success, so that, knowing the ground on which we stand, we can effectively plan a better future.

OTTO VON HABSBURG

Acknowledgements

We are very grateful to a number of people who have supported or shown interest in a projected biography of Emperor Charles and Empress Zita. Special thanks are due to Rev.Fr. Brian Harrison O.S. who first interested us in the story of the late Emperor, and to Pater Stephan Sommer of the Kaiser Karl Gebetsliga to whom we are also indebted for permission to use primary extracts from the Gebetsliga yearbook.

We owe a special debt of gratitude to Dr Otto von Habsburg who patiently answered all our questions and gave us much information giving graciously of his time even though deeply involved with his work as a member of the European Parliament and with his special commitments at a time of rapid change in Central Europe.

We thank Mrs Susan Bogle for her translation work and the invaluable brochure which produced many of the illustrations, the staff of the London Library, the Catholic Central Library, and the Austrian Cultural Centre Library for their assistance and the library of Brompton Oratory. We thank also *The Wanderer* newspaper (USA) for the extracts from the memoirs of Rev. Francis McNutt, Mrs Angela Gracey and Mr Harold Brooks-Baker of Burke's peerage for much useful information on the Habsburg and Bourbon family tree, Mr Gordon Brook Shepherd for permission to quote from his book *The Last Habsburg*, Mr and Mrs Karl Lavrencic and Miss

Alenka Lavrencic for background information on the traditions and multi-ethnic concept of the Habsburg Empire, Dr William Griffiths for the information on St Zita.

Thanks are also especially due to Archduke Lorenz of Austria for much assistance and advice about his grandfather's life; to Baron and Baroness Joseph Doblhoff for much invaluable background and insight and so much generous help and encouragement; to Professor Roger Scruton for permission to use material appearing originally in the *Salisbury Review;* to Mr Alexander Tomsky for his special knowledge of Poland and Czechoslavakia; to Mr Christopher Peake for books on the Habsburg family; to the staff of the Innsbruck Hofburg for their patient help; to Rev Roman Cholij for information on the Ukraine; to Countess Monika Draskovich for anecdotes and encouragement; to Princess Daria von Thurn und Taxis for explaining, among many other things, *Standesgnade;* to Mrs Judith Flenley for patiently translating letters; to Rev John Parsons for access to his legendary and encyclopaedic knowledge of European history; and to Countess Tatiana Holstein-Ledreborg for a number of interesting tales and much patient sympathy at trying moments.

Finally thanks must go to The Sisters at St Cecilia's Abbey, Ryde, Isle of Wight for their warm hospitality during a happy afternoon spent with them, and permission to use the photographs in their possession of Emperor Charles' funeral in Madeira; and to the library staff of the Goethe Institute, London, for help with book enquiries.

Introduction

We think of Austria today as a small country in the centre of Europe. Once, however it was the heart of a great empire, and one which had a unique part to play in Europe's history. Unique also was its ruling family – the Habsburgs. The period of this family's rule straddled the transformation from Holy Roman Empire to Austro-Hungarian Empire. The last member of this dynasty – Charles – is today something of a forgotten figure. In worldly terms Charles was not a 'success'. Forces beyond his control conspired to defeat him in his most cherished aim – the establishment of peace among the European nations.

What was this Holy Roman Empire? It began in 800 AD with the crowning of Charlemagne by Pope St Leo III. This took place in Rome on Christmas Day of that year, after Charlemagne had defeated the pagan barbarians threatening the peace of Rome. The Roman Empire in the West had ceased to exist in 476 when Emperor Romulus Augustulus was ousted from power by Odoacer the mutinous barbarian captain of his mercenaries. The focus of Imperial power was now centred on the Eastern Empire in Byzantium, which became the seat of great Emperors like Justinian.

The Eastern Empire retained this supremacy until Charlemagne, King of the Franks, established himself as the foremost Christian monarch, and principal force in Western Europe. His might and power were ultimately put at the service of the Church and of Western Christendom. It was for this reason that the Pope crowned him Emperor of the Romans, as the Church and Christendom in the West had ceased to be able to rely on the Eastern Roman Empire to defend them.

Rome was under constant threat from the descendants of the barbarians living in the northern part of the Italian peninsula and had almost no security and stability at all. The situation had continued for some time and while the Eastern Emperor could not or would not do anything to alleviate it, it was up to the King of the Franks (a vast and disparate nation converted to Christianity some 300 years earlier) to come to the aid of Rome and the beleaguered Christian Church in the West. It is said that Charlemagne was unwillingly crowned Emperor while praying in the Cathedral Church in Rome. Pope Leo had deliberately crowned him 'Emperor' and 'Augustus', the ancient Roman Emperor's titles. According to Einhard[1], Leo had previously had his eyes and tongue torn out, and had suffered many other injuries. It is certain that except in the lands of the Franks, and certain parts of Britain, the Church was suffering considerable persecution. There was a constant threat from pagan barbarians in the Italian Peninsula and in Eastern Europe, and from Moors in Africa and Spain. It is worth remembering that were it not for Charles Martel, an ancestor of Charlemagne, all of Europe would very likely have been overrun by the Moors in the South (who reached as far as Tours) and probably in due course by barbarians from the East. Add together the subsequent weakness of the Eastern Empire which was reduced by the Moors and their successors the Turks, and one can see that Christianity could well have ceased to exist entirely. It is therefore understandable that Leo and the majority of churchmen in the West looked upon Charlemagne as something of a saviour.

This was the start, or perhaps one should say the re-starting, of the Christian Roman Empire in the West.

It was the remarkable achievement of Christianity not only to convert the pagan barbarians who had invaded and sacked the Christian Roman Empire in the West, but also to rebuild that Empire through the agency of these same, now christianised, barbarians.

The Eastern Empire had continued to exist after the collapse of the Western one and the Eastern Emperor retained the title of Roman Emperor by default. However there was now an occupant of the old title of Western Roman Emperor. In due course Charlemagne came to accept his position as successor to this ancient title.

This new Empire included within its ambit many nations and peoples who had not been embraced by the old Roman Empire. The Christian gospel was able to reach areas that had been inaccessible by use of the sword alone. One such people became in due course the very heart and centre of the new Empire: the Germanic races. These 'barbarians' had undergone an immense transformation through the civilising influence of Christianity. In the course of time they came to preside over an empire of great peace and prosperity that was held together more by family ties, fidelity and loyalty, than by sword and plunder as in the old pagan times.

In various forms (and in name at least) this Christian Roman Empire was to last a thousand years. Through many vicissitudes the notion of the Christian Roman Empire continued to be the guiding principle around which the nations of Central Europe were organised. This remained the case even though at times the Emperor was not the most powerful monarch in the region and indeed may have been overshadowed by more powerful rulers who were technically his vassals. However the imperial symbol was a potent force for unity which helped to hold together an empire of varying cultures, races and national outlooks.

Some time after Charlemagne's death in 843, his lands, which covered most of Western Europe, were subdivided among his grandsons. In the west lay the kingdom of Charles, in the east the kingdom of Louis (Ludwig) and in the centre the kingdom of Lothar (Lotharingia, later shortened to Lorraine). The Imperial Crown continued but its power was diminished, until the accession of Otto the Great. Otto once again was a powerful emperor, as Charlemagne had been. However the importance of the imperial idea had all along been firmly established. Whether the Imperial Crown was worn by a ruler with a large and substantial empire or as a petty king did not determine the symbolic value of the conception. The principal importance lay in the ideal relationship between the so-called 'two swords', that is, the temporal and the spiritual.[2] In this respect the Emperor, the Christian Caesar Augustus, represented the temporal sword, whether or not the holder of the Crown was the most powerful ruler in Christendom. To this extent the Imperial power was seen to have divine sanction parallel to the ecclesiastical power. It mattered not whether the Emperor was elected to or inherited the Imperial power - since democracy, too, enjoyed divine sanction and had been preserved and exalted by the monasteries - but whether the process was lawful and had the sanction and blessing of the Church. The Church, it its turn, depended upon the Emperor and Empire for its material well-being, and, in worldly terms, for its survival. There was a mutual interdependence of sovereignty, whether or not other Christian rulers accepted it. This was a marked departure from the pagan conception where the strongest man ruled, regardless of the laws of God or man.

The power of those who were either elected to or inherited[3] the title of Emperor (ratified by papal sanction) waxed and waned with the fortunes of human affairs. The next great consolidator of the Empire was the Emperor Saint Henry II who established a new dispensation of widespread peace and justice. This happy state of affairs outlived him to some extent, but since he died childless an election became necessary and Conrad II succeeded him. Subsequently the Hohenstaufen dynasty came to dominate the Imperial throne. It was during this period that the Investiture contest became the principal political question of the day. This was the battle between the Papacy and Empire over who had the prime right to approve the appointment and 'investiture' of Bishops. Eventually it was decided that the right of ratification lay with the Papacy but that for the 'temporalities' (ie wealth and power) of the Bishop, loyalty was owed to the Emperor or King.

During the same period Imperial politics were dominated by the Crusades, with the expeditions of Emperors such as Frederick Barbarossa. Later still, another Frederick (Frederick II), called *stupor mundi* ('the Wonder of the World') for his brilliance of intellect and great abilities, fell into conflict with a papacy which itself had suffered no small corruption. This time was also marked by the claims of the Emperor to sovereignty in Italy and more particularly in Rome, in part due to the expanded power of the Empire, and in part to his conceptions of past Roman imperial grandeur. The anti-imperial party in Rome (often allied with the Papacy) came to be called the Guelf party and the imperial party, the Ghibellines.[4] However the imperial pretensions to rule Rome were confounded shortly thereafter with the defeat and death of Frederick II. Then came the period known as the Interregnum and it is at the end of this period that we see the election of Count Rudolf of Habsburg, a powerful nobleman from the part of the Empire which today is in Switzerland. He was the first of the great Habsburg line of emperors, and came to power in 1273.[5]

His family came to remain on the throne until the fall of the Empire and beyond to its re-formation as the Austro-Hungarian Empire. The most illustrious and powerful of the Habsburg rulers was Charles V, who by virtue of his parents' marriage acquired all the lands traditionally belonging to the Empire and also all the lands of the Spanish Empire including those in the recently discovered New World of Latin America. It became a characteristically Habsburg tradition that nations and territories were acquired by the Empire through marriage, in marked contrast to the military conquests of other empires.[6]

One pre-eminent exemplar of the Habsburg tradition of acquisition by marriage was the famous Empress Maria Theresa, who succeeded to the Imperial throne although barred as a woman. Her father had persuaded the European sovereigns, before his death, to accept her as ruler. Although the Empire was weak, she nonetheless strengthened it by judicious political skill. She married Francis, Duke of Lorraine and Grand Duke of Tuscany, and cleverly made him

Emperor in 1745, the first Habsburg-Lorraine Emperor. It was an outstandingly successful period. However her anti-clerical son, Josef II, fell in with the prevailing climate of thinking dominated by philosophers such as Voltaire, and heralded the beginning of the end for the ancient order in Europe. By the end of Josef's reign the Empire and the whole of Europe were in a dangerously corrupt state and at the brink of disaster. Complacent scepticism and fashionable cynicism ruled. The disaster came in 1789 with the French Revolution.

The Holy Roman Empire officially ended in 1806 when it was declared defunct by Napoleon Bonaparte. The Bonapartist conquest of Europe, although shortlived, succeeded in redrawing the political map of the continent, a feat which had not been achieved by the earlier revolution in France. The stable order that had existed in Europe for centuries was no more.

After the defeat of Bonaparte, the Congress of Vienna attempted to restore some stability to Middle Europe, but the twin forces of revolutionary fervour and nationalism which had emerged from the French revolution, continued to destabilise the region.

A remnant of the old Empire was kept in existence by the Congress however - Austria-Hungary. It was ruled, as the Holy Roman Empire had been ruled, by the Habsburg family. A measure of stability was maintained in the face of nationalist agitation until 1848 when revolution once again swept across Europe threatening further upheaval.

The Empire survived this unrest and the new Emperor was the eighteen-year-old Franz Josef who was to rule until the First World War. His reign was one of remarkable stability in the face of many trials, threats and attacks. Nationalism had inflamed the passions of the Hungarian leaders who forced upon the Emperor the historic compromise which resulted in the dual monarchy and the separation of the Empire into two halves. The 'lever' of nationalism was however being manipulated by those with a wider agenda, whose aim was not merely the exaltation of the nation-state at the cost of Imperial ideals, but a wider assault on the idea of Christian government as a whole.

Thus ultimately the various compromises with nationalism were seen by the agitators not as elements of a final solution but as stepping stones towards a position from where they could seize power for themselves.

However the success of their plans was by no means inevitable. Similar plots had existed down the centuries and these had been successfully overcome by the use of force or finely-tuned political compromises. The Habsburgs' success in suppressing the revolutions of 1848 are an illustration of this. Without the existence of the central European empire it would have been necessary to have another equally comprehensive political system if stability were to be assured. This would, *ipso facto*, not have been the end result of a process of organic development, but of arbitrary impositon such as eventually emerged from World War I and which failed so miserably to ensure a lasting peace.

As one commentary has put it: "The Habsburg Empire was in fact a response to the quite specific problem of overlapping nationalities in eastern and central Europe. Thus Bohemia and the Western part of Hungary had substantial German populations; there were both German and Rumanian populations in eastern Hungary; the region of Trieste was populated by a mixture of Italians, Germans and Slovenes, and the story goes on. Indeed the problems raised by these mixtures of populations (in present day Yugoslavia, or Rumania or Hungary) have still not finally been solved. The core of the Habsburg monarchy was not, however, a heap of randomly accumulated territories. Its people shared, first of all, a common geographical region around the Danube - which had for centuries served as an important thoroughfare uniting the peoples on its banks.

They shared also a common enemy in the Turks and 200 years of warfare against the Ottoman Porte had contributed not a little to the development amongst them of a feeling of a common fate and history. The peoples of the monarchy shared further the presumption of belonging to a common political entity, a presumption bolstered not least by the allegiance of Habsburg dynasty itself .... It is of course true that the Empire of the Habsburgs collapsed, not least as the result of an unfortunate war, before a political solution could be found to the growing problem of the conflicts between the various nationalities of the Empire (or rather between the Imperial authorities and certain vociferous and influential minorities with nationalistic tendencies).

This should not, however, be taken to imply that no such solution was possible. And nor should it be taken to imply that there is no possibility of a general political and philosophical justification of the kind of order that was manifested by the Habsburg Empire."'

Here we must look back to the beginnings of the Empire and of that ideal conception of the purpose of the Christian monarchy as protector of Christendom, the temporal arm in balance with the spiritual. The two concepts, each distinct, are inter-related and interdependant. The spiritual symbolism of the Christian monarchy is well illustrated in the coronation ceremonies of the kings and princes of Christendom, which in turn derive from that of the Emperor. The crown is worn not as a symbol of dominance but of service and sacrifice, and is symbolically linked to the crown of thorns worn by Christ Himself. As Jesus Christ was an anointed Saviour (which is the meaning of His name) so too the Christian monarch is anointed, significantly on the breast and palms, recalling the wounds of the nails and the lance. In like manner the sceptre resembles the reed with which Christ was beaten and which had been placed in his hand. The orb signifies the dominion of the Messiah over the world. Thus the vocation of the Christian monarch or emperor was not to lord it over his fellow men "as do the kings of the gentiles" but to serve, so that "he that is greater, let him become as the lesser .... and he that is the leader as he that serveth" (Luke 22:25-26).

Linked to this is the idea of the *'Standesgnade'*, the notion of grace for one's state in life - in this case the state of a monarch - which Christian rulers must possess. This idea was a particularly favoured recurrent theme amongst the Habsburg rulers, and indicates their commitment to these high ideals of monarchy. From all these symbols, translated into reality, comes the popular feeling of the sacredness of the imperial and royal estate of Christian kings and princes. Additionally for the Habsburg monarchs, there lay other calls to service in other courtly and chivalric symbols such as the knightly Order of the Golden Fleece, representing a nobility of vision similar to that of the English Order of the Garter. Both are in imitation of the vows and promises of the famous Order of the Knights Hospitaller of St John.

In opposition not only to the conception of Christian monarchy, but indeed to all kinds of Christian leadership, there had arisen a new spirit of national chauvinism. It was in many ways a contradictory spirit in that it was dissenting and rebellious to the lawfully constituted authority. However it nonetheless demanded a much greater servility and subservience from those whom it in turn conquered. Thus the Hungarians chafed at having to deal with the court at Vienna, whilst in turn trampling upon the rights of minorities within their half of the Empire and forcing the Magyar language on the minority Slavic races such as the Croats and Slovaks. This chauvinistic spirit conspired to doom all efforts at stability, unity and eventually even peace.

With the beginning of the First World War the dismemberment of the Empire became a real possibility and it would seem for this reason that the occurrence of the war served the ends of nationalism rather than the security and stability of the Empire in whose name it was at first officially prosecuted.

Beginning as the understandable reaction of a monarchy whose heir-apparent had been assassinated, the momentum was quickly taken from the Austro-Hungarian government, and the initiative was carried into a wider arena where it was used by those who were plotting and planning on a much broader canvas, and who had far-reaching ambitions to redraw the political map of Europe.

The goals for which the nationalists had striven had finally been attained, and Europe lay in ruins, ravaged by war and famine. The small nation-states that resulted from the post-war settlement were not in a position to survive on their own unless given support by the Allied Powers to do so. The major powers, weakened by war and disease did not have the strength or courage to give them this support. The old empires had gone, and in their place were new all-embracing supra-national powers who were waiting in the wings to devour the wounded body of Europe. Harsh, ideological, dictatorial and inhuman, they replaced the organic stability of a system centuries old.

It is worth noting that Vienna at the beginning of the 20th century was a city with a rich cultural mix. Many of the figures most prominent in its intellectual life were Jews, who along with others thrived in the atmosphere of a city aware that it was the Royal capital of a multi-ethnic empire. It was to be part of Europe's tragedy that this tolerant and creative atmosphere was to vanish with the destruction of the Empire, and give way to the vicious rule of National Socialism and its savage anti-semitism: a marked contrast to all that had gone before.

The Austro-Hungarian Empire is frequently and too glibly described as an anachronism in its final days, with words such as "tottering" and "weak"[1] used about its internal bonds and the loyalty of its people. The facts speak otherwise. The Empire did successfully hold onto the affections of millions of people in a way that has not been achieved by subsequent attempts at trans-national and trans-racial groupings. This hold was based on notions of mutual tolerance and trust. Yet the Empire in its final days did face grave problems. Not least among these was the humiliating defeat it had received at the hands of Prussia in the latter half of the nineteenth century. This defeat left Austria-Hungary in a weak position when Prussia, now leading a united Germany, pressed her claims as an ally in the events leading up to the summer of 1914. The new Prussian government (led by Bismarck) combined the most strident nationalism, based upon German racialism, with imperial aspirations and a determination to supplant Austria-Hungary's ancient pre-eminence. In contrast to the Austrian tradition of acquisition by marriage, Prussia was set upon a course of acquisition by brute force. It looked alarmingly like a return to the uncivilized methods of paganism, which Christian rulers had been urged to eschew.

Another obvious difference between Prussian Germany and Austria-Hungary was the two governments' attitude to the Roman

Catholic Church. Under Bismarck the German government undertook a war of attrition (known as the *Kulturkampf*) against the Catholic Church particularly in the south of Germany. Austria in contrast maintained good relations with the Papacy, a tradition that Emperor Charles was to continue.

France's position with regard to Prussia (and Germany) must also be understood. France had suffered badly in the Franco-Prussian war of 1870, and memories of this defeat and of the long siege of Paris must have still been vivid as the new century opened. A further complication on the European scene was Austria's relationship with Italy, which remained tense following the bloody suppression of the 1848 revolutions which had seen Italian agitators clamouring for territory long held by Austria in Lombardy and Venetia.

This was the world inhabited by Karl von Habsburg, who as the great-nephew of Emperor Franz Josef succeeded to the throne in the place of his uncle (Archduke Franz Ferdinand who had been asssassinated at Sarajevo in 1914) in 1916 in the midst of the First World War. It was his unenviable task to rule that Empire in the most difficult period in its history.

Perhaps only now, as the century draws to its end, can we see him in his true historical context. The solution to today's problems cannot be found if their roots in the past are ignored. As the Rev Aidan Nicholls OP writes:

"A re-evaluation must be undertaken of these pre-nationalist polities which, for all their limitations, embodied the principle of identity-in-difference in some recognisable form. In a European Catholic perspective one obvious candidate for re-evaluation would be the Danubian monarchy, brought to an end in 1919 by a coalition of factors, one of these being Woodrow Wilson's doctrinaire nationalism.

Is it altogether a coincidence that this particular moment in the history of Europe, constituted jointly as it is by the formation of the European Community in the West and the ending of the Soviet system as we have known it in the East, and the consequent prospect of what Mr. Gorbachev has called 'our common European home', is also the moment when the Church authorities are preparing to raise to her altars the servant of God Charles of Hapsburg, the last Hapsburg Emperor, under the title 'patron of Peace'?"[3]

Notes:

1. *The Life of Emperor Charles,* by Einhard, written in the ninth century AD.
2. *Luke 22:38* "Here are two swords. And He said to them it is enough".

Luke 20:25 "Render therefore to Caesar that which is Caesar's and to God that which is God's..."

3. Eventually the system of electing the Emperor was codified into written law by the Golden Bull of 1356 under the Emperor Charles IV. The seven most important nobles in Germany elected him and were thus called "Electors" ('kurfürsten' in German) this becoming the highest title any noble could have. They were the three Archbishops of Mainz, Cologne and Trier and the "Electors" of Saxony, Brandenburg, Bohemia and the Palatinate (the Elector Palatine).

4. 'Guelf' and 'Ghibelline' came from the German dynastic names 'Welf' and 'Waiblingen' and are the italianised version. The 'Waiblingen' were the supporters of the Emperor. 'Welf' was the name of a dynasty of rulers some of whom became Kings of Hannover and whose modern descendants are the British Royal Family. 'Guelphs' subdivided further into 'White' and 'Black', the 'whites' being supporters of a balance between Empire and Papacy. Dante, the great Italian poet, was a 'white Guelph' in his political views.

5. Rudolf, although powerful, was not among the great magnates of the day. He was chosen precisely because of this. The magnates, like the King of Bohemia, thought they could ignore or manipulate him. In fact Rudolf was not so lightly dealt with. Although he hated war he was compelled to commit his forces against the expansionism of the King of Bohemia who was much richer and more powerful. Rudolf defeated him and then received the King's huge entourage for the surrender. Rudolf was dressed as a humble foot soldier in a grey tunic to receive the magnificent but defeated King of Bohemia. Despite his victories the first Habsburg Emperor retained his humble and peaceful demeanour throughout his reign, which was a reign of prosperity and justice.

6. It was said "Alii bella gerent, tu, felix Austria, nubes" – "Others make war, but thou, O happy Austria, simply marry!"

7. Wolfgang Grassl and Barry Smith "The Politics of National Diversity" (*Conservative Thoughts,* Ed. Roger Scruton, Claridge Press London 1988).

8. *New Blackfriars,* Oxford 1990.

Emperor Franz Josef.

Chapter One

When its last Emperor was born, the Austrian Empire was geographically the third largest country in Europe and the fourth largest as regards population. In addition to Austria and Hungary, it covered large parts of the countries we know today as Czechoslovakia, Rumania and Yugoslavia, together with slices of Poland and Italy. Its people included Austrians, Czechs, Moravians, Slovaks, Ruthenians, Poles, Slovenes, Croats, and Magyars. The Empire's official name was Austria-Hungary. The Habsburg family had ruled since 1273. A dual-monarchy had been established in 1867 through which the Emperor ruled over two territories, Austria and Hungary, each with its own official systems of voting and government practices - the Hungarian half including a large number of races who were thus in effect subject to the Magyars, as the Hungarian race was called.

To describe the Empire is to conjure up a vanished world, a world where modern maps are of little if any use. Two world wars, the creation of new republics and the imposition of new boundaries have destroyed all the certainties of the Europe of the 1880s.

The last emperor was born on August 17th 1887: his full name was Karl, Franz, Josef, Ludwig, Hubert, Georg, Maria von Habsburg-Lothringen. he was the great nephew of the ruling Emperor, Kaiser Franz Josef[1].

Karl—in the English form, Charles—was born at Persenbeug Castle, about fifty miles from the Empire's capital at Vienna. His father was Archduke Otto von Habsburg and his mother Archduchess Maria Josefa, born a princess of the little German kingdom of Saxony, part of the German empire ruled by the Hohenzollerns. They had married in October 1886 at her father's court in Dresden.

1

In 1887 the Emperor Franz Josef had ruled the Empire for nearly forty
years, having received the crown in 1848. His son, Rudolf, was the heir
and seemed set to inherit the crown in due course. The Empire had seen
plenty of political and military upheavals but seemed for the moment
secure - a fixed part of Europe's geography. The *Encyclopedia Brittanica*
for that year described it as having an area of about 240,000 English
square miles: "It is surrounded on all sides by other countries, except
where it borders upon the Adriatic, which is about one-fifth of the entire
extent of its boundaires. Of the rest, about one-third on the W. and N. is
formed by the German empire (Bavaria, Saxony, and Prussia), a third on
the S. and E. by the Turkish empire and the Danubian principalities, and
the remaining third by Russia in the N.E. and Switzerland and Italy on
the S.W. . . . . As compared with France, Austria has a form nearly as
compact, but its frontiers are by no means so well defined or so strongly
protected by natural barriers."

The child born at Persenbeug did not seem a very significant addition
to the Imperial family, although his arrival was greeted with general
pleasure as he was his parents' first born. His grandfather was Archduke
Karl Ludwig, the Emperor's second youngest brother who was at that
time technically second in line to the throne. It seemed unimaginable that
the throne would ever eventually pass to little Charles. If Crown Prince
Rudolf died without issue, the crown would go through Karl Ludwig and
on to his eldest son Franz Ferdinand, the baby's uncle.

The birth and christening of Charles were family affairs, celebrated
without undue attention being paid by the rest of the Empire or wider
Europe. Archduke Karl Ludwig and his wife were staying at Persenbeug
for the arrival of their first grandchild, and the christening was held in the
great hall of the castle. Unusually, the grandfather was also a godparent.
The ceremony was performed by the Bishop of St. Polten on August 19th,
which happened to be the day after the Emperor's own birthday.

Persenbeug Castle still stands today - unusually among Austria's
castles in that area it was not ransacked in World War II and it still
remains in private hands.

Charles was to have two childhood homes - Persenbeug on the Danube
and the Wartholz mansion at Reichenau at the foot of the Rax mountains,•
about thirty miles south-east of Vienna. This had been built in 1872 by
his grandfather. His father's career as an Army officer however meant
that the little family travelled around to many places and only used these
two castles from time to time. His parents' marriage was not a
particularly happy one, but a strong influence was his mother's staunch
adherence to her religious faith, and his small world seemed solid and
secure.

Major events were however about to change this. Charles was two years old when a scandal broke which shook the whole of Austria and was to have profound repercussions for his young life. In 1889 the Emperor's eldest son Crown Prince Rudolf died suddenly at Mayerling, his hunting-lodge located some twenty miles from Vienna. His death continues to be the subject of speculation, and has given rise to a number of books, plays, and films. One theory is that there was a suicide pact between Rudolf and his mistress, Baroness Marie Vetsera. The pair had not known each other long however and Rudolf had not been in particularly poor spirits in the preceding weeks. Attempts to hush the matter up created further mystery: Rudolf was first said to have died in a hunting accident, then to have suffered a heart attack. Rumours spread abroad and heavy press censorship failed to prevent them from buzzing around Vienna. Perhaps the truth of the tragedy will never be known. The work of the Empire's enemies, notably in France, an unsuspected instability in Rudolf's mind, the bizarre involvement of unknown criminal forces, were all discussed as possible reasons for his death.

The suicide theory is not as strong as it may seem. Its supporters argue that Rudolf shot Marie Vetsera at her own request, and then killed himself. But Marie was only one of a number of women in Rudolf's life. It may be that in his desperate love for her he was prepared to give up his life and all that it promised, including the throne and the opportunity to take action on political changes in which he had long been interested; but this is on the face of it unlikely.

One theory - recently revived with the centenary of the tragedy (1989) - was that it was the result of a political plot by foreign agents. Rudolf was known to be opposed to his father on a number of issues, notably on liberalising voting patterns and allowing more scope for activities of national groups within the Empire. According to this theory, influential forces in France and elsewhere saw this as an opportunity to play the son against the father and thus weaken the position of the whole Empire. Rudolf refused to agree, and when approached with a suggestion that his father might be deposed and he himself installed, denounced it as traitorous. He then had had to be killed for fear he would reveal it all to others.[2]

The story of Mayerling is relevant to Charles' life not only because Rudolf's death was part of the chain of events that brought him to the throne, but also because the tensions and possibilities that surrounded Rudolf would eventually surround him, too.

In 1889 the most immediate effect of the Mayerling tragedy was a sense of moral outrage that the heir to the throne could have been found dead with his mistress, and a profound disruption of the idea of order and dignity on which the Habsburg rule of the vast multi-national empire depended. The trappings of ceremonial did not stop the gossip and rumours. Rudolf's body was brought back to Vienna and was buried in state in the Capuchin church crypt among those of his ancestors.

Marie Vetsera's body was buried privately in an obscure graveyard and her family forbidden to speak of the events surrounding her death. Only much later was she given a tombstone.

The hunting lodge at Mayerling was later pulled down on the Emperor's orders. Today a Carmelite monastery near the site has a memorial chapel to Rudolf.

The great personal anguish and sense of loss which Franz Josef had to endure were masked by his iron self-discipline and dedication to his duties as monarch. He had to bring these qualities to the fore more than ever to avert a sense of confusion throughout the Empire. He set about doing this and it was effective; but scars remained.

Franz Josef's personal austerity and sense of order were fundamental to his life and were to become legendary. Rudolf's death buffeted the monarchy: contrary to the hopes and perhaps the expectations of its enemies the throne remained secure, but it did become surrounded by an aura of sorrowful mystery. This was to be enhanced by the murder of the Empress Elisabeth, Franz Josef's beautiful beloved 'Sisi', nine years later. She was stabbed by an assassin while on one of her many trips abroad - in September 1898.

Rudolf had no heir which meant that after the Mayerling tragedy Archduke Karl Ludwig, Charles' grandfather, was now heir to the throne.

All the confusion went over the head of the toddler in the nursery at Persenbeug or Wartholz - but its effect was to bring him much nearer to the Imperial Crown. Meanwhile plans for his future were being discussed.

Charles seems to have been a delightful little boy. A particularly attractive memory was recalled by one visitor, Countess Wittgenstein. She remembered him aged about three, going upstairs with his rather stout nanny who was having difficulty with the journey and puffing and wheezing, "Now Nanny" he said, very politely, "why don't we stop and rest a moment?" and sat down happily half-way up the stairs while she caught her breath.

His aunt, the Archduchess Maria Josefa, youngest daughter of Karl Ludwig, saw a good deal of him during those very early years before he disappeared into the masculine world of tutors and packed timetables. Many years later she was to remember him as "a sweet and loving child, slim and finely proportioned. With his golden-blond hair and striking blue eyes he had, although a very healthy child, something very tender and soft about him."

"This was also true of his character. Although he was able to be merry and play happily with his toys, he was neither wild nor unruly. I can recall nothing bad, disobedient or angry that I ever saw in him. The same went for everyone who knew him as a child and as a boy. He was an uncommonly conscientious and truthful child - and also very unselfish and thrifty."[3]

This carefulness about money was linked to a warm generosity: he was discovering that not everyone in the world was as well provided for as he was. He found by running small errands he could earn little tips which he could save and give to the poor, and later when he was given his own small patch of garden he sold its produce to the grown-ups in the castle and the money also went into the poor-box.

These things can make him sound rather priggish - but there is no evidence that he was acting in a smug or ostentatiously pious way: on the contrary he seems always to have been a cheerful, straightforward and open-hearted child with no silly pretensions. The poor whom he was anxious to help were those he saw around him - in the village and local community - and the incentive came from his own generous and essentially uncomplicated nature and the religious and moral principles in which he was being trained. He was happy about life and keen that others should be, also.

His favourite games tended to revolve around playing at soldiers: he was surrounded by all the trimmings of army life and automatically became interested in drill, music, and marching. From an early age he knew he would be a soldier when he grew up. There were gentler pursuits: his soft toys included a collection of monkeys of which he was particularly fond, the first one having been a present from his grandmother. He played happily with these for hours, each monkey having its own name and identity. He invented a private world for them in which they spoke "Affiesprache", monkey-talk, which only he and they could understand.

It wasn't all games and nursery life. He was taught to read and write by his Irish governess, Miss Bridie Casey - and thus was fluent in English as well as in German by the age of six. Before he entered his teens he would also study French, together with Hungarian and the other main languages of the empire he was to rule. As an adult, he spoke seven languages fluently.

The young Archduke's serious education began at the age of seven, when he was moved from the nursery to the schoolroom and came under the direction of a tutor, Count George Wallis. A punishing schedule was drawn up, involving a full programme of studies and activities for each day. The emphasis was on laying the foundations for a wide range of knowledge. Modern languages, history, geography and the classics were included along with religious instruction.

In April 1895, when he was seven and a half, his brother Max was born. Years later members of the household were to recall with amusement that Charles' reaction was one of complete bafflement and surprise. No one had told him the baby was on its way. How had the child arrived? Who had brought it? Whose was it? He was enchanted by the baby but completely mystified. He finally decided that one of his father's staff had brought the child to the castle as a present. That night, he was so excited about his baby brother that he could not sleep.[4]

The initial enthusiasm grew into a close affection. Max was later to recall that Charles was always his hero - the person in his life he most admired and looked up to, and his ideal as he was growing up.

Charles himself was getting closer to the throne. In 1897 - when he was nine, nearly ten - his grandfather, the Archduke Karl Ludwig, became very ill following a visit to the Holy Land. After the death of Crown Prince Rudolf, the Archduke had been heir to the throne, so his illness was a serious matter, and as his condition worsened, increasing attention was paid all over Europe. The Emperor visited his bedside. In London *The Times* reported on May 19th "The Archduke, who was in excellent health until his recent tour in Egypt and the Holy Land, had made arrangements to attend the opening of the Millenium Exhibition in Budapest. Thence he intended to proceed to Moscow where he was to represent the Emperor-King at the coronation ceremony [of the Tsar Nicholas]. It was therefore arranged that these duties should be performed by his younger brother, the Archduke Ludwig Victor.

"The condition of the Archduke Karl Ludwig, which had shown signs of improvement during the past two days, took a turn for the worse last night. At ten o'clock his Highness lost consciousness, and remained in that state for nearly two hours. The physicians in attendance were immediately summoned and have since then not left the Palace. The archduke fainted again this morning and several times during the day. He has now received the last sacraments.

"According to particulars published in the clerical organ *Das Vaterland* which are evidently derived from the Archducal family, his Highness contracted his illness during a three-day tour on horseback to the Dead

Sea. The overexertion, combined with the cold night air, led to an indisposition the first symptoms of which were fever and loss of appetite, followed by dysentery. The Archduke was accordingly obliged to hasten his return but, although still unwell, he was able to give audiences for a few days after his arrival in Vienna. During the last few days he suffered from great nervous depression. According to the latest accounts, the doctors no longer entertain any hope."

Archduke Karl Ludwig died that night. It seems likely that the actual cause of his death was not merely over-exhaustion following his travels, but an infection caused by drinking impure water from the Jordan while in the Holy Land.

His death meant that the heir-presumptive to the throne was his eldest son, Franz Ferdinand, little Charles' uncle. Franz Ferdinand was unmarried, so after him the next in line to the throne was his brother Otto, Charles' father, and after that Charles himself.

At the time of Karl Ludwig's death, Franz Ferdinand was himself unwell - he was in fact suffering from tuberculosis - and Europe's newspapers speculated that he might within a short while follow his father to the grave. *The Times* correspondent reported on May 21st "The condition of the Archduke Franz Ferdinand d'Este, now the heir-apparent, is such as will probably prevent him from attending his father's funeral. The news of the Archduke Karl Ludwig's death reached him, as I stated yesterday, prior to his arrival in Vienna, and it appears that it gave him a terrible shock which, owing to his weak state of health, had unfavourable consequences."

Archduke Karl Ludwig's funeral at Vienna's Capuchin church was attended by the Emperor and all the Imperial Family but Franz Ferdinand, who was too ill to leave his bed. He had spent the previous two winters abroad, in the hopes that a warmer climate would help to heal his lungs, and was now widely regarded as an invalid. Attention was focused on Otto, Charles' father, whom *The Times* described as being "comparatively little known outside a very narrow circle in both halves of the Monarchy". The paper reported "He has hitherto displayed greater interest in sport and recreation than in politics" and went on to note that after him the crown would go to "his eldest son, the youthful Archduke Karl".

Charles' father had in fact acquired a reputation for high living for which "sport and recreation" was perhaps something of a euphemism. He had little in common with his pious, serious-minded wife Archduchess Maria Josepha, whose interests focused on home and family, church and charity work. Young Charles' education was aimed at ensuring that he would steer a steadier path in life than some of Austria's royals were apt to manage. In particular there was an emphasis on religious formation and on an understanding of constitutional matters, and of history.

He was emerging as an immensely likeable boy. The generosity that had been evident in the small child remained with him as he grew up. Countess Sophie Wallis, wife of his tutor, was later to recall one typical incident when she met him at a local shrine: "Archduke Charles had come with his tutor, my husband, to make a little excursion to Maria Taferl, and I had also been permitted to meet up with them there. After the little pilgrimage we stood in front of the church and waited for the return journey. Archduke Charles had all his pockets full of small souvenirs that he wanted to bring home as presents. Suddenly he whispered to me, soft and low 'Please - could you lend me two guilders? I simply must give something to our gardener, and his wife who works in the kitchen. I need one more small souvenir - and I haven't got any more money'. It was certainly not really correct for me to fulfil this request and my husband quickly warned him 'You've bought enough, and that really must be all now'. But we recognised the little boy's wish - he only intended to give pleasure to some one else. So I gave him the guilders and he thanked me with great joy and quickly bought the little present for the people of the house."⁵

Count Wallis himself wrote later: "He never told a lie. Anything in the way of wilfulness was completely foreign to him. Absent-mindedness, here and there a little forgetfulness, untidiness among his things, were the 'biggest offences'. Seeing him praying in church remains a memory - his greatest joy was in being allowed to be an altar-boy. A result of his clear conscience was a sunny, happy nature that was obvious in his appearance. He seemed to be cheerful about everything."⁶

Charles was prepared for his First Confession and First Communion by Father Norbert Geggerle. He took his faith seriously and was to receive the sacraments regularly throughout his life.

Holiday breaks included visits to other royal and aristocratic families: these included the Bourbon-Parmas, who had a home in Austria, at Schwarzau, in the countryside south of Vienna. This was a large family which could very easily accommodate two extra children in the nursery; years later one of the Bourbon-Parma daughters, Princess Zita, would recall Charles' watchful care of his little brother Max and the thoughtful way he looked after him at meals and in general activities. Zita was four years Charles' junior - mostly he played with her older brothers rather than with her.

Charles did not remain in the closed world of a castle upbringing. When he was twelve, he was sent to school in Vienna - to the city's Schottengymnasium where he studied alongside boys from a wider range of backgrounds, and earned popularity for his easy friendly ability to mix without showing off about his royal connections. Because he was a royal archduke, the boys called him "Arch-Charles" - but he was an ordinary, cheerful member of the school and joined in all its activities. He was a pupil there for two years and it was during the second of these that a major event in his family leapt into the headlines and focused attention on the future of the Habsburg dynasty.

The Archduke Franz Ferdinand had experienced a remission of the serious disease which at the time of Karl Ludwig's death had seemed to be threatening his own life. The longstanding trouble with his lungs cleared and it began to be apparent that he was going to have a normal and active life. As heir to the throne of Austria-Hungary his clear duty was to seek a wife - but his choice, when it came, startled everyone.

Despite hopes that he might pay court to a daughter of some suitable princely house, he instead fell in love with Sophie Chotek, a young woman from a minor aristocratic family whom he met at a ball in Prague. Although of noble birth and perfectly respectable in every way - from a good home, charming, educated and pretty - Countess Chotek was not suffiently high born to be Empress[7]. The aristocratic network of the Empire was clear-cut but delicate . The Habsburg family line was the root and basis of the entire structure, and marriage with a person of unequal birth was an idea that posed immediate and significant problems. A sustained family argument now began, with the ageing Emperor Franz Josef making it clear from the beginning that there never could be any question of the marriage proceeding in the normal way. Franz Ferdinand, deeply in love and already a mature man who had conquered disease, travelled widely, and formed his own ideas about the future of the Empire he hoped one day to rule, held firmly to his commitment. In the end a compromise became necessary. The Emperor sanctioned a morganatic marriage, in which Countess Chotek would be denied the rank and title of an Archduchess and later of Empress, and all children of the union would be barred from succession to the throne.

On 28th June 1900 a formal ceremony was held at the Hofburg Palace in Vienna. All the senior members of the Habsburg family gathered together with the Archbishop of Vienna, Cardinal Anton Grushcha, and the Primate of Hungary, Cardinal Lorenz Schlauch. It was a warm sunny day and the ceremony began on the stroke of noon, the Emperor standing in front of his throne in the Private Council Chamber.

The details were described with some awe in the newspapers. Drumbeats and a solemn trumpet call rang out. In what *The Times* in London called "a grave tone and with unwonted emphasis", Emperor Franz Josef announced: "Ever desirous of doing what is best for members of my Archducal House, and with a view of giving my nephew a new proof of my special affection, I have given my consent to his marriage with the Countess Sophia Chotek. It is true that the Countess Sophia Chotek is of noble descent, but her family is not one which, consistent with the customs of our House, can be regarded as of equal birth . . . . . This marriage is to be looked upon as a morganatic marriage, and the children which with God's blessing may issue from this union cannot therefore participate in the rights of members of the Archducal House. . . . " The Minister for Foreign Affairs, Prince Agenor Goluchowski, then read from the steps of the throne the formal statement in which Franz Ferdinand publicly accepted every detail of the terms of the morganatic arrangement. His voice rang out loudly through the hushed room: "We, Archduke Franz Ferdinand Karl Ludwig Josef Maria of Austria . . . . make clear our firm and well-considered decision to join in marriage with the high-born Countess Sophia Maria Josephina Albina Chotek . . . . " The Archduke would be renouncing the throne for all his descendants, for all time, and promising that he would never attempt to weaken the agreement or destroy its force. Franz Ferdinand himself then came forward. He went down on one knee in front of the Emperor, before going to a table to the right of the throne where a crucifix stood between two lighted candles. Placing his right hand hand on an open Bible held by Cardinal Grushcha, he formally and publicly read aloud his declaration, first in German and then in Hungarian. The royal line of the Habsburgs was passing from his descendants to another branch of the family, for ever.

The young Charles, still a schoolboy, was not present at this dramatic ceremony which sealed his own future. But it was clear to everyone what its implications were for him. The morganatic arrangement meant that his father, Otto, was now next in line to the throne So from the summer of 1900 onwards, he knew that he was being trained to be Emperor of Austria-Hungary.

By an extraordinary coincidence of dates, it was to be another June 28th, just fourteen years later, when the next tragic and dramatic event of the saga was to occur. On that date, 28th June 1914, Franz Ferdinand and his wife Sophia were to be shot by the assassin Gavril Princip in Sarajevo, plunging Europe into war and bringing Charles his inheritance in the most bitter of circumstances.

In 1900, the solemn event in the Geheime Ratsstube of the Hofburg gave way two days later to a cheerier event in the chapel of Reichstadt Castle in Bohemia, when Franz Ferdinand and his Sophia were finally married. The bride wore a white satin gown with a long train and the traditional veil and myrtle crown. The groom wore his uniform as a cavalry officer. The wedding was a simple one followed by a family reception: the Emperor and other senior male members of the Habsburg family were not present. The day was seen as a triumph for romantic love. *The Times* reported: "In placing the rings on the fingers of the bride and bridegroom the chaplain said that millions of people cherished the hope that they would enjoy uninterrupted happiness." At the reception a goodwill telegram from the Emperor was read out announcing that the bride was to be given the courtesy title of Duchess of Hohenburg. The bridgegroom's mother, Archduchess Maria Theresa, presided as hostess. A local choir came to sing, and the Fire Brigade and town veterans association turned out to parade and salute the newly-weds. The couple then departed for their honeymoon by train, and the bride's smart travelling outfit and black straw hat with a silver ribbon were later described in detail by the *Vienna Illustrated*.

It had been the major event of the year in the Empire, and it focused attention on the young student Charles, who would be carrying the monarchy into the far distant days of the twentieth century, while Franz Ferdinand's own children would be denied the Throne.

It seemed in the nature of things that Charles would probably inherit the crown when he was in his mid-forties. At present the old Emperor Franz Josef was still reigning, and then Franz Ferdinand would follow him in due course - for Charles himself the responsibilities of the crown were still distant. But his training was nevertheless a matter of importance. It was planned that after school he would travel - around the Empire and also further afield to other parts of Europe. He finished at the Schottengymnasium without taking his formal public exams - it was felt incorrect for an heir to the Throne to compete against others in this way. Then he set off on a long trip which took him to several of the different courts of Europe, while continuing his studies under Count Wallis and his other tutors. His home base was now Reichenau, the family having left Persenbeug in 1899.

In the spring of 1904 it was decided that he should go for a month to a fashionable health resort, Brixen, in the South Tyrol. Here he met Count Arthur Polzer-Hoditz, who was later to be head of his Private Office during memorable and tragic days in war.

The two had first met a couple of years previously, at a dance for young people in Vienna where the middle-aged Count recalled the Archduke as "still quite a child, a friendly, fair-haired boy with blue eyes". Now Charles was a sixteen-year-old, already expressing his opinions on a variety of topics and showing a good knowledge of history and politics. Polzer-Hoditz was later to recall: "We took walks according to medical orders, made excursions on foot and wheel in the surrounding districts, played tennis, hunted for antiquities in the villages around Brixen, and generally whiled away the month's "cure" in all the ways we could think of. I hurt my eyes through an accident, and the young Archduke came to see me several times a day to help to fleet the hours I had to spend in a darkened room . . . . . For all his *joie de vivre* he liked serious conversation. I was often amazed at the clear and straight forward judgements he expressed on men and things. His judgements were always charitable, never malicious"[8]

In 1905 Charles took up a commission in a Dragoon regiment, and immediately began garrison life as an ordinary subaltern, taking his turn at various duties. He was now a young man out of the schoolroom and able to start enjoying adult life, although he would not be formally deemed to have come of age for a couple of years yet.

Home meant Reichenau in the mountains and it was here that he came when on leave, although there were also visits to the Hetzendorf palace in Vienna, not far from the Emperor's own official residence of Schönbrunn. Another base was at Schloss Miramar where his mother, Archduchess Maria Josefa, played hostess to frequent house-parties. Charles' parents were now largely estranged from one another - although never officially separated or divorced they led separate lives.

Polzer-Hoditz has left a description of a ten-days holiday at Miramar in the September of 1905, which began with Charles meeting the guests in the special "court waiting-room" at the local station, built exclusively for the use of the castle family and their visitors. It is an account of an apparently unchanging way of life - pleasant, cheerful and ordered "Archduke Karl, in white hunting-dress . . . . helped us to get our luggage, which had been registered through to Trieste, out of the luggage van and drove us through the shady winding roads of the park to the Schloss. We breakfasted on a terrace facing the sea. In the morning we made an excursion by motor-boat to Sistiana. At 11 o'clock Mass was celebrated in the Castle Chapel; at 1 o'clock we dined. In the afternoon we drove to Trieste Harbour, climbed the lighthouse, had tea on board a motor-boat, and, after a ramble through the streets of Trieste, drove back to Miramar at sunset. Afterwards we had supper on the terrace by moonlight. Next day we went to the Brioni Islands. We had some interesting plan for every day."⁹

It all seems to belong to a world safely cocooned from Europe's political ferment and seething tensions, and it was all to be savagely disrupted within a decade with the outbreak of World War 1.

Miramar had an intriguing history - and over the years was to acquire an eerie reputation. It was built by Archduke Maximilian, younger brother of the Emperor Franz Josef. As a young man he was sailing in the bay of Trieste when the boat threatened to capsize. His life was saved when the craft ran safely aground on a small promontory just outside the city. In commemoration he decided that one day he would build a castle there - and so Miramar was erected. It was designed as a place of charm and magic. Its gardens had numerous paths and grottos and the windows of the house had a clear view of the Adriatic. Lanterns lit the main balcony looking westwards over the ocean. Inside the castle itself, the Archduke's study was designed to echo a naval theme, panelled as if it were a galleon. Archduke Maximilian's life ended in tragedy when, in 1867, he accepted the Throne of Mexico in an idealistic venture which ended in death by firing squad when local Mexicans rejected his claims. Left behind at Miramar were various mementoes such as a marble-topped table, a gift from Pope Pius IX, on which he had signed the formal acceptance of the Mexican Throne.

Later generations would pass on the story that anyone who spent a night inside the castle would die in tragic circumstances far from home. In the late 1940s, at the end of the Second World War, an American general who was allocated the castle as his quarters refused to sleep under its roof, and instead had a tent erected in the grounds.

At the little railway station described by Count Polzer-Hoditz, the old imperial waiting room can still be seen. The station itself has not been used since the 1950s and is described by a current guidebook as consisting now mainly of "timbered pavilions strewn with wisteria".

Notes:

1. Kaiser, meaning Emperor, is a German word derived from the Latin word Caesar which was used to describe the Roman Emperors from the time of Octavian (Caesar Augustus). It was properly used by the Holy Roman Emperors and was latterly used by their successors, the Austro-Hungarian Emperors. In the 19th century, the newly emergent German Empire, established by Bismark's conquests, used the title for its king, who now became a new Prussian Kaiser in contrast to the Catholic, Austrian Kaiser whose Empire had been established organically over centuries more by marriage than conquest. In time the Prussian Empire grew into a great military power and defeated the Austrian Empire (at Koniggrätz, 1866) and dominated Europe. Both Empires ended after World War I.

2. Empress Zita, in a rare public interview in 1988, said that the death at Mayerling was not suicide but part of a political plot. A biography of Emperor Charles published the same year (Erich Feigl, Vienna, 1988) goes into some detail in the same vein.
3. Memories of the Archduchess, quoted in *Kaiser Karl Gebetsliga* yearbook, Lilienfeld, Austria, 1988.
4. Memoirs of Markgräfin (Marchioness) Crescence Pallavincini, lady-in-waiting to Archduchess Maria Josefa, published 1926.
5. Memories of Gräfin (Countess) Wallis, quoted in *Kaiser Karl Gebetsliga* yearbook, Lilienfeld, Austria, 1985.
6. Memories of Graf (Count) Wallis, quoted in *Gebetsliga* yearbook 1985. *op. cit.*
7. The concept of 'ebenwördig' ('equal rank') may at first seem strange and unfair but there were reasons for it. It was important that a future Empress had been brought up to be equal to the trials, difficulties and obligations of her state in life. An unsuitable candidate could seriously weaken the monarchy and therefore the whole state and constitution. Countess Chotek was the exception that proved the rule although it could be said that the system was perhaps a little inflexible in excluding a woman from such a pre-eminent Bohemian family which was even older, arguably, than the Habsburgs. Nevertheless, the principle was important and was aimed at avoiding the kind of match sometimes sought and secured by unscrupulous and ambitious people and which have had such a disastrous effect on some modern monarchies.
8. Polzer-Hoditz *The Emperor Charles*, Putnam, London, 1930.
9. *ibid.*

Chapter Two

While Charles was growing up at Persenbeug and Reichenau a little girl from a big family which also moved in royal circles was growing up, too. She was Princess Zita of Bourbon-Parma. This French family had formerly ruled in Italy and was now spread across Western Europe.

The Bourbon-Parmas had ruled the duchy of Lucca and Parma from 1748 until the time that the territory was seized by Victor Emmanuel to form part of his new united Italy. They were a branch of the ancient Bourbon family whose history can be traced back to the 10th century and who were connected to many European nations.

Zita's father was Duke Robert of Bourbon-Parma; his father had ruled the tiny duchy but had been murdered in a grim assassination in an open street in 1854. For a few years during his childhood Duke Robert was nominally still ruler, with his mother acting as regent, and then finally the family had to flee and a chapter of Italian history was closed.

Essentially French in culture and understanding, the Bourbon-Parmas had homes in Austria and France as well as in Italy and were linked by marriage to many of the royal houses of Europe. Duke Robert who was born in 1848 married twice. Both his wives presented him with large numbers of children, and the resulting family of offspring must surely have created something of a record. He had no less than 24 children and although three died in infancy the family was still a huge one which, together with all its staff of cooks and cleaners and nurses and maids and gardeners, must have formed a very substantial community.

Duke Robert's first wife was Maria-Pia of Sicily, whom he married in 1869 and by whom he had twelve children: Maria Luisa, Ferdinand (who died aged one year old in 1872), Luisa, Enrico, Immacolata, Guiseppe, Teresa, Pia, Beatrice, Elias, and two babies who died in 1881 and 1882, Anastasia and Augusto. This marriage had begun with a wedding ceremony performed by the Pope himself - Pius IX, the famed "Pio Nono" - in the Sistine Chapel.

Maria Pia died in Biarritz on 29th September 1882, leaving her husband with a young family. His second wife was Maria Antonia of Braganza, daughter of the King of Portugal. Zita was the fifth child of this marriage. She was born on May 9th 1892, and given her unusual Christian name at the suggestion of her godmother, her aunt Adelgunde, the wife of Prince Henry of Bourbon, Duke Robert's brother.

The name Zita was that of a popular Italian saint who had lived in Tuscany in the 13th century and who continues to be the object of much local devotion. St Zita, born about 1218 in the village of Monte Segrati, was a domestic servant and became the patron-saint of all cooks and domestic workers. An unusual choice of patron for a child who was born a princess and would later become an empress, but an edifying choice and one which was to prove popular in Zita's adopted country of Austria later on. St Zita is said to have been well known for her cheerful willingness to help everyone, although initially her diligence made her unpopular with the other servants and her lavish gifts of spare food to the local poor infuriated her employers. She was extremely devout and spent much time in prayer. In later years her employers allowed her to do as she pleased and she devoted her time to looking after prisoners, destitute, and anyone in trouble. One legend told of her is that she gave away large quantities of beans from her employers' store cupboard - she worked for a prosperous local weaver and his family - during a time of famine. He had been planning to sell them at a huge profit. When he came to check the cupboard she prayed and God miraculously filled up all the jars to the brim. Similarly, it is said that one day she stayed too long praying, and hurried home expecting to find all the bread burnt, but instead the loaves were golden-brown and just ready. Tradition in the Lucca district still maintains that whenever St Zita was praying, angels from heaven hurried down to look after her kitchen work. She died in 1278 having served the same family for forty-eight years, and is buried in the church of San Frediano, where she used to pray every day.

Her feast-day is April 27th, and perhaps it was this proximity to Princess Zita's own birthday of May 9th that suggested the choice - together with the obvious thought that this saint was a particularly popular one in the Lucca duchy where the Bourbon-Parmas had ruled for so long. Princess Zita was one of only three of Duke Robert's children who were actually born in Italy - at Pianore, the family home.

Before Zita, there had been Adelaide, born in 1885, Sixtus (1886), Xavier (1889), and Francesca (1890) - known as "Cicca" by the family. Later would follow Felix, René, Maria Antonia, Louis, Henrietta, and Gaetan. These children of Duke Robert's second marriage were very different in character, personality, and achievements from their elder half-brothers and sisters, and would go on to make their mark in many fields of life.

The family had two homes - Pianore, on the Italian Riviera between Viareggio and Lucca, and the Austrian mansion of Schwarzau, about twenty miles south of Vienna. Schwarzau was set in its own grounds on the edge of the Neunkirchen forest. The family spent half the year there and then moved (using a special train for the purpose) to Pianore, for the rest of the year taking with them books, household goods, the children's horses, and all the substantial accoutrements of such a very large family.

The Bourbon-Parmas were Catholic, and from her baptism onwards Zita's life would be lived out within the framework of the faith. At her baptism she was given a great collection of names: Zita, Marie della Grazie, Adelgonde, Michaela, Raffaela, Gabriella, Guiseppina, Antonia, Luisa, Agnesa. They honoured family traditions and lineage as befitted a grandaughter of King Michael of Portugal and the 17th child of the last reigning Duke of Lucca and Parma also a descendant of the Bourbon Kings of France.

It must have been a serene and secure childhood. Duke Robert's second marriage was a happy one, and the family life seems to have been characterised by cheerfulness and good companionship. Frequently guests from the world of books and universities stayed at Schwarzau, and there were regular visits from cousins and other children. It was on such a visit that Archduke Charles and his little brother Max came to Schwarzau, sharing in the Bourbon-Parma children's games and meals and family life. He became a good friend of her brothers Xavier and Sixtus: in childhood this meant games and sports together, and during the teenage years this progressed to long talks and a sharing of ideas and opinions. The Austrian royal family had in any case close links with the Bourbon-Parmas, and Kaiser Franz Josef had himself visited Schwarzau two years before Zita's birth, for the christening of Francesca, his godchild.

It was a way of life so vastly different from our own that trying to comprehend it is almost impossible. This was a Europe in which the idea of a monarchy was taken for granted and in which the idea of an internationally-linked aristocracy was also simply part of the scenery. A big mansion set in its own grounds and populated with children, parents, servants, relations and guests was an ordinary part of life for people in Zita's milieu. This was regarded as the normal way for such a building to be used. Nobody imagined that within a short time it would become a museum or be turned into a school or hotel or conference centre. The estates were part of the local economy and the social and class strucures with their delicate interweavings seemed utterly ordinary and part of the natural scheme of things.

In one of the salons at Pianore hung a huge painting of the coronation of the Bourbon King Louis XIV. Over the door of Duke Robert's study his name "Robertus Parma Dux" was carved in marble. Rich foliage fringed the wide terraces which ran round the mansion. As many as forty guests might sit down to a meal together. But for the children, life was essentially simply and well-ordered: years later the Empress Zita would recall that "a sweet trifle at the table was a high point" and that things were uncomplicated and carefree.[1]

From an early age, all the children became fluent in a number of languages. French and German were the main languages spoken at home. Italian was used with the local people at Pianore, and English with various visitors. Portugese was spoken to certain relations, and of course Latin was used in church.

One photograph shows Zita as a serious, slim, dark-eyed child dressed in a high-necked cotton ruffled dress with wide sash, lining up with her sisters and sailor-suited brother. Their childhood activities were country ones: playing out of doors, riding, swimming, and excursions. The main events in life were the grand moves, every six months, between Schwarzau and Pianore and vice versa - a thrilling journey for the children as they took part in the great drama of an entire household being packed on to a specially-commissioned train which was then drawn across the mountains.

Of the young Archduke Charles, Zita would later remember "We were children in the same family circle", seeing one another from time to time, living the same lifestyle in the serene and protected world of a Europe at peace.

At the age of eight, Zita began catechism lessons under Father Travers, who had similarly instructed her brothers, and in June 1902 she made her First Communion in the private family chapel at Pianore. The next year brought a major change in her life, when she went away to boarding school. She was sent with Francesca to a Salesian convent at Zangberg in Upper Bavaria—across the border from Austria into Germany. Her first term there started on September 16th, 1903. A photograph survives showing her with Cicca, both wearing school uniform capes and berets.

The school offered a broad general curriculum with all the usual subjects such as maths, history, languages, art and music. Zita learned to play the piano, although she actually preferred the organ, which she played at home in the holidays for Sunday Mass in the family chapel at Schwarzau.

The two young princesses were at school in the Autumn of 1907 when a telegram came summoning them home. Their father was seriously ill. He died on November 16th, and the funeral was at Viareggio, the local town of the family home at Pianore. This was the first death Zita had known, and the first break in her family circle. The homes at Pianore and Schwarzau were maintained, however, and the rhythm of life went slowly on. Zita's education and that of her sister was being supervised by her grandmother, the Queen of Portugal, who in her widowhood had become Abbess of a Benedictine community. The next plan was that the two girls would go on to another convent, St Cecilia's on the Isle of Wight. If an English religious community seems a strange choice for the completion of the education of a Catholic princess from mainland Europe, then the background to the community at St Cecilia's will make things clear. Its origins lay not in England at all but in France, where a Benedictine community of nuns was flourishing at Solesmes in the late 19th century. The French government, however, in a spate of anti-church and anti-clerical enthusiasm, passed laws to suppress such communities out of existence, and many fled abroad so that they could continue their traditional lifestyle in peace. Thus it was that several such religious orders fled to Britain - a strange reversal of events in a Europe which had seen Catholics from England fleeing for refuge to France only a few generations before. The Isle of Wight just off England's south coast was an obvious choice for a new home for the exiles. Monks from Solesmes settled at Quarr, where they built for themselves a new abbey adjoining the ruins of a medieval one destroyed under Henry VIII. The sisters, after a brief stay at Cowes (Northwood) chose a site on the other side of the town of Ryde. There they bought a house which had belonged to a local businessman, Appley, and bore his name.

Ryde was - and still is - a busy resort, with bow-fronted Georgian and neo-Georgian houses facing on to the sea front and lining a main road which leads up the hill. It is the island's port for the ferry from Portsmouth, and the mainland can be clearly seen across the Solent, along which a busy traffic of shipping passes.

The nuns created a convent for themselves which still stands today at the end of Appley Rise, with a chapel topped by a tower with a bell ringing out the Angelus at midday and evening, and extensive gardens and grounds making the community self-sufficient.

To this convent had come Zita's older sister Adelaide, following her grandmother into the Benedictine way of life in the strict enclosure of the cloister.

St Cecilia's was a "contemplative" convent where the nuns engaged in prayer and study of the Scriptures and Church Fathers. Its sisters did not run a big school as other religious communities often did, but a small group of girls were nevertheless given their education there, sharing in some of the prayers and especially the music of the nuns in the chapel. As a teenager Zita became absorbed into this little world, the people of Ryde and the holiday trippers certainly not imagining that in the convent overlooking the Esplanade was living a young woman whose husband to be would, in a few years time, be deemed their official enemy in a major war.

Adelaide had become Mère Benedicta in the convent. Zita was allowed to see her from time to time during recreation periods. Later Cicca would become a nun, too, as Mère Scholastica, and later again a younger sister, Maria Antonia, would join them in the convent.

Music was important at St Cecilia's and Zita's time there widened her knowledge of this and of Church liturgy in addition to offering her a chance to study Latin, history, and philosophy. It also surrounded her with a Catholic tradition of piety and belief that was to foster and develop her faith. What had begun in a Catholic family atmosphere with a crowd of brothers and sisters grew and flourished in an austere framework in which doctrine was taught with strict adherence to orthodoxy and familiar prayers were re-echoed with renewed understanding.

There were special events in the routine of convent life - saints' days, the Church's round of the seasons, anniversaries, and ceremonies such as those surrounding the death of the first abbess, Madame Cecile Bruyers, in 1909. St Cecilia's, like the family back at home, was a community of faith united by strong bonds of common heritage.

It seems that Zita herself considered joining this religious life. She became an "alumnate" at St Cecilia's in 1909. When she returned home it must surely have been with the sense of conviction that if God had not chosen her for this particular role, he must have some other specific task in mind for her. She would never waver from adherence to the Catholic faith and would continue to rely on the sacraments and the teachings of the Church through a life that was to offer changes and drama of a quite staggering kind.

Once back home at Schwarzau, the Princesses Cicca and Zita were ready for the adult world of balls, country weekends, and social life. They were still close and shared their social activities as they had shared all their growing-up experiences. But life was now to offer them very different futures. Cicca would eventually return to St Cecilia's, taking the name Mère Scholastica and live out the rest of her life within the religious enclosure.

In 1922 political changes made it possible for the community from Ryde to move back to France and Zita's sisters who by then had joined the convent continued their Benedictine lives there. Mère Benedicta died in 1959, Mère Maria Antonia in 1977 and Mère Scholastica in 1979. The abbey at Ryde is now occupied by a thriving English community of sisters who keep a few mementoes of the Bourbon-Parma links in the form of books and photographs and letters.

But for Zita life was to offer a very different alternative, and a world of wider horizons. At Viennese balls and dances she would meet again the young Archduke she had not seen since he came on childhood visits to Schwarzau.

Notes

1. Erich Feigl, *Kaiserin Zita, Legende und Wahrheit*, Vienna, 1978.

Chapter Three

In 1906 Charles' father Otto died at the early age of 41. He had been ill for some time, and was being nursed in the Augarten Palace in Vienna where for part of the year Charles was also staying recuperating after damaging his foot, skating.

Charles had been close to his father despite the gulf between his parents. His mother was at Miramar in October 1906 when news came of a serious worsening of her husband's condition: she hurried to Vienna but returned to Miramar when his condition seemed to improve. Neither she nor Charles were with him therefore when he died on November 1st. Charles, his mother and his younger brother Max returned to Vienna having been summoned a second time, but they were tragically too late.

In London *The Times*, reported the Archduke's death, commenting that he had been "before ill-health made physical activity impossible, a brilliant cavalry officer, and one of the most popular member of the Imperial and Royal family". Otto had not been particularly well-known or influential outside his own circle and his interest in politics or social concerns was minimal: but his image of unstuffy jollity was an attractive one which had appeal to his friends and acquaintances.

Charles himself was deeply saddened by the loss of his father and there was nothing forced about the solemn way in which he participated in the requiem ceremonies. Vienna was plunged into official mourning for the funeral on November 6th. The Duke of Teck was the formal representative of the British Royal family at the ceremony in the Capuchin church. Thousands of spectators lined streets which had been hung with black flags, and all traffic was suspended whilst the procession, with Charles

22

leading the mourners, wound its way from the Hofburg through the Josefplatz, Augustinierstrasse, Albrechtplatz and Tegethhoffstrasse. A double line of troops formed a guard of honour the whole way.

The death marked the beginning of a new era in Charles' life: now he had to start preparing himself for the throne in earnest. The Emperor Franz Josef had given his approval to a programme of political education drawn up by Count Wallis after consultation with Count Polzer-Hoditz. The scheme included a study of law and economics - including details such as Hungarian constitutional law in all its complexities. To engross himself in this, Charles arranged to live for a period of some months at another family castle - Hradcin, the Royal Castle of Prague, about 150 miles from Vienna.

Prague was at that time the third largest city in the Austro-Hungarian Empire. The palace of Hradcin dominated the town from its splendid position on the heights of the left bank of the river Moldau. It was a rambling collection of buildings with a total of over 400 rooms adjoining the cathedral of St Vitus.

Here Charles settled down to work. Already the previous year Emperor Franz Josef had pronounced himself pleased with his great-nephew's mastery of the difficult Hungarian language: now the next two years were to be dedicated to absorbing the information, ideas and background of Hungary and the other territories and races of the complex empire. The rooms that he occupied in Hradcin included the one which had seen the famous "defenestration" which began the Thirty Years War. Differences between Catholic and Protestant Councillors in the beginning of the 17th century had erupted when the Catholics arranged for a staunchly anti-Protestant Archduke, Ferdinand, to succeed to the throne. Protestant councillors, led by a Count Thurn, decided to throw the Catholics from the windows of the palace. On the 23rd May 1618 the two Catholic councillors, Martinic and Slavata escaped with their lives after landing safely on a dung-heap when they were thrown from the window of this very room.

Charles liked to point out the historical link and tell the story to visitors. He was surrounded by history, as well as simply studying it.

His twentieth birthday in 1907 was celebrated in style with the announcement that he had now formally come of age. He was photographed in military uniform seated among his tutors, whose work was officially deemed to have been completed. He took his place as an adult Archduke in the Royal Family, with Prince Lobkowitz being appointed his Head of Household and Count Ledebuhr gentleman-in-waiting. Then, after a further spell in Prague to complete his studies he returned to the Dragoons and regimental life.

The next year saw Franz Josef's Diamond Jubilee as Emperor - sixty years on the throne - an event duly marked by commentators all over the world analysing the state of the empire's strength and stability. In Britain, the *Cambridge Modern History* noted that a decade earlier at the time of the Golden Jubilee "Europe had viewed with fear and distrust the future of the monarchy, which seemed inevitably doomed to dissolution at the death of Francis Joseph. But ten years have elapsed since then, and the prognostications are wholly different. The acute crisis has been dispelled solely by the internal forces of the monarchy. The external dangers, that is to say pan-Germanism and pan-Slavism appear much less serious than at that time.... There is still violent struggle between the nationalities but the inevitable solution is in sight. The union between Austria and Hungary has, in reality, been strengthened by the new Compromise and the new Eastern policy. It seems as though all the Austrian, Hungarian, and Austro-Hungarian questions could be settled from within. It is in this that the progress consists; herein lies the great security for the future." It went on to note, in words that now have a sad ring to them bearing in mind the break-up of the Empire within the next decade, that the peoples of the Empire were becoming conscious of their common interests and the value of their unity under the crown: "Herein lies the great internal change: herein lies its mighty new strength; this is the great, the enormous result of the reign of Francis Joseph."[1]

Franz Josef was an institution: millions of his subjects had never known any other monarch and he was an unchanging face on the European scene. His own way of living and working exemplified a notion of order and a commitment to the self-discipline and moral dedication on which he sought to base his rule.

He rose every day before 4am, and after washing and shaving knelt to pray at his prie-dieu before a crucifix. Morning and night prayers were a fixed part of his routine which dated back to his earliest childhood and his mother's teaching. He lived in two rooms in his vast palace, using others only for official occasions, keeping all his papers and personal items neat and tidy. After a light breakfast he worked for hour after hour at his desk, reading and signing papers, silently poring over documents relating to every aspect of the internal and external state of the nations he ruled. When the rest of Vienna rose to a new day he had already been labouring for several hours: if he were ever asked about this he would no doubt have simply said that such a state of affairs was natural and right for a monarch.... but it is impossible to imagine anyone starting a conversation in which Franz Josef's role and tasks in life were compared to anyone else's.

For the jubilee the entire Habsburg clan gathered at Schönbrunn. The city of Vienna was illuminated and massive festivities were planned for the population. In the palace itself, the children of the Habsburg family - the Emperor's grandchildren and great-nephews and nieces - presented a ballet which was choreographed by Archduke Ferdinand Karl (one of his nephews) after which they all trooped up to give him flowers and kiss his hand[2]. The next day at a formal gathering the heir to the throne, Archduke Franz Ferdinand, gave a ceremonial address to the whole family in the Alexander Apartments at the Hofburg. That evening, there was a gala presentation in the Opera House - a glittering spectacular attended by all of Viennese society.

The white-whiskered face of the Emperor gazed out from commemorative postcards as it had ten years earlier in 1898 when the slogan on the souvenirs had been "Funfzig Jahr mit weiser Hand schirmet er das Vaterland". The Emperor was depicted with plump cherubs strewing him with garlands and laurel wreaths while a guardian angel stretched a golden wing protectively over him. Around his figure the painter had included all the coats of arms of the various nations and territories over which he ruled.

The anthem of the Empire, "Gott erhalte, Gott beschütze unsern Kaiser, unser Land...." was widely sung across the land[3], but beneath the celebrations the Empire was criss-crossed with tensions, chiefly arising out of nationalism then becoming an increasingly dangerous force.

In his memoirs, Count Polzer-Hoditz recalls a conversation with Charles at the time of the Jubilee. The young Archduke had played a major part in the celebrations, introducing and concluding the children's pageant in front of the Emperor. He took a gloomy view of the way things really were amongst the complex and conflicting groups joined together under Habsburg rule. Polzer-Hoditz recalls: "This was the first time that the usually so happy and optimistically inclined Archduke expressed dark views about the future.... He spoke of the tradition of his House, which consisted in adherence to the federalistic principle. We had, he said, departed too greatly from that principle, which we would have bitter cause to regret." Charles had been discussing things with Franz Ferdinand, whose ideas for the future included offering much more scope for representation of the various minority groups within the Empire. He did not reveal the content of these confidential discussions but had for a long time held strong views of his own which the points raised by his uncle and others only served to enforce. He believed that the only possible way forward lay in creating a truly federal system of essentially independent nations, linked under the crown to form an effective partnership. He had even gone so far as to see that some of these could even be republics, if the people particularly wanted this form of government, and he saw the Crown as a uniting factor bringing together nations for mutual prosperity and protection within the splendid heritage of a Christian monarchy.

Any such notions would have to wait for the day when their proposer was in a position to put them into effect. Meanwhile, the Empire continued in the way that had now been established for six decades, while the various nationalist groups agitating for more power, influence and authority jostled and pushed for space and looked abroad for allies.

In Vienna, there were too many people who, unconcerned with the real problems faced by the Empire preferred instead to concentrate on gossip and fantasy. Envy of the Royal family perhaps had something to do with it, but this was combined with a lack of vision and purpose in the role and destiny of the society in which they were living. The rumours could be silly, but dangerous. They could - and later would - be taken seriously by the Empire's enemies. Polzer-Hoditz gives an example, concerning a hunting expedition at the end of December 1908, organised by Archduke Charles: "The Archduke, the Court Master of the Hunt Edward Grunkranz, and I drove in a sledge to a hunting-lodge which Prince Liechtenstein had lent to the Archduke. There we had a snack and then took up our positions. We brought down a few head of big game, and when the light began to fail, descended to the valley, where the sledge was waiting to take us to the station. We had supper in the restaurant car. On our arrival in Vienna, the Archduke Charles drove me home, and then drove himself back to the Augarten. A day or two later, Count Wallis told me there was a rumour going about in Vienna that we had a regular orgy all night at the Liechtenstein hunting-lodge with a musical comedy-star, and that there had been scandalous goings-on. The rumour had reached the Emperor and the Archduke Franz Ferdinand. Wallis heard it from Count Paar. I immediately wrote a letter to Wallis, in which I described the harmless events of our hunting expedition, and asked him to give my letter to Count Paar. The Emperor who, I afterwards found, had in any case put no faith in the rumour, now learned the true story. But the report of dissipations with musical comedy stars spread and continued to be believed by the population of Vienna. At the request of the Archduke, I had an investigation made, and discovered, among other things, that a musical comedy actress had borrowed an expensive piece of jewelry from a jeweller, and had told all her numerous friends, male and female, that it was a present from the Archduke. A fresh crop of marvellous tales grew up around this rumour, and people began to gossip about the Archduke's dissipated way of life. Thus the seed of malicious rumour was sown, and this seed, diligently watered, partly by credulous persons and scandal-mongers, and partly by enemies of the dynasty, finally grew into a poisonous tree which twined itself around the figure of the future Emperor."

It was all the more cruel and malicious because Charles' life was not only blameless but marked by an unusual dedication and spiritual commitment.

Charles was acutely aware of the responsibilites he would inherit on ascending the throne. He was serious about fulfilling his vocation: as a member of the Habsburg house with its special duties and responsibilites to the peoples of the Empire, and as a future monarch.

He had already been invested with the Order of the Golden Fleece, the ancient order of chivalry given by the Emperor and dating back to the early days of Christendom. He was given this honour in 1905 as a token of his position within the Royal family and the Empire. To some people the Order would have represented simply a colourful and exciting link with the distant past; to be worn with a sense of pride in having been singled out for such a particular honour. Charles took a different view: he saw the thing essentially in a spiritual light and was anxious to uphold the terms and conditions under which it was given. Not without difficulty, he ploughed his way through the rules of the order - written in old French - and tried to see how they could be applied to his own life.[4]

The religious faith implanted in his childhood was growing within him: it was to play a fundamental part in the next major decision he would make - that of marriage.

The choice of bride was something potentially fraught with difficulties. His uncle Franz was now domestically very happy, and starting to raise a family in great contentment with his Sophie, but the pair were constantly subject to awkwardness and embarrassments centered on the morganatic status of their marriage. Charles was on good terms with them and found the atmosphere of their home congenial - they were a devoted couple, faithful to their marriage and delighting in their children - but no one could pretend that the future, when Franz Ferdinand ascended the throne, was going to be easy.

A formally arranged dynastic marriage - such as that of the hapless Rudolph with Sophie of Belgium - was not a notably better option. Love, personal commitment, and veneration for marriage itself were the priorities a modern prince might legitimately hold in his mind in seeking a bride. But how to make the right choice within the narrow band of potential candidates? And when should the choice be made?

Later accounts of the lives of the Imperial couple - notably official booklets published for their coronation in 1916 - would claim significantly that it was at a ball at the German embassy in Vienna in 1910 that they first met again after the long gap in their acquantaince, and there romance blossomed. But in fact dynastic alliances are not formed quite so spontaneously as that. Doubtless the Bourborn-Parma girls had long been regarded as eminently suitable spouses for the members of other Catholic royal houses of Europe. With the example of his uncle before him, Charles was clearly concerned to make the right choice in the matter of marriage.

Providence intervened to bring together Charles and Zita of Bourbon-Parma: meeting in the time-honoured way as children in the same family circle and then having the friendship change and deepen when their paths crossed again once they were both grown up, made everything easy.

They met at Franzenbad, where Charles - who was now based with his regiment at Brandeis on the Elbe river - was visiting his aunt Annunciata. Later the Empress Zita would recall: "We were glad to meet again and became close friends. On my side feeling developed gradually over the next two years. He seemed to have made up his mind much more quickly, however, and became even more keen when, in the autumn of 1910, a rumour spread about that I had got engaged to a distant Spanish relative, Don Jaime, the Duke of Madrid.

"On hearing this, the Archduke came down post-haste from his regiment at Brandeis and sought out his grandmother, the Archduchess Maria Theresa (who was also my great-aunt) and the natural 'confidante' in such matters. He asked her whether the rumour was true and when told it was not, replied: 'Well, I had better hurry or else she really will get engaged to some one else.' "[5]

Certainly Zita, an unusually beautiful young girl with her dark hair swept up crowning her head, good posture and a warm smile, was capturing much attention at the grown-up balls and dances she attended. Photographs of the period show her as an unaffected, cheerful young woman. Her background and training had given her some formation in the duties of a princess, but she was untouched by the glamour or glitter of a city life among fashionable people.

Emperor Franz Josef had for some time been urging on Charles the importance of finding a suitable bride. Charles had never really had any doubts about who it was to be. "The little Zita", the girl he had known long before on visits to her father's castle, the princess enjoying her first dances. A young woman whose serious commitment to her religious faith matched his own. She was to be the one.

The Princesses Cicca and Zita (Cicca had not yet entered the convent and the two were still close companions) were invited to a ball given by Charles' mother. Later they went to stay at St Jacob, the hunting-lodge owned by his grandmother. It was here, during a week of beautiful May weather away from military duties and official work that Charles was able to get to know Zita.

They spent long hours talking together and it was here that he proposed marriage to her. They were away from the nods and smiles and interest shown by others at balls and dances, and could be themselves.

It is said that when Charles went to Princess Zita's mother, the Duchess of Parma, to ask formally for her daughter's hand, the Duchess expressed concern about Zita who was still so young, taking on the responsibility of being so near the throne. But Charles reassured her that the Emperor was still in good health and Franz Ferdinand was in the prime of life. There was no need to fear that the young princess would be Empress too soon.

In the Austria of the 1900s there was none of the intrusive insistent press scrutiny of each developing aspect of a Royal romance that has been a feature of royalty in the 1980s. Zita's name was not known to the public until the engagement was announced, and then the only photographs released were formal ones. The enthusiasm generated was genuine, however. Zita was beautiful, merry and clever - her experiences in a large family had given her a friendly manner which combined with serene dignity to give her a charming character and from the day of the announcement the Royal family seemed touched by a note of genuine happiness and security for the future which it had not known for a long time.

When the announcement was made from Pianore on 13th June 1911 the young couple posed for photographs on the terrace of the mansion. Charles wore a formal frock-coat and Zita tucked her arm under his: they looked very correct but also unpretentiously happy. It was the birthday of Charles' mother, Archduchess Maria Josefa. Some commentators noted that it was also the feast-day of an important Italian saint, St Anthony of Padua: a good day for a former ruling family of an Italian duchy to mark this new and significant chapter in its history. Others looked into the past to find the last alliance of a Bourbon-Parma and a Habsburg monarch, that of Princess Isabella to Kaiser Josef I in the 18th century.

In one sense, however, the position of the radiant young couple was a potentially embarrassing one: Franz Ferdinand, the heir to the throne, had children who were all barred from reigning under the terms of the morganatic settlement. Charles and his young fiancee were thus to acquire the Habsburg crown for their own family. The prospect was therefore raised of two rival power bases.

The fact that it fortunately did not turn out like that was due to Charles and Zita's own personal stance. Charles saw the crown as an obligation and a solemn responsibility under God, rather than as a worldly opportunity, and he would therefore never allow it to become a matter of political intrigue.

Above all, his religious faith made him put a high premium on genuine humility and on the simple life. He had a genuine sense of purpose which he brought to all his duties. Marriage was to increase his obligations and he had no intention of allowing it merely to add to his status.

Inevitably however it thrust him into public prominence. The newspapers - not only within the Empire but throughout Europe - focused attention on the young couple on whom the hopes of the Habsburg dynasty were now based. The Emperor was well satisfied. Everything about Zita: her faith, manner, upbringing, family background and dynastic connections, made her suitable as a future Empress, and the popularity with which she was received served only to confirm this view.

The papers described her as combining the merits of the Bourbons with the charm of the Viennese: she was unprejudiced, vivacious and clever, "a tender daughter and sister".

Meanwhile the young couple talked and planned. The wedding was set for 21st of October. It would not only be a major event for the Empire and for the Crown but also a family occasion shared with the local people. Before it took place there were other duties and experiences for both the bride and groom: for 19-year-old Zita a special audience with the Pope with a mysterious prophetic quality about it, and for Charles an unforgettable visit to England in his first major engagement overseas as second-in-line to the throne.

Notes:

1. *Cambridge Modern History,* Cambridge University, Press, 1908.
2.3.4. Polzer-Hoditz, *The Emperor Karl*, Putnam, London, 1930.
5. Gordon Brook-Shepherd, *The Last Habsburg*, Weidenfeld and Nicolson, London, 1968.

Chapter Four

The summer of 1911 saw a major event for all Europe's royalty: the coronation of Britain's King George V in London. It was announced in Vienna that Archduke Charles would be Austria-Hungary's official representative at this ceremony, thus underlining the importance of Charles' status and overcoming any awkwardness that might have arisen had Archduke Franz Ferdinand pressed to go. Franz Ferdinand's morganatic marriage was continually presenting foreign governments with protocol problems. For such a major event as a coronation (with balls and receptions of every kind) it would have produced virtually insurmountable difficulties. Technically, Archduke Franz Ferdinand's wife was not entitled to be given royal status: but how could this be avoided without an endless series of what appeared to be offensive snubs to the lady? At what events could she be present? Where should she be placed in line-ups, at the dinner-table, in a procession, in a formal photographic session?

The young Archduke Charles presented no such difficulties. Indeed, he would prove to be an excellent representative of the Empire he would one day rule. Newly engaged to a beautiful princess whose miniature picture he carried in his pocket, he was charming and cheerful, and exuded an air of youth and confidence. It was a happy image for the old Empire to offer to the world.

The chief foreign guest at the celebrations would, of course, be the German Emperor, Kaiser Wilhelm, the eldest son of Queen Victoria's eldest daughter. It was he who had been with Queen Victoria when she was dying ten years before at Osborne on the Isle of Wight, and he had

31

been a chief mourner at her funeral. His links with the British Royal family were strong and close: he spoke English like a native and was comfortable with British food, clothes and manners. For him, in a more intimate way, this London coronation was a family as well as a state affair.

While Charles set off for England, where he would join royalty and dignitaries from across the globe in this magnificent celebration of pageantry and monarchy, the young Princess Zita, with members of her family, was heading for Rome. It had been announced that they would be given a special audience by Pope Pius X, to honour the Princess' engagement. The union between a Habsburg archduke and a Bourbon-Parma princess brought together Europe's leading Catholic royal houses.

It was not Zita's first visit to the Vatican. She had been there as a child for the Silver Jubilee celebrations of Pope Leo XIII in 1903. As a ten-year-old she had been awed and thrilled by it, later recalling "the splendid ceremony, the chants, the grandeur of it all". Now she was returning as a young woman, to meet a different pope, and one who would have a special message for her.

First the Pope celebrated Mass for members of the family in his private chapel, and then he entertained them in the library. He opened the conversation by telling the young Princess "I am very happy with this marriage and I expect much from it for the future . . . . Charles is a gift from Heaven for what Austria has done for the Church". The young Archduke's piety and loyalty were evidently very much in his mind. Later in the conversation, Princess Zita was placed in an awkward position when the Pope (forgetting for a moment the true state of affairs) referred to Charles as the heir to the throne. Gently, she pointed out that he was not the direct heir: first came his uncle, the Archduke Franz Ferdinand. At this however the Pontiff looked serious and repeated that Charles would soon be on the throne. The young Princess, startled, said that surely Franz Ferdinand was not going to abdicate - but the Pope, looking troubled and thoughtful, said in a low voice "If it is an abdication...I do not know . . . . ", as if he could see ahead to something that was about to happen. It was a strange conversation, which none of those who heard it ever forgot.

It must have been a rather thoughtful young princess who left the Vatican at the end of the interview and returned to Schwarzau with her mother to continue the preparations for the marriage. But she had plenty to do. The wedding arrangements were not just a matter of buying new clothes or talking about guests and festivities. She was spending much of her time in serious study of the new languages she now had to learn:

Hungarian and Czech both vital for a future empress of the Slavs and the Magyars. Her marriage would change not only her status but also her nationality, and give her a whole new range of duties and responsibilities in different parts of Europe.

Although Princess Zita's father had died four years earlier, Schwarzau remained the family home and would shortly be welcoming a great parade of distinguished wedding guests, including the Emperor. The marriage ceremony would be the Empire's most important domestic event of the year. Local people prepared pageants and celebrations, menus were drawn up for the banquet, and a wedding-gown of royal beauty was designed and fitted for the 19-year-old bride.

Meanwhile over in England Charles was witnessing - and sharing in - the magnificent and awe-inspiring ceremonial surrounding the crowning and anointing of the British King Emperor. Did his thoughts turn, as he sat in Westminster Abbey among the other royal dignitaries, to his own coronation as King Emperor of Austria-Hungary which beckoned somewhere in the distant future? Probably he would not have dwelt on this idea, as it must have seemed many years away. His uncle Franz Ferdinand was a hale and hearty man with an apparent zest for life who showed no inclination towards either early death or abdication.

London was host to a huge number of foreign royals for what was to be, although no one involved in it was to know, the last gathering on the world stage of the royal houses of Old Europe before the wholesale social disintegration that was to come in the aftermath of the 1914-18 war. As just one among so many foreign guests Charles did not attract particular attention - although as every detail of coronation news and gossip was of interest to the people of Britain, the press did offer bits of information about him. *The Lady* magazine in its special coronation edition of 15th June 1911, reported that "The housing of the coronation guests has been a matter of grave consideration . . . . . The Archduke Charles Francis Joseph, who represents Austria, will, I believe, be at 41, Belgrave Square, the house of Mr E.V. Sturdy, and Lord Herschell will be one of those in attendance on him."

The following week's edition with its lavish and slightly breathless descriptions of all the celebrations gives some idea of the splendours in which Charles participated. There was a "splendid ball given by the Duke and Duchess of Sutherland at Stafford House . . . . to which a vast concourse of Royalties with their suites came on from a dinner party at Buckingham Palace . . . . The Royalties began to arrive about half past eleven and of course those we looked for most were the German Crown Prince and Princess who arrived together, the latter tall, erect, smiling and very smart, with a beautiful tiara pointed with pearls in her hair . . . . . Then there were Princess Louis of Battenberg, Princess Frederick Charles of Hesse, the Hereditary Princess of Saxe-Meiningen, the Princess Militza of Montenegro, and the Crown Princess of Bulgaria. Amongst the most interesting men present, of course, were the Grand Duke Boris of Russia who represented the Czar, the Hereditary Prince Youssof Effandi representing Turkey (who, by the way, is second in precedence amongst the coronation guests and, I was told, had never been to a ball before!) and the Infante Don Fernando of Spain, the handsome Italian Prince, the Duke d'Aosta and the Archduke Charles Francis Josef of Austria representing his uncle the Emperor, a handsome young prince who, by the way, was formally betrothed the day before he came to England to the Princess Zita of Bourbon-Parma, a daughter of the late Duke of Parma and sister of the present. The bride-elect is only 19 and very pretty, and she is the 12th child in a family of 20 brothers and sisters, all born of the same parents!" [sic].

This ball was only one event among many. In addition to the coronation itself, there was a "Shakespeare Ball" at the Albert Hall, a huge reception at Clarence House given by the Duke and Duchess of Connaught, and a dinner and reception given by Sir Edward Grey at the Foreign Office. Sir Edward Grey, Liberal MP and Foreign Secretary, was to play a decisive role in the events that would shape Charles' future - and the future of so many young men in Europe. Born in 1862, he was to be Britain's longest-serving Foreign Secretary, having taken up the office in 1905. In 1914 it would be Grey who, despite his hatred of war, was to tell Parliament that there was an obligation to hurry to the aid of Belgium - thereby precipitating what was to become four long years of fighting.

In the June days of 1911, however, Europe seemed very much at peace and the mood was festive and celebratory. Charles received congratulations on his engagement, and took part in all the spectacular events, including the Naval review at Spithead which greatly impressed him. He shared in the warm and friendly atmosphere of a nation enjoying itself. He was, of course, a fluent English speaker as he had been taught the language as a child by his governess Miss Casey.

Charles returned to Austria to find wedding preparations well under way and that the plans for the great event at Schwarzau were taking shape. He and Zita were able to enjoy some happy times together. These included attendance at the "Austrian Flying Week" organised at Wiener Neustadt by the Empire's newly-created air force. This had been arranged to take place in the week before their wedding. They were given a great ovation: this attractive young couple represented everything that was new and fresh and optimistic in the old Empire. Charles in uniform and Zita in a wide picture hat and elegant outfit, accompanied by Cicca, walked around the airfield looking at everything and meeting everyone involved. A few days later they would be greeted by air cadets from here putting on a special display for their wedding.

Years later the Princess Zita would recall the seriousness and dedication with which Charles approached their marriage. "Now" he told her the evening before the ceremony "we must help each other to get to Heaven". For him, matrimony was first of all a sacrament and a means of grace.

The wedding day combined royal splendour with family happiness and local pride but it also broke with tradition in a number of ways. For a start, part of it was recorded on film - perhaps the first time that cine cameras were used at a royal wedding. The involvement of the air display among the celebrations also introduced a throughly modern note.

The surviving film clips show a smiling family gathered together on the terrace after coming out of the church: a radiant bride in an exquisite gown, tiara and veil laughing with a bridegroom who, seeing the camera at work, hurries the group into a semblance of order. The celebratory mood is evident as children run about - the bride's youngest brother Gaetan, hurrying across to greet her. Adults congratulate the bridal couple and chatter to one another. Even the Emperor is seen beaming, and the sun shines down on a scene of informality and pleasure.

The Times of October 23rd 1911 gave its readers a taste of what the day had been like: "Bright Autumn weather favoured the wedding of the Archduke Charles Francis Joseph with the Princess Zita of Parma at Schwarzau am Steinfelde yesterday. Notwithstanding its importance from the dynastic standpoint, the occasion bore an almost patriarchal character and was marked by an at least apparent absence of the rigorous etiquette that usually governs Austro-Hungarian Court and State functions . . . . the Emperor Francis Joseph reached Schwarzau at 11 o'clock yesterday morning and after greeting the Duchess of Parma and her children gave the signal for the opening of the ceremony . . . . the Archduke Charles Francis Joseph in the uniform of a captain of Dragoons proceeded to the chapel between the Emperor Francis Joseph and his mother the Archduchess Maria Josefa". The ceremony was in French, "the answers of the bride and bridegroom were clear, those of the bride being so emphatic and joyous as to draw a smile from the Emperor."

Presiding over the wedding was Monsignor Bisleti, the personal representative of the Pope, and London's Catholic weekly magazine *The*

Tablet reported that he "was also the bearer of a present from the Pontiff to the Royal pair, and an autograph letter in which His Holiness expressed his paternal affection and good wishes". The Papal gift was a silver-framed religious picture. To commemorate the special day the Monsignor who was a long-standing family friend of the Bourbon-Parmas, was given a decoration by the Emperor: the Grand Cross of the Order of Leopold. Some flavour of the cosmopolitan nature of this remarkable Royal gathering is given by the fact that Mgr Bisleti's address during the French wedding ceremony was given in Italian. The whole proceedings were of course taking place in Austria in the presence of guests who included King Friedrich August of Saxony, and Admiral Nicholas Horthy who would one day be the Regent of Hungary.

The bride's dress was of Duchesse satin patterned with Bourbon lilies. It was high-necked with a wide sash waist and was trimmed with antique point-lace. Delicate silvered embroidery interwove Austrian and French themes. She wore a spray of orange blossoms and myrtle in addition to carrying a large bouquet. Her Valenciennes lace veil was held in place by a tiara on top of her swept-up hair. This tiara was a gift from Emperor Franz Josef. Many years later it would be worn by another Habsburg bride - when Charles and Zita's son Otto married Princess Regina of Sachsen-Meiningen at Nancy in France in 1951. But that day was four decades and two world wars away from the sunny day at Schwarzau.

Zita's white prayer-book was a gift from the sisters at St Cecilia's and bore a design hand-painted in gold-leaf. The two wedding rings lay on it, overlapping, with the names "Karl von Osterreich - Zita von Bourbon-Parma" written underneath, and a dedication taken from a favourite prayer of Charles: "To thy protection we fly, O Holy Mother of God . . . . "

Charles, in his Lorraine Dragoons uniform, was wearing his various medals including the Order of the Golden Fleece (whose rules he had so assiduously studied when it was first bestowed on him) together with the Jubilee Medal issued by Franz Josef a few years before to mark the 60th anniversary of his reign.

A magnificent lunch was served in the castle's Theresiensaale with the guests seated at five long tables. The Emperor made a hearty and affectionate speech in which he wished the pair long life and good health, and told Charles that in Zita he had truly found a partner for life's journey. The newspapers reported that his speech ended with a stirring "Gott schütze und schirme Erzherzhog Karl und Erzherzhogin Zita, Sie leben hoch, hoch, hoch!"

Overhead, flowers were tossed down on the happy scene by air cadets from the nearby Wiener-Neustadt academy, putting on a spectacular display of greetings.

Later, when the bridal pair left - by car, another royal innovation - for Reichenau where they would spend their honeymoon, the road out through the town was lined with cheering, waving local people. They had played their own part in the celebrations on the day before the wedding when, wearing local costume, they presented flowers and sang songs to the bride. There had also been fireworks and a torchlight procession. Zita was being given her first taste of what would always be hers from now on: a public life as a major figure in Austria's Royal family.

Now followed a halcyon time. Photographs taken at Reichenau during the honeymoon show a relaxed young couple in country clothes strolling jauntily arm in arm through the village accompanied by a large umbrella. They made a little private pilgrimage to the shrine at Mariazell where they prayed for a blessing on their marriage. They later went on to Dalmatia, for a stay on the coast. Then Charles had to rejoin his regiment and they became an army couple, living out of the public gaze in the secluded atmosphere of peacetime army life. One story is told of this first winter of their married life: during a car journey they had to stop while some repairs were carried out, and they took shelter in a nearby house where the housewife gave them hot drinks and chatted comfortably. When she heard where they were headed she was pleased - her son was a young soldier in the regiment. Would they take his clean washing back to him for her? And also this small envelope of money that he needed? The Archduchess cheerfully took charge of the laundry, and the Archduke promised to deliver the money safely. Only later, when both had been handed over to the young soldier - the money with some extra added - did the story emerge, and the country woman realise who her guests had been. The story got told and re-told. The friendliness and naturalness of the young couple who were second in line to the throne was beginning to win hearts.

Initially the Dragoons were at Brandeis on the Elbe where Charles and Zita made a home in a local castle. Then came a posting to the far eastern border of the empire: Kolomea in Galicia. Here was the frontier with the vast Russian territories ruled over by the Tsar[2]: the local people were Poles and Ukrainians. The archducal couple moved here in the early spring of 1912, Charles travelling with the regiment by horse and Zita going ahead by train. It was a long way from Vienna with its politics culture and glamour, and they lived in an ordinary small house sharing fully in the routines of regimental life.

Then in the summer Charles suffered an accident during a major army exercise. He was thrown off his horse after it had slipped and his head hit the ground. He lay unconscious and badly concussed. He was sent back to Vienna and given a period of sick leave which he spent at Reichenau. It was October - their first wedding anniversary - before he was fully well again.

A new chapter was in any case beginning in this Autumn of 1912: Zita was expecting their first child. On 1st November Charles was promoted to the rank of Major and given a new posting to a different regiment: the 39th Infantry, based in Vienna. The Emperor further announced that they would be given one of the capital's royal palaces, Hetzendorff, as their home. They were being brought into the centre of things, after a happy year of domestic and military life without political pressures. The period of living as an ordinary army couple had been enjoyable but was now ending. There was no running away from royal duties.

The baby was born at Reichenau on November 20th: a little boy, in perfect health, third in line to the throne. He was christened with the Emperor's names among others: Franz Josef, Otto, Robert, Maria Antonia, Charles Maximilian, Henry, Sixtus, Xavier, Felix, Réné, Ludwig, Gaetan, Pius, Ignatius, in a ceremony performed by Cardinal Nagl using water from the Jordan. The Emperor stood as godfather at the baptism which was on November 25th.

The boy - always to be known as Otto - was welcomed into the world with massive local celebrations at Reichenau, the local people organising singing and festivities with the whole town en fête. Members of the Royal family including Charles' mother and two of Zita's brothers went out to greet people.

Hetzendorff was a beautiful palace - well known to Charles from his boyhood - and as the young couple settled into it with their baby they brought a breath of life to the royal scene in Vienna. A couple of years later one commentator looking back noted "At Kolomea his boyish simplicity and the girlish charm of the Archduchess Zita won all hearts, and when they left the Galician garrison to take up more responsibilities in Vienna - the Emperor Franz Josef fitted up for them the old castle of Hetzendorff near Schönbrunn - they had become the most popular of the younger members of the Imperial family."[3]

The Archduchess Zita was, of course, the first lady at court, because of the morganatic status of the Duchess of Hohenburg, Franz Ferdinand's wife. But both Charles and Zita were determined not to let their home become a focus of attention that would detract from either the Emperor or from his immediate heir. They managed to keep aloof from much of the political bickering that was part of Viennese court life. Franz Ferdinand had his own specific ideas about the way the Empire should be run, and was not shy about trying to lay the foundations for what he hoped to achieve once he inherited the throne. He believed very strongly that it was impossible to keep things as they were, with the Hungarians dominating the other races in their half of the Empire, and groups pulling in so many different directions with their national tensions and aspirations. With well-placed appointments and a good network of reports he was making his plans for the Empire's future. There was inevitably tension between him and the Emperor. Charles could have been in the unfortunate position of being caught between the two, or of making a third centre of power at Hetzendorff. He managed to avoid either of the two extremes, and remained on good terms with both his uncle and the Emperor.

Charles Polzer-Hoditz was later to recall that Franz Ferdinand found his position as heir extremely difficult because of the Emperor's unwillingness to keep him informed on topical matters: "The Archduke Franz Ferdinand complained . . . . that he had so little influence on the Government, and often did not hear of important decrees, even such as might have a future prejudicial effect, until after they had been published. He used regularly to add 'When I am Emperor, I shall have Charles with me in the Hofburg and let him work with me'. The heir to the throne, he went on, must be informed on all points; moreover he had the right to advise on measures which might have a decisive effect in the future. Only in this way could a change of rulers be effected without violent upheavals."[4]

Franz Ferdinand was now very happily settled in his domestic life at Belvedere Palace, not far from Hetzendorff. He and Sophie had three children: a little girl born in 1901 and named Sophie after her mother, and two boys, Maximilian and Ernst, born in 1902 and 1904. The Archduke was a doting father, and all the drama attached to his marriage plans proved to have been well worth while as his family life brought him great contentment. "Sophie is a treasure" he had written to his mother after the wedding, and a few years later in the same vein "You don't know, dearest Mama, how happy I am . . . . I cannot thank God enough for my good fortune . . . . . She is everything to me, my wife, my adviser, my doctor, my friend - in one word my whole happiness . . . . . And our children! They are at once my wonder and my pride. I could sit the whole day admiring them, I love them so much. And in the evening at home, when I smoke my cigar and read my newspapers, and Sophie knits, the children play about, and everything is so delightful and cosy!"[5]

Charles' family life, too, was giving him great joy: he and Zita were finding in their home and in their happiness together a source of peace and comfort that was to remain constant throughout the years ahead. The baby Otto was to be the first of a large family of children - eight in all - and Charles enjoyed being a father.

He and Zita had a relationship that was unusually close and binding: as one commentator was later to put it "Both shared the same deep faith, the same simple tastes, the same love of home and - not so far behind these three in enduring value for a marriage - the same sense of humour."[6]

They had taken with them to Vienna their happy sense of enjoyment of simple things - family togetherness, country activities, outdoor walks - that had hallmarked their courtship and early married life. From the beginning they had shared in common their strong religious faith and it continued to be a major focus of their life.

On a superficial level things seemed fairly serene in the Vienna of 1912/13. The future of the monarchy was assured by Franz Ferdinand, and Charles and his new baby showed a line of succession stretching far ahead. The old Emperor was the object of much veneration and respect. The city was famous internationally as a focal point of intellectual, artistic and social life. It exuded an air of prosperity and gaiety, of self-confidence and colour and life.

But there were many tensions within the Empire, and all sorts of forces pulling it in different directions. Budapest was the other centre of power in the Empire and the Hungarians had their own specific ideas about their future destiny. Their vibrant sense of Magyar nationhood did not sit easily alongside the national aspirations of other groups within the empire: Czechs, Slovaks, Slovenes, Croatians, Rumanians. Unlike Austria, Hungary did not have universal suffrage and the Magyars controlled the Hungarian parliament. The countryside was dominated by the large estates of the major landowners.

Within the Austrian part of the Empire pan-German sentiments were common among certain groups. They saw friendship and alliance with the neighbouring German Empire - presided over by William II and ruled from Berlin - as the cornerstone of foreign policy, and therefore viewed the Slavs as a likely source of dissent.

Most people in the Empire thought of themselves as Christians, and regularly celebrated the feasts and ceremonies of the Christian year. Amongst certain sections of the population however there was a feeling of detachment from the teachings of the Church and even some cynicism about them. Religion was too often thought of as being a part of folklore and traditional culture, not something that could have a significant impact on individual lives. This meant that newer alternatives - nationalism being one - quickly captured the hearts and minds of articulate people.

Tensions within the Empire were matched by those outside. This was a time of major rivalries: between Britain and Germany, each struggling to outdo the other in the size of its Navy; between Germany and France, in animosity which dated back to the Franco-Prussian war of 1871; and between Germany and Russia, with the latter worried about the former's growing industrial might and potential.

Above all, tensions were growing on the fringes of Austria-Hungary, amongst the Slavic races. Slavs within the Empire who sought a greater status were urged on by Slavs outside. In the past, most had thought more about their loyalties to the Empire than about their loyalty to their particular nation. This now changed. This particularly applied to those Slavs living in the Hungarian half of the dual monarchy. They suffered from the national chauvinism of the Magyar-dominated government. In contrast the minority nations in the Austrian part of the empire (where ethnic autonomy was respected and encouraged far more) tended to be more content. The Slavs in the Hungarian part of the Empire were sometimes more fervently loyal to the imperial idea which seemed to protect their interests better. Alternatively, they abandoned the Empire entirely and became separatist. The old loyalties: to Church and Monarch, to local landlord and to a simpler view of life which took no account of international status, were drowned out by the louder nationalistic voices clamouring for attention. The right of each specific group to a defined status within the Empire, the importance of asserting claims on language, culture and trade, the rivalries thrown up in a world where communication and speed of spreading information were raising new questions . . . . all these challenged the old certainties on which a central European empire had been based.

In Vienna, where the aged Emperor lived and worked with spartan personal dedication, all sorts of radical ideas were present beneath the surface. Challenging ideologies were springing up to oppose the traditional view of life: new ideas in psychology, in the education of the young, in politics, in religion. The Habsburg rule continued to promote and honour the ideal of inherited monarchy ruling over a family of peoples. By moving to Vienna the young Archduke and Archduchess and their family had come to symbolise the future of the dynasty, and were therefore already a powerful image of hope for continued Habsburg rule. But was it powerful enough? Cosy domesticity was not all that was being demanded of the monarchy at this time of rapid change. There was also a need for political vision, for acceptance of the need to adapt, and for leadership of an inspiring kind that could bring together creative forces. Leadership which saw in the Empire a rich set of possibilities for prosperity and peace.

Charles had often spoken about the future of the Empire with Princess Zita while they were engaged. Now, as he saw at first hand the various ideas that had been adopted by the various factions in Vienna, he came to realise the pressure seething within the wider Empire. He could not be unaware of the dangers and problems that lay ahead.

His own idea, of transforming the Empire gradually into a federation of self-governing states, was by far the most radical and visionary on offer in Vienna or anywhere else in Europe. His politics were less concerned with trying to play off one power group against another - as Franz Ferdinand was inclined to do in weighing up the varying demands of the Magyars and the Slavs - than with genuinely seeking a solution that was fair and just to all. When he finally became Emperor he would sum up his attitude towards the various races in the Empire by saying "A father has no favourites among his children". It was a view which was straightforward, and it is characteristic that when searching for a phrase with which to describe his idea he automatically found it most comfortably in one relating to family life. Family life meant not only domesticity but an appreciation of the value of each individual, an acceptance of eccentricities and faults, a commitment to mutual help and support, a sense of solidarity and teamwork to overcome difficulties - all things needed on the world stage as well as at home.

Notes:

1. Interview with *Jesus* magazine (Italy), 1988.
2. The Russian Orthodox ruler of the Russian Empire was also heir to a tradition which sought to link that Empire with the ancient Roman Empire. The word Tsar also derives, like Kaiser, from Caesar. The Russian claim stemmed from the traditions of the Eastern Roman Empire . When the capital, Constantinople, fell to the Turks in 1453, the Russian rulers claimed to inherit the Roman mantle. Russian Orthodox theologians developed a theory in which Moscow was designated "Third Rome" following after Constantinople and the first and real Rome.
3. *The Times*, June 29th, 1914.
4. Charles Polzer-Hoditz, *The Emperor Charles*, Putnam, London, 1930.
5. Quoted in *Franz Ferdinand - Der verhinderte Herrsher* by Friedrich Weissensteiner, Vienna, 1983.
6. Gordon Brook Shepherd, *The Last Habsburg*, Weidenfeld and Nicolson, London, 1968.

Chapter Five

1914 began on a happy note for the family at Hetzendorff Palace with the arrival, on January 3rd, of their second child, Adelheid. Otto, now over a year old, was already a much-photographed little boy. The young family's presence in Vienna created a happy picture of hope and security for the future of the monarchy.

Franz Josef had ruled for 66 years and was the oldest monarch in Europe. Over the border in Germany the Emperor William reigned supreme. He had inherited the throne while still a young man from his father, Friedrich III, who had died from throat cancer after a tragically short reign of only three months. Very confident, something of a show-off and fond of dressing up in his different uniforms, he was very proud of his Army and in awe of his generals. Kaiser Wilhelm was a complex character with a rather simplistic view of Europe and the world. He seemed unconscious of giving offence when he made loud assertions on topics that others found sensitive and he was certainly unaware of his own limitations and lack of long-term vision.

To the East, the Romanovs ruled in Russia. The young Tsar Nicholas and his German-born Tsarina, Alexandra (a princess of Hesse and granddaughter of Queen Victoria) must have envied Charles and Zita their healthy baby son. Their little boy Alexis, the Tsarevitch, or heir to the Russian throne, had been born with an incurable blood disease and would need constant care to bring him safely to adulthood. The huge Russian empire faced many problems. In the cities there was much squalour and poverty, and the great gulf between the social classes was a continuing source of tension. The situation provided rich opportunities for the promotion of the ideas of political revolutionaries.

Extraordinarily similar to the Tsar in physical appearance was his cousin George, King of England. Both wore identical pointed beards and had wide-set clear blue eyes: when they were photographed standing side by side they looked like twins. But their two countries were very different. George had only very limited powers as a monarch. He had a vast overseas empire: Britain was united with Canada, Australia, New Zealand, India and large parts of Africa including the Cape. He and Mary, his Queen, had received confirmation of their enviable and settled position with the acclaim of their people at their coronation three summers before.

The spring and early summer of 1914 were unusually pleasant and sunny. Vienna's aristocratic families were busy with summer plans for what looked like being a particularly enjoyable year. Charles and Zita had plans, too - they wanted to visit, together, St Cecilia's Abbey on the Isle of Wight where she had been so happy and where Cicca now lived. It would be a private visit where they could escape from official pressures.

At the end of June Archduke Franz Ferdinand was due to visit Bosnia to view the major military manoeuvres which would take place there. In his capacity as Inspector-General of the Empire's armed forces, he would spend two days watching the troops on exercise, and would then take the opportunity of visiting Sarajevo, the capital of the district. Thus he would be able to make the Royal presence in the area whilst forming some idea of local views and feelings, in what was strategically an important region.

As a strong supporter of minority races in the Empire and in particular of the Southern Slavs, the Archduke was known to oppose the rigid Dualist structure of the Empire with its heavy dependence on the landowners of Hungary, and its cumbersome inability to respond to the aspirations of the varied national groupings. His visit would give him an opportunity to form impressions of the Bosnian situation at first hand. On the 23rd June he and Sophie left Konopischt, their castle which was some 30 miles from Prague, and headed south. They left behind them their children who were to await their return. Their son Max was due to take his exams at the Vienna Schottengymnasium - where Charles had been educated - and then the whole family would enjoy a month together at Chlumnetz, their other castle in Bohemia, before a visit to the Tyrol. On 27th June the Emperor left Vienna for his annual stay at Bad Ischl, the spa in Gmunden, Upper Austria, which his visits had made fashionable. Charles and Zita were also out of the city, at Reichenau, where they were enjoying the quiet country life they loved best.

The manoeuvres of the XV and XVI Corps of the Army began at 2pm on June 25th and ended at midday on the 27th: they were very successful and the Archduke left the troops a warm congratulatory message and sent the Emperor a telegram reporting on a happy trip: "An excellent spirit and a high standard of education and efficiency," he noted "Hardly any tiredness, everyone fresh and awake. Tomorrow I visit Sarajevo . . . . "

June 28th was a warm sunny day which brought crowds out on to the streets of the town to greet the Royal pair. But there was tension in the air - there had been rumours and counter-rumours of various plots planned by different factions against the visit. In an instant these exploded into high drama. From somewhere in the crowd a bomb was suddenly thrown at the Archducal car. It fell on the roof and rolled off, exploding behind the vehicle and seriously wounding a member of the entourage, Colonel von Merizzi, who was in the next car. Sophie was grazed on the neck by pieces of the flying cap of the bomb that hurtled through the air. While von Merizzi was rushed to hospital the Royal couple were driven swiftly to their next destination, the Town Hall, which was only a few hundred yards ahead. Here lunch with official speeches had been arranged, but any chance of a happy mood had been destroyed. "Of what use are your speeches?" the Archduke is reported to have said to the Provincial Governor, General Potiorek, "I come here and bombs are thrown at me". All the formalities seemed empty, and the programme was hurriedly changed: the Archduke and the Duchess wanted to visit Colonel von Merizzi in the hospital where he had been taken. Count Polzer-Hoditz describes what happened next: "The chief chamberlain, Count Rumerskirch, then put to Potiorek the shrewd question where the garrison hospital was situated, and whether it could be reached without driving through the town. It was decided to drive, not through the town, that is, not along Franz Joseph Street, where the crowd was awaiting the passing of the Archduke, but along the Appelkai, which was now quite deserted. In front of the Rathaus, before they entered the cars, this decision was repeated to the chauffeurs several times, with the express order 'not along Franz Joseph Street, but along the deserted Appelkai". The Archduke's chauffeur had instructions to follow the car in front. But when it came to the place where the roads forked, the leading car did not, as it had been expressly ordered to do, drive straight on along the Appelkai, but turned aside, against orders, into the crowded Franz Joseph Street. The Archduke's car followed. Count Harrach [who was in the car with the Archduke, having already announced his intention of acting as his bodyguard in case there were any more assassination attempts] at once drew attention to this. Potiorek rose and shouted excitedly to the chauffeur "What are you doing? We are taking the wrong road. We were to go by the Appelkai". The chauffeur turned round to General Potiorek and came to a halt. Hardly had the car stopped when an arm holding a Browning pistol thrust out of the crowd lining the street close to the car. Shots rang out. At the first shot, the Duchess' head fell forward, and she slid to the ground by her husband's side; at the second shot, the Archduke put his hand to his neck and said "Sopherl, I beg you to live for the sake of our children! . . . "[1]

The assassin in the crowd, Gavril Princip, had known his moment. The Duchess was dead on arrival at the hospital, to which the car now sped. The Archduke died very shortly after arrival, without recovering consciousness.[2]

The terrible news hurtled across the Empire by telegram. To Ischl, where the aged Emperor was stunned by this latest blow in a life haunted by tragedy; to Chlumnetz, where the couple's young children were initially told only that their parents had been badly wounded, with the full news broken gently to them next morning; and to Reichenau where the telegram from the Archduke's aide de camp reached Charles and Zita as they were sitting at lunch in a little summer house in the mansion grounds.

The effect on them was shattering. Although their own immediate sympathy was for the couple's orphaned children, and then for the effect on the Empire of this horrific double-murder in broad daylight in the streets of a provincial capital, the long-term implications were in fact to affect them personally more than anyone else. They had seemed so safely remote from the awesome responsibilities of the throne, so secure in their quietly happy family life at Hetzendorff and Reichenau. Now everything was to change.

From this moment Charles was the direct heir to the 84 year old Emperor. At any time the full imperial mantle could fall on his own 26-year-old shoulders. Zita was only 22. Just four years earlier she had been a virtually unknown young woman studying in obscurity in a convent off the coast of Hampshire. Now she was at the centre of the European stage.

Charles telephoned the Emperor immediately at Ischl, and the latter announced that he was at once making his way to Vienna. Charles went there, too, to meet him at the station. By this time news of the tragedy had swept across Austria as newspapers rushed out editions bearing dramatic headlines and photographs of the murdered pair. Huge crowds gathered to see the young heir to the throne greet his monarch and travel with him back to Schönbrunn.

That night violence erupted in Sarajevo as Croats - supporters of the monarchy - demonstrated against the Serbs who were widely held responsible for the crime. The Empire's national anthem was sung by the Croatian crowds. The bodies of Franz Ferdinand and Sophie lay in a chapel surrounded by candles and flowers before being taken by train and warship back to Vienna. The long journey brought them to Austria's capital late on July 2nd. Darkness had fallen by the time Charles met them at the station amid the full drama of blazing flares, silent crowds and formal military mourning. Throughout the whole journey there had been gestures of homage and sorrow at the various stopping points by the public authorities and the armed forces. Now the two coffins were brought to the Hofburg to lie in state. From 8am on the Friday, July 3rd, people filed past to pay their respects. The queue stretched from the entrance of the chapel in the Schweirhof round the stately Josefplatz along the Augustinerstrasse and up the Ring to the outer Burgtor. Inside the building, candles in massive silver candelabara lit the scene. At Franz Ferdinand's head his general's hat, sash and sword lay displayed while nearby on a cushion lay his two jewelled coronets, a reminder that he had been heir to a double monarchy.

Pinned on a similar cushion near the Duchess' head were the poignant symbols of her femininity: a pair of white gloves and a black fan. The only formal floral decorations present were two big crosses from their children. In the evening after the crowds had gone there was a brief ceremony before the chapel was closed for the night. Ten Archers of the Life Guard in red tunics, white breeches and high boots, and ten Imperial Hungarian Guards in scarlet and silver laced tunics with leopard skins across the shoulder marched in and took up places beside the bodies. At a given signal their swords flashed from their scabbards and their headresses were put on and they stood motionless at attention. A few moments later the Emperor, in uniform, entered a small gallery on the right of the chapel close to the altar. Charles and Zita stood alongside him. Other relatives quietly filled the remaining galleries. The Cardinal Archbishop led the short service during which the coffins were blessed with holy water and incensed while prayers were sung.

The main funeral ceremonies later would include a full requiem Mass in Vienna - echoed by other services in all the major capitals of Europe as monarchs and government representatives met to pay their respects. The burial was at Arstetten, the Archduke's castle in Lower Austria not far from Persenbeug. Here Franz Ferdinand had some while before quietly made arrangements for his tomb. Jokingly, he had announced that he did not want to be buried in the traditional Habsburg vault in the Capuchin Church in Vienna because "I would never have any peace there with all the electric trams rattling overhead all the time". But undoubtedly his real reason was that in the Capuchin vault, he would lie separately from his beloved Sophie, whose body might be placed in a different part of the mausoleum because of her morganatic status.

In these first days after the shooting, the general mood of other governments and commentators across Europe was one of sympathy for the house of Habsburg, generally focusing on the dramatic lonely figure of the aged Emperor. His brother the Emperor Maximilian of Mexico had been assassinated by a firing squad of revolutionaries. His only son had died in still unexplained circumstances at Mayerling. His wife had been murdered by a casual assassin in Switzerland. In Britain *The Times* commented: 'After all the awful blows that have fallen upon him as a sovereign and as a man, it was fondly hoped by all who have watched the vicissitudes of his troubled life that the head of the House of Habsburg, the oldest of European Sovereigns, might be suffered to close his days in peace.... Brother, son and wife were torn from him, one after the other, by violent and sudden deaths. Now the pistol of a Slav assassin has taken the nephew who was to succeed him and the mother of that nephew's children. There are men and women in all states of life to whom fate seems ruthless, showering upon them one pitiless blow after another. But few amongst these children of misfortune can have had to suffer a succession of calamities so grievous as the stricken old man who sits upon the proudest throne on the continent.... "

The Catholic weekly *The Tablet* went further, mourning the loss, in Franz Ferdinand, of a man it considered to have been a strong hope for the future: "By this senseless crime is lost to the world a Prince upon whom Catholic Europe had learned to build her highest hopes.... a devoted Catholic and an eager soldier, a serious and earnest student of statecraft, as well as of the higher arts of war.... Whatever he set himself to do he seemed to do successfully, and his strong personality soon made itself felt as a power, first in the Empire and then in Europe."[3]

On the mainland of Europe, the death had stirred dynastic feelings among all the people who looked to the Habsburgs as a symbol of stability and security. Prince Hubertus zu Lowenstein who was a child in Bavaria at the time remembered many years later the fires being lit on the mountain-tops to celebrate Midsummer on June 24th and then the dramatic news four days later of the deaths at Sarajevo. His father ordered that the family's flagpole, which was flying the Bavarian blue and white flag, should instead fly the black and yellow flag at half-mast: "This was the flag of the House of Habsburg, and when I saw it waving in the gathering dusk, I knew that something terrible, beyond description, must have happened . . . . When I went out into the park, fires were burning again, not on the summits this time, but on the alpine meadows, half way up. Walls of fire - in mourning, and as a sign that the heir to all the crowns of Habsburg was dead."[4]

This crime, seen initially as a mere domestic tragedy for Austria-Hungary, was to set in motion a chain of events that was to engulf millions of lives. From the beginning, Serbian involvement in backing, encouraging or even organising the assassination, was strongly suspected.

The murder seemed to many people outside the Empire as a dramatic event which would nevertheless be absorbed by a dynasty which had seen so many other sorrows and extraordinary happenings. In the event however it had a much wider significance. The Empire had for a long time felt the pressure of lying between two other major powers - Imperial Russia on the one side and Imperial Germany on the other. The connivance of Serbia in the killing of the heir to the throne was not something that could be ignored or glossed over. For centuries, there had been tension in the Balkans where the Catholic Croats met the Orthodox Serbs who took their focus from the East. Austria-Hungary felt herself consciously to be a central meeting-point which gave the Slavs their doorway to the rest of Europe. A meeting-point that was only made possible by her own strong allegiance to the idea of European Christendom as a whole. The Empire's strong and deeply-rooted Western values, and its notion of unity-in-diversity with regard to the way its varied peoples lived, was threatened by the vastness of Russian territory. A small central European empire bringing together Slavs, Magyars, Southern Slavs and Viennese naturally felt the pressure of this massive presence on its Eastern borders: when this pressure was manifested in the killing of the heir to the Empire's throne, the Empire's own future demanded a response.

Today the standard historical view sees the Austro-Hungarian Empire over-reacting to a crime inflicted by a much smaller nation, Serbia. In order to understand the real issues at stake it is necessary to recognise the conflicting tensions present on the map of Europe in 1914.

This standard view is well summed up by a 1960s historian: "Austria was having trouble with her Balkan minorities who wanted to leave the Austro-Hungarian Empire and join independent Serbia in a Greater Serbia. Russia gave these minorities her tacit approval: Serbia gave them outright assistance. In July 1914, when a Serbian nationalist killed Archduke Francis Ferdinand, heir to the Austrian throne, the Austrians decided to punish Serbia and end the minorities problem for good. Russia promised all-out support for Serbia and called up her Army. Germany was already committed to help Austria in any Balkan dispute with Russia. Because France, her enemy since 1871, was allied to Russia, Germany felt she must act quickly and set in motion a plan for capturing Paris. The first step called for the invasion of neutral Belgium. That, if nothing else, brought in the British, who had guaranteed Belgian neutrality since 1839. What had started out as a punitive measure by an aged and insecure Emperor against his small-sized Serbian neighbour became, without plan or design, a World War between major powers - the Allies (Britain, France, Russia, Italy, Japan) on one side; and the Central Powers (Germany, Austria, and Turkey) on the other . . . . "[5]

This scenario merely gives the sequence of events, however, and does not satisfactorily explain the underlying realities which led to the war. Germany had its own rivalries with Russia, and perhaps inevitably saw the Austro-Hungarian Empire as ineffective in standing up for a pan-Germanic view. Germany's own aggressive stance and sense of identity was coloured by the fact that German unity had been brought about under Prussia: this state was dismissive of neighbouring Austria-Hungary's whole vision of Europe which rested on the rich traditions of its multi-ethnic links and loyalties welded together under Habsburg rule. What Germany wanted was a clear-cut chance to assert herself as the leading power in Europe, and thus to challenge Russia. The German agenda did not include a desire to foster a polyglot empire, able to draw together diverse nations and races in the heart of the continent, which was what the Austro-Hungarian Empire was all about. Germany had been opposed to this concept largely on religious, nationalistic and racial grounds.

The history of the North German kingdoms and Empire had run along parallel but opposing tracks to that of Austria-Hungary. Highly nationalistic, the make-up of the German Empire was in sharp contrast to the multi-racial empire of the Habsburgs. Almost symbolic of the attempts to supplant the Austrian empire by the German was the usurping of Haydn's famous birthday tune used for the Austrian Imperial Anthem "Gott erhalte". The replacement of the opening words "God defend and God protect our Emperor and our land", with "Germany, Germany over everything" was offensive to pious Austrian ears and represented an altogether alien philosophy of empire. This philosophy, based as it was upon ideas of national and racial superiority, monoglot, German, and of necessity expansionist, was to reach its awful conclusion in the appalling racial doctrines of the National Socialists .

With the strong sense of nationalist identity which was to be found in Germany, there was naturally a sense of rivalry with Britain. This was despite the fact that the two countries' royal families were closely linked by marriage and therefore should have been friends. Their rivalry had now been evident for a long time: over their respective navies, their world status, their colonial ambitions in other continents notably Africa, and the influence they had on other nations in Europe and around the globe. Germany envied Britain her world-wide Empire, her links with the USA, her sea power. Britain saw Germany as a massive power in Europe sweeping other nations out of the running, threatening the equilibrium of the Continent which Britain had worked so hard to establish and maintain. Neither had a real concern for Austria-Hungary, both tending to see it as something that could nevertheless be used for their own purposes.

France, which could have been Austria-Hungary's ally against German expansion, no longer had any sort of Catholic government and was led instead by people who had been trained to think that the age of monarchies was past and that all crowned heads claiming an ancient lineage could be a source of trouble. Italy - recently unified and now strongly nationalistic under its anti-clerical and anti-Austrian rulers - was equally ill-disposed towards the Empire .

Other factors in the scenario included pan-Germanism in Austria - essentially a negation of what the best of the Empire was all about, and easily fed by neighbouring Germany for obvious purposes - and the peculiar mood of many in Europe who wanted to believe that an old era was ending and were eager to participate in something new, without being quite sure what it was. The rapid industrialisation in Russia, the arrival of air travel - in however primitive a form - the long years of peace during which new rivalries had grown to be added to those of the previous century - all these played a part in creating a set of tensions between nations, a feeling of adventurous uncertainty among youth, and a notion that Europe was about to embark on a new era for a new century.

Charles played no part in the critical decisions that led up to the most fateful one of all, the sending of an ultimatum to Serbia. Trained as a soldier - and a loyal patriot - he knew what his duty would be if war came, but it was not part of his personality to long for that day or to see in the prospect of battle any real fulfilment of a country's ultimate purpose. Peace was to him the most desired of blessings and war a tragedy to be avoided if the welfare of the Empire permitted it.

Of course he shared the general indignation at his uncle's savage death - shared in it more deeply than many of those who were expressing themselves most ferociously on the subject. He had been close to his

uncle and had talked with him often and long about the future of the
Empire which was their responsibility, and of the hopes for the welfare of
people living under Habsburg rule. He had been a frequent visitor at
Franz Ferdinand's home, a welcome guest along with Zita at the family
table with Sophie and the children. The double murder was something to
which he could not but react with horror and anger. But he had as yet no
political role. It was not his signature which would be appended to any
official document committing Austria-Hungary's government or troops
to any specific action. When events began to slide towards war he had no
authority to stop them. All he could do was wait, support his Emperor
loyally, accept his own responsibilities, and pray earnestly that when the
time came for him to be the one taking the decisions he would act with
prudence and justice.

Others were more hot-headed. A pro-war faction took only a fortnight
to gain the upper hand fully. This faction then maintained their control
until the Emperor's signature had been obtained to what they finally
needed - a series of demands which effectively made it impossible for
Serbia to draw back from war. By the end of July the thing had been
accomplished. There was a sense of gleeful anticipation of an hour of
reckoning. The *Neues Wiener Tagblatt* of July 26th opined "The desire
to have finished with it is so powerful among our people that the news of
the presentation of our demands is looked upon as a release. Everybody
felt thus: 'If Serbia gives in, then we are safe, at any rate for a time. If she
does not give in, we will create tranquillity for a long time to come."' By
that evening, Serbia's final response - conciliatory but deemed to have
fallen short of what Austria-Hungary had demanded - had been published, and feelings poured over into exuberance. In Vienna, they found
voice in a strong feeling of pan-Germanism, with crowds singing "Die
Wache am Rhein", a stirring German, rather than an Austrian, military
chorus. Meanwhile in Berlin crowds swept down the Unter den Linden
shouting "Down with Serbia!" and even "Down with Russia!" -
although that country was at that time technically not involved in the
negotiations.

In Vienna as the news spread crowds marched to the War Ministry and
gathered around statues of national heroes. A large group sang patriotic
songs in front of the Foreign Ministry, waving black and yellow flags and
cheering any officer in uniform with wild enthusiasm. They tried to
march to the Russian Embassy to cause a disturbance there, and to the
Serbian Legation, but were prevented by police, and so contented
themselves by thronging down the streets to the German Embassy, to
cheer wildly.

At the official level diplomatic relations between Austria-Hungary and Serbia were now broken, the Serbian minister left Vienna, and the way was clear for the next inevitable move which was partial mobilisation of the Empire's forces. This was now ordered amid scenes of excitement at barracks and railway stations as the troops gathered to depart to their war postings. All ordinary life was now disrupted. Normal travel was suspended as the entire rail network was commandeered for war use. On 28th July the official gazette in Vienna issued the final and irrevocable statement: "The Royal Government of Serbia not having given a satisfactory reply to the Note presented to it by the Austro-Hungarian Minister in Belgrade on July 23rd 1914, the Imperial and Royal government of Austria-Hungary finds it necessary itself to safeguard its rights and interests and to have recourse for this purpose to force of arms. Austria-Hungary therefore considers itself from this moment in a state of war with Serbia." Serbia had in fact sent a more conciliatory note at a later stage but this, for reasons still mysterious, arrived too late.

Over the border in the Hohenzollern empire on August 4th the German parliament met in the Reichstag in Berlin in a mood of high enthusiasm for war. Emperor William addressed them and announced "From now on, I no longer know any parties, only Germans." He repeated what was now widely believed all across Germany - that the country had been the victim of an unprovoked attack, and that the war was an entirely defensive one. The newspapers had been paving the way. In the southern parts of the country there had been headlines announcing that French planes had been attacking across the border while Germany remained passive. Over to the North and East, Russia was seen as the great enemy and banner-headlines there highlighted the perceived threat from the Tsar's armies. After the Emperor William's speech there followed a report by the Chancellor Bethman-Hollweg which while giving a rather confused picture of the actual events which had taken place over the preceding days allowed the newspapers to assert confidently that Germany had been surrounded by enemies and forced into defending herself to protect her borders. The truth of course was otherwise.

Austria had an enthusiastic ally - one that was to cause heartbreak and tragedy in the months and years to come.

By the middle of August it must have seemed to Charles and Zita that the happy days at Hetzendorff and Reichenau before June 28th belonged to a different world. Charles rejoined his regiment in Galicia, and by his birthday on August 17th was away at the front where the fighting had begun in earnest against the Russians. Russia had by now committed herself fully to her ally Serbia in the rapidly escalating conflict. Their home at Hetzendorff was closed for the duration of the war and Zita went with the two children to Schönbrunn to be with the Emperor. This 18th century Royal palace, built by the Empress Maria Theresa in French style had seen much history. Napoleon had made it his headquarters in 1809, and his son, the Duke of Reichstadt, had died in the Empire Room. With origins dating back to the 14th century, and a total of 1,141 rooms, it would provide a dramatic setting for this next chapter of Habsburg history.

Charles had always loathed the idea of war and could not share in the excited idealised conceptions of it that now began to pour out in prose and poetry in magazines and newspapers. The savage realities of fighting seemed to be something that those who campaigned most energetically in favour of battle chose to ignore. Charles was under no illusions. "I am an officer with all my body and soul" he told Zita "But I do not understand how anyone who sees his dearest relations leaving for the front can love war."[6]

He was certainly seeing plenty of these tragic scenes. An eye-witness of one such departure, from Gmunden, would later recall: "I remember vividly the visit of the new heir to the throne, the young Archduke Charles, who inspected the troops going to the front. There was a solemn high Mass said in the parish church, a rather beautiful late Gothic building. Many of the congregation cried. There was no wild enthusiasm when we accompanied the young soldiers, their caps decorated with green twigs, to the railway station."[7]

Perhaps because of the very obvious geographical vulnerability of the Empire, people were aware that the war was going to be a source of sorrow and confusion as much as glory and splendour.

The Empire still represented a much older tradition of government, diplomacy, and war than some of the others that were now embarking on this massive conflict. Some of the flavour of this is conveyed by the reminiscences of an American priest, Father Francis MacNutt, who was living in Austria at the time. He was in fact a friend of the Royal family and of Charles in particular.

"Whatever the politicians in Vienna and Pest may have foreseen, nobody else appeared to imagine that the punitive expedition into Serbia was going to provoke a world war. As the declarations of war rolled in daily—from Russia, France, Belgium, and finally England—the gravity of the situation became apparent.

"We were plunged suddenly into the excitement of mobilization. Endless trains loaded with soldiers followed one another with intervals of but a few hours between, and at all the stations were throngs of people offering food and drink and flowers to the troops. How precious such provisions were soon to become, none of us realized!

"In our open car, I toured the neighborhood with Countess Wolkenstein-Rodenegg, making arrangements with the authorities at various points for the establishment of Red Cross centers. The high roads were well guarded by soldiers, the entrance to every village being barricaded and provided with a military patrol, where travellers had to show their passes. Improvised soldiers—raw country bumpkins—in their excess of precaution against possible spies, several times levelled their muskets full at us from a couple of yards' distance, until I protested to the commanding officer, saying I should report him unless he put a stop to such risky displays of superfluous zeal.

"It is interesting to recall the attitude in Austria toward 'enemy aliens' who found themselves within the Empire, because it so markedly contrasted with that of other nations. When war was declared on Serbia, the Commander-in-Chief of the Serbian armies was taking the cure at Gleichenberg. Instead of seizing and interning him, the Emperor gave him a special railway carriage to carry him over the frontier into his native country, where he assumed command of the forces. If this was foolish, it certainly was chivalrous; nor can we imagine Hindenburg at Vichy, Ludendorf at Harrogate, or Kitchener at Wiesbaden being thus treated. In Brixen, Lord Grimthorpe was taking the *Kneipkur* at the Guggenberg Anstalt; he finished his cure, unmolested, and departed without hindrance for England where, I imagine, he never dared say how well he had been treated. Also, a sister and niece of the Russian General Rennenkampf were likewise there, and were not only left perfectly free, but were allowed to spend the following winter in Meran."[8]

The position of Archduchess Zita's family was now an extraordinary one. They had grown up to feel cosmopolitan, and were strangely placed in this bitter new Europe of opposing armies. Her brothers Xavier and Sixtus badly wanted to join the French Army - as Bourbon princes they saw their natural destiny as fighting for France in time of war. Sixtus had been born in Switzerland - at Wartegg Castle, another Bourbon home - and after education with the Jesuits at Feldkirch in Austria had studied history and jurisprudence in Paris. Now he wanted, romantically but perhaps rashly, to hurry to serve France in the tradition of his ancestors. He and Xavier left Schwarzau for Vienna where they called on Charles and Zita on August 10. Charles was on the point of leaving to join his own regiment. Sixtus announced his plans. Despite the fact that they were now technically becoming enemy aliens the two Bourbon-Parma brothers were given permission to leave the country by car via

Switzerland and they arrived in Paris at the end of the month. However, their ideas about hurrying to France's aid were not shared by that country's republican government: they discovered that they were in fact banned by law, as members of a former ruling Royal house, from serving in the French army. Only some while later, after much lobbying of their other Royal relations, were they eventually accepted into the Belgian army, where they were to serve with distinction.

Two other brothers Felix and René' had taken a very different position. They automatically went to join the Austro-Hungarian army on the outbreak of war: they had grown up in Austria, their sister was married to the heir to the throne, and they felt more loyalty to the Empire than to any other particular state in Europe. The four brothers Xavier, Sixtus, Felix and René were photographed together - a solemn group - before going their various ways. By special agreement with the Army authorities, Felix and René were never sent to fight on the French front and so the family was spared the horror of having brothers ordered to attack one another in the field.

Zita was not to meet Sixtus and Xavier again for many months. They would meet again in the most dramatic of cicumstances in early 1917 when the fighting had dragged on for 2 bitter years and the feverish enthusiasm of the summer of 1914 was long over. This meeting would be a highly secret one after a dash by the two brothers back to Austria to meet Charles and Zita (by then Emperor and Empress) for the launch of a peace bid.

All this was however unthinkable in the heady days of the August outbreak of war.

At this stage of the war the dividing lines did not seem as clear-cut as they were to appear later: most Frenchmen felt that they were fighting Germany rather than Austria and old friendships, loyalties and links were not yet broken. Only later would the savagery of what was happening present a different scene. Sixtus himself would always remain convinced that a France/Austria partnership, linking Western Europe via the Empire to the Slav lands of the East, was in the best interests of all of Europe.

A tragic situation, with close relatives on opposing sides, developed during the war for several members of Royal families. To give one example, Britain's Prince Maurice, youngest son of Princess Beatrice (Queen Victoria's youngest daughter) was later to be killed serving with the British Army at Ypres, two weeks after his cousin, Prince

Maximilian, had been killed a few miles away serving with the Germans. The links between the British and the various German Royal families were extremely strong. The Prince of Saxe-Coburg Gotha, for instance, was completely English. He had been educated at Eton, and was the brother of Princess Alice, Countess of Athlone. He had only accepted the title - which of course had come into the British Royal family through Prince Albert - because it had come down to him when others in the family had not wished to accept it as they, being now members of the British Royal family, did not wish to live in the German state. As in other cases, a special agreement was made whereby he would not fight on the Western Front against his own countrymen. Some people who had previously been good friends, however, did have to face each other: the 3rd Hussars regiment from Britain, for instance, found themselves drawn up in battle against the 3rd German Hussars, only a few weeks after officers of both regiments had enjoyed convivial mess dinners during a courtesy visit earlier in that spring of 1914.

Zita's childhood home at Schwarzau was turned into a hospital for the wounded, and her mother joined the Red Cross as a nurse in order to be able to run it. Charles' mother, the Archduchess Maria Josefa, also joined the Red Cross and was soon immersed in nursing work.

Charles was first posted to the Army headquarters at Przemsyl where he served for several weeks, and then in September he was given a new role as liaison officer representing the Emperor on all the different battlefronts. This meant that he would be based in Vienna but would travel to the various regiments. When in Vienna he would be working alongside the Emperor: he was effectively being trained so that he could be ready and take over the reins of government himself at a moment's notice. Franz Josef knew that he would be giving his great-nephew the most difficult and heavy of burdens, and was at least trying to ensure that the handover would be as smooth as possible.

War fever had gripped Europe that summer: in Britain the posters were proclaiming "Your King and Country need you!" and young men were joining up, anxious not to miss the chance of being heroes, telling each other "It'll all be over by Christmas!". By the Autumn things were beginning to look different: by Christmas itself trench warfare had begun and casualty lists were growing.

But the mood in Austria-Hungary continued for these first few months to be optimistic. Pictures of the Royal family were sold as popular postcards: one was captioned "Three Generations" and showed the aged Emperor seated in full dress uniform, with Charles and little Otto - wearing a frilled smock and clutching on to his father's legs - standing alongside. Another, showing Otto in the same pose but this time alone with the seated Emperor, was on sale to raise funds for various war charities including the Red Cross. In the spring a new one appeared showing Zita arm in arm with Charles in the palace gardens watching while Otto with a small watering-can toddled along in a straw hat holding the Emperor's hand, under the caption "God save our Beloved Kaiser" and with a verse saying that the pretty picture showed a scene which secured both the present and the future.

But the tragedy of Austria's whole involvement in the war had begun even while the enthusiasm of the populace was at its height. As a later historian was to summarise it, "No formal military convention had ever been concluded between Germany and Austria-Hungary, nor had the two allies worked out a common war plan . . . . All Count Conrad, the Austrian Chief of Staff, knew was that the Germans intended to concentrate most of their forces in the West for a big offensive against France and would not intervene in the eastern war until they had defeated the French . . . . "[10]

The first wartime meeting between Charles and the Emperor William took place in January 1915 at the German military headquarters at Charleville. It achieved little in the all-important matter of establishing some clear war aims and working directly and specifically for the long-term objective of peace, although the talks were frank and the two men communicated well on a personal level. Charles, however, had no authority to act on his own initiative except under specific orders from Franz Josef: his own personal plans for peace, and dramatic ventures that sprang from his revulsion against the slaughter and conviction that the fighting must be brought to an end, would have to wait until the responsibility for ultimate decision-making was his.

Emperor Franz Josef was keeping Charles fully briefed on every aspect of the war situation and the two worked closely together, Charles reporting fully after every visit to the front. When he was back in Vienna he had official work to do of an increasingly urgent nature and there were long hours of meetings, paperwork, and reports. His little family was growing: a son, Robert, was born on February 8th 1915, and another son, Felix, would arrive the following year, May 31st 1916. Both were born at Schönbrunn. The Royal family continued to be popular with ordinary people, perhaps because they recognised in Charles a genuine front-line soldier and in Zita a wife and mother with relatives on the battlefield.

In the East, the front zig-zagged, victory favouring first one side and then the other. The swift, decisive war that so many had imagined and expected was to prove illusory. In March 1915 a fresh Russian breakthrough gave them Lemberg and then a few days later Przemysl, where Charles had earlier been posted and which had been considered an Austro-Hungarian fortress. Vast quantities of ammunition, food, and medical supplies were captured, and 126,000 officers and men taken prisoner. Bells of victory rang throughout Russia and the Tsar made a triumphant entry into Lemberg. However, in the first week of May the Russians were thrown back and the territory regained - by the end of the month the Tsar's army had been almost completely turned out of the whole area, and they continued to retreat all that summer, losing everything that they had earlier won.

While these battles were being fought by the Austrians along the border with Russia, a new and sudden move along their Italian frontier changed the course of the war and introduced a whole new dimension, one which was to have a particular personal significance for Charles and Zita.

The unified state of Italy, which had thrown Zita's father, Duke Robert out of the little duchy which his family had ruled for generations, had always coveted large areas of the South Tyrol which lay within Austria's borders. In the early months of 1915 a secret Treaty of London guaranteed to Italy a large tract of this land if she would enter the war on the Allied side. Hungry for these enticing spoils of war she declared war on Austria and on May 23rd threw in her lot formally with the Western Allies. Nationalist feeling was aroused in Austria. The battle against Italy brought out passions stronger than those which surrounded the fighting in the East. Eventually, in May 1916 Charles was sent to command front-line troops in a major offensive which would gain the main strategic objectives in the territory for Austria and create a temporary victory. He was put in charge of a specially-created unit, the 20th Army Corps, for this offensive, which involved some of the bitterest fighting of the war.

A lover of peace who would shortly stake his whole future and reputation in an attempt to bring the war to an end, Charles was nevertheless a professional soldier and a man of courage and resourcefulness in battle. By the end of May the Austro-Hungarian troops had pushed southwards, temporarily securing the territory and sending a message of cheer to the people back at home. Then a sudden new development far away on the Empire's eastern front - the Russians had made a significant breakthrough in Galicia - brought Charles a fresh posting there where he saw renewed action. This new Russian offensive which had begun in the first week of June was carried out by General Brusilov. "Fighting continued until the beginning of September," historian Richard Charques writing from Russia's viewpoint, notes.[11] "Relatively well nourished, the onslaught achieved swift and dramatic gains on both flanks. Brusilov's feat, assisted in part by the half-heartedness of the Slav elements in the enemy ranks, was indeed remarkable and demonstrated in striking fashion the Russian power of recovery. The Russian armies penetrated deeply into enemy territory and captured in all some four hundred thousand prisoners. Lacking staying power once more, their advance was halted by German reinforcements thrown into the battle and the offensive petered out." This offensive had done incalculable harm to Austria-Hungary, however. Many men had been lost - dead, wounded, or captured - and the quickening of the pace of the war had emphasised the vulnerability of the Habsburg empire, with its need to battle simultaneously on so many fronts.

While fighting both in Italy and along the Empire's Eastern border Charles had to deal with paperwork sent to him from Vienna: it was essential that he be kept in as close contact as possible with political developments and decisions. He also represented the Emperor at top-level meetings with Austria's ally, Germany, meeting the German Emperor William again in October for discussions on the progress of the war and on peace hopes. Over eighteen months had passed since their first meeting in January 1915 - months in which thousands upon thousands of young men had died in savage fighting.

Peace was the all-important goal now. The war had escalated beyond all recognition, the suffering being endured was appalling, the causes for which the nations had originally gone into battle were being obscured by layers of hatred and misery built up over the weeks and months of drawn-out slaughter.

The items on the agenda covered a wider range and were even more urgent than they had been at the first meeting: the importance of a clear statement of war aims, the pressing need for some concrete proposals to be put forward as peace terms to the Western Allies. Although the two men got on well personally, they differed so much in outlook and mentality that it was virtually impossible that communication between them could prove fruitful. William was all too evidently excited by the spectacle of his generals leading his army into battle, and emotionally incapable of listening to prudent advice or accepting political realities while surrounded by enthusiasts who were offering more thrilling alternatives. He wanted to be encouraged by talk of victory and cheered by morale-boosting news, not reminded of difficulties. Although not an inhumane man, he simply failed to share Charles' anguish at the suffering that was being endured by men in their thousands, strung out across

Europe in the grim trenches that now marked the battle-lines.

Nor was his Germany in any way similar to the multi-racial Austro-Hungarian empire with its innumerable tensions and local loyalties. To William, everything seemed agreeably straightforward: his enemies were those who opposed Germany, who sought the downfall of his nation or its place in the world and who wanted to assert themselves over him. He failed to recognise the wholly different perceptions and attitudes of the varied peoples grouped around the Danube basin. The loyalty that he demanded was not the same as that afforded the Habsburg crown by Croats, Czechs, Slovenes and Slovaks. In any case William was by now completely under the control of his generals. Initially dazzled by the war, he had increasingly become remote from its realities, allowed little say in tactical decisions by his military men who at an early stage had become dismissive of his leadership with its vacillation between euphoria and panic. He was becoming little more than a bombastic figure-head. "If people in Germany think I am the Supreme Commander they are grossly mistaken" he is said to have confided in a moment of candour. "The General Staff tells me nothing and never asks my advice. I drink tea, go for walks and saw wood . . . . "[12]

Thus Charles' first attempts to work out peace formulas stumbled on the blocks of his German ally's ideas and attitudes. It was a disappointed man who sent a report back to the Emperor and then returned to his own military post on the Eastern front.

Notes:

1. In fact these were not absolutely his last words: a moment later, when he was asked by an aide if he had been hit he murmured "Oh, no" before slumping forward. Polzer Hoditz's report comes from his book *The Emperor Charles*, Putnam, 1930.
2. The uniform he was wearing when he died is now displayed in the museum behind his old home, the Belvedere Palace in Vienna.
3. *The Tablet*, 4th July 1914.
4. *Towards the Further Shore* autobiography of Prince Hubertus zu Loewenstein, Gollancz, London, 1968.
5. Barbara Sapinsley, *From Kaiser to Hitler - the life and death of a Democracy*, Grosset and Dunlop, USA, 1968.
6. Interview with Empress Zita, *Jesus* magazine, Italy, 1988.
7. Prince Hubertus zu Loewenstein, *op cit*.
8. *A Papal Chamberlain: the Personal Chronicle of Francis Augustus Macnutt*, quoted in *The Wanderer* newspaper, USA, Aug. 3rd 1989.
9. Prince Felix subsequently married Grand Duchess Charlotte of Luxembourg who had succeeded to the Grand Duchy after her sister, Marie-Adelaide, had abdicated. Both Prince Felix and his son, the reigning Grand Duke John, served in the British Army during World War II. He arrived back in Luxembourg in Autumn 1944 with the liberating Allied armies and was later rejoined by his wife, Charlotte. This remarkable woman was accused by nationalistic French republicans after the First World War of

being pro-German especially when she became engaged to Prince Felix who had served in the Austro-Hungarian Army. She therefore held a plebiscite of the people who voted 90 per cent for retaining her as reigning Grand Duchess and only ten per cent for a republic much to the disgust of the "democratic" and republican Prime Minister of France, Clemenceau, who had hoped to annex Luxembourg into republican France. The "Tiger"- as he was called - had been outwitted by his prey, it seemed.

10. Hajo Holborn, *A History of Modern Germany 1840-1945*, Eyre and Spottiswode, London, 1969.
11. Richard Charques, *The Twilight of Imperial Russia*, Phoenix House, London, 1958.
12. Theo Aronson, *The Kaisers*, Cassell, London, 1971.

Chapter Six

On November 11th, 1916, Charles received the telegram that he had known must come. The Emperor was seriously ill and Charles was urgently needed in Vienna. The message reached him at Schassburg, and he set out immediately for the Empire's capital.

Everyone knew that the end of an era was approaching. On November 17th an official announcement was made in Vienna that Charles would "have charge of affairs of the realm conjointly with the Emperor". Franz Josef's last illness had begun with a bad cold, which had affected his lungs. His iron self-discipline never deserted him, and right up to his last days he worked on official papers and tried to keep to his usual self-imposed strict regime. Only a few concessions were made : when he said his prayers, for example, he found that he could no longer kneel at his prie-dieu and so was persuaded that it would be acceptable if he remained seated in his chair, with the prie-dieu in front of him.

Finally on November 21st the end came. In the morning he had received Charles and Zita in his room and had worked on some documents about army recruitment. By the evening however it was clear that he was slipping away. He had been persuaded to go to bed two hours before his usual time because he was so weary. Charles and Zita were summoned by his staff, and were in the room when he died in his sleep. His two daughters, Princess Gisela of Bavaria and the Archduchess Marie Valerie were also present, together with various high officials. All those present were praying the Rosary.

As he knelt in prayer, Charles must have felt the responsibility of his new position descend heavily upon his shoulders. When everything was over the small group left the room in silence. When, in an ante-room, people finally spoke, he found himself being addressed by a new title. Offering their condolences and respects, those present greeted Charles for the first time as "Your Majesty".

The people of the Empire, although they had known that their old Emperor was coming to the end of a long life, were still shocked at his death. He had reigned for so long that it must have seemed impossible to imagine a world without him. He had been something unchanging, a name which had echoed strongly from distant days in the previous century and provided a strong and certain link with the past.

Now he would be laid to rest in the crypt of the Capuchin church, among the bodies of his ancestors. While arrangements were made for the state funeral, attention was focussed on the young couple who were now taking on his mantle.

They were very much alone. Charles had not had a lengthy period of preparation before assuming the massive responsibilities of the crown. He had until two years previously been able to rest in the knowledge that he would be Emperor only in the distant future, with his uncle Franz Ferdinand taking on the burden before him. Since 1914 he had been caught up in war. He had no tried and trusted team of advisers, and had built up no set of court officials with whom he could work out new plans and ideas. Such people as he had worked with over the years were dispersed across the Empire at their various appointed tasks, working under the urgency and pressures of war. His own training had been essentially that of a soldier and although in the past months he had increasingly been taken into Franz Josef's confidence and given what training in statecraft was possible, he had to face the unknown future with very little guidance.

His first declaration to his people struck a formal note, and lacked any direct personal appeal. It did however include a phrase in which he pledged himself to "do everything to banish in the shortest possible time the horrors and sacrifices of war, to win back for my peoples the sorely-missed blessing of peace, insofar as this can be reconciled with the honour of our arms, the essential living requirements of my lands and their loyal allies and the defiance of our enemies". In spite of the stilted language and necessary use of ritual phrases it was a cry from the heart. The new young Emperor was to spend the whole of his reign in pursuit of a just peace.

But he was not going to be allowed to do so in a climate of openness to such a possibility. In Britain, *The Times* of 23rd November, commented acidly "There is no reason whatever to suppose that the young ruler will rise in character or in statecraft above the somewhat low average of Habsburg rulers". It went on: "When Francis Joseph succeeded to his uncle's throne in his 19th year, he had already shown qualities that seemed to render him not unfit for his task. He was a young man, but a man. The Archduke Charles Francis Joseph not only in his 19th but even in his 25th year was a boy, and in some respects a young boy. Two years of war may have hardened and sobered him, but great surprises would be felt by those who knew him between 1908 and 1913 if he were to show in any respect the qualities of a great monarch."

The new young Empress was dismissed with some gentle praise: "The Empress Zita is a simple, unaffected woman of great charm and attractive appearance". This is ironic in view of the way she was to be routinely presented by the British press and Foreign Office, in due course - as a scheming woman full of Bourbon intrigue and wielding considerable international influence.

The funeral of Franz Josef took place a few days later, on November 30th. At two o'clock the procession left the Chapel Royal, where the body had been lying in state, and wound its way slowly through the wintry streets, lined with troops and packed with silent crowds. It made its way to the massive St Stephen's Cathedral, where Charles was waiting together with a vast congregation.

Everyone present - and everyone reading the descriptions of the event in all the newspapers across Europe and America the next day - was aware that with this burial came the ending of a whole chapter of European history. But surely no one could possibly have imagined that the next full Habsburg funeral using the same Royal hearse would be that of the Empress Zita, 70 years later, in an Austria which had seen another world war and had been officially a republic for decades. In 1916 old Europe was tottering but still intact. While battles raged at the front, Imperial Vienna was still functioning as a royal capital and Charles was heading a group of official mourners who included the Kings of Bulgaria, Bavaria, Saxony and Wurtemberg, together with over 50 archdukes and archduchesses of his own Royal House and over 40 other princes and princesses.

The Cardinal Archbishop of Vienna officiated at the funeral, assisted by four other cardinals, ten bishops and 48 priests. When it was over, the coffin was slowly carried out of the church and the massive final procession to the Capuchin church for the burial began. Now Charles led the mourners through the streets. Dressed in uniform, his head bared above his long military overcoat with its formal black armband of mourning, he looked an impressive figure. With him walked Zita, dressed completely in black, and with a veil covering her face and falling to below her waist, while the train of her long skirt trailed behind her. Between the new young Emperor and Empress walked a golden-haired child, tightly holding his mother's hand and looking solemnly at everything that was happening. His white kilted coat bore a broad black sash and his bare head turned occasionally towards his father or out towards the crowds. It was small Crown Prince Otto, taking part in his first and unforgettable solemn public ceremonial.

At the Capuchin church all the ancient ceremonies associated with a Habsburg burial were carried out with due solemnity. The church door was firmly shut when the procession arrived, and from inside a monk enquired in a loud voice who begged admittance. The Court Chamberlain called out the Emperor's full name with all his Imperial titles, honours, and decorations. There was a dramatic pause before the answer came back from inside: "We do not know him". Only when the question was put for the third and final time and the answer given was simply "a mortal sinful man", was the great door opened. The body was admitted for burial and greeted by monks holding lighted tapers, who escorted it down to the crypt below. The whole entrance ceremony was a dramatic representation of the passing to a new kingdom where titles and those who hold them are judged by a more searching standard in the presence of a greater King. Seventy years later Zita's body would be brought to the same church in the same fashion, this time watched on television across Europe, with commentators pointing to the haunting echoes of Franz Josef's funeral in this vanished Europe of Imperial days.

Franz Josef's funeral had brought home to everyone in Vienna the fact that a new reign was beginning. During the long ceremonies, attention had focussed on the new Emperor and Empress, walking along with quiet dignity watched by the thousands who lined the streets. They represented youth and hope alongside a continuation of tradition.

The next major ceremony of Charles' life would take place not in Vienna but in Budapest. Although he had automatically inherited the throne of Austria-Hungary, his relationship with the second half of that Empire could not be considered sealed until he had been anointed and given its crown. The crown of the Magyars - St Stephen's crown - held a most precious and important place in the history and traditions of the Hungarian nation. In accepting it, a king of Hungary formed a special and spiritual bond with the Magyar people. This was not mere symbolism: until he was crowned Charles could not rule, nor would the monarchy be secured.

But being crowned as King of Hungary posed problems. Charles knew only too well that the aggressive sense of Magyar nationhood with which the Hungarians wished to associate the crown was at variance with the legitimate hopes and aspirations of the many other races occupying the same territory. His personal wish to be a father to all his peoples, having no favourites and treating all justly, directly challenged the passionate Hungarian nationalism of the day. For years, the owners of Hungary's great estates had reacted furiously to any suggestion of change in the way the country was run, and specifically to any opportunities for other races in what they deemed exclusively Magyar territory.

For Charles, the problem was a deep one. To him, the coronation would hold a profound religious significance. For Count Tisza, Hungary's Prime Minister, the ceremony was essentially a celebration of nationalist pride. When Charles opened talks with him on the whole question of the coronation, Tisza argued in favour of having the ceremony as soon as possible. But Charles was less sure. He was particularly concerned about the wording of the oath that he would have to take. This bound him to protect "St Stephen's lands" and seemed to imply a total commitment to Magyar domination. Could he in conscience swear it when he had every intention of giving the other races their full say in the Empire's affairs?

Finally the constitutional arguments won the day. Charles *must* be crowned: if he failed to become King of Hungary the Empire would be faced with a massive internal crisis just when it was fighting a desperate war on two fronts. Hungary's agricultural resources were badly needed to feed the army - and the hungry people of the Empire's towns and cities.

The date was fixed for December the 30th - barely a month after Charles had become Emperor. All the festivities, banqueting, and celebrations that normally surrounded such an event as this would of course not be happening. Charles was emphatic on that point: no time should be spent in balls and feasting while men were dying on the battlefronts. For him personally the religious significance of the ceremony was in any case the most important thing.

The crown of St Stephen linked him with the very beginnings of Christianity's arrival in Hungary. Stephen inherited the throne of the country in 997 from his father, Geza, who was the country's first officially Christian king. Stephen took his new faith seriously: he had been ten years old when both he and his father were baptised and he deliberately took the name of the martyr Stephen mentioned in the Scriptures as being stoned to death for witnessing to his faith in Christ. Charles knew the story of Stephen's life very well: the battles fought and won against pagan nobles, the founding of monasteries, the establishment of Hungary's first proper church structure with bishops and dioceses. The ancient coronation robes which Charles would wear, and the ceremony in which these would be given to him, all dated back to those distant days of the 10th century or had origins that were lost in the centuries in between. They represented a heritage of faith that was splendid, and solemnly rooted in bedrock to an ancient tradition.

Years later the Archbishop who crowned Charles would recall "He prepared himself conscientiously for this great ceremony. He examined every detail and pondered the inner meaning of it all. Like a priest before his ordination - that was how devout and prayerful the King was before his coronation. I often had the opportunity of speaking to him during the period of preparation beforehand, and I remember observing him at the rehearsal as well as at the coronation itself. It was moving to see how the difficult burden of the feelings of responsibility had imprinted itself on his young soul.

"It was neither the ornamentation nor the pomp that interested him, it was only the duty, that he was undertaking before God, before the nation and before the Church. He wished to be worthy of this, for which he had been chosen."[1]

On Tuesday December 28th, *The Times* in London duly reported that the Imperial pair were setting off from Vienna to Budapest for this great ceremony. By the strangest of coincidences, the main headline on the same page was of a submarine raid on a remote spot that would one day play the most poignant part in their lives, and be for ever associated with Charles' story - Funchal in Madeira, where he was later to be exiled.

Meanwhile Budapest put on a fine display of Magyar nationhood for the coronation. All the members of the aristocratic families who qualified to attend the solemn ceremonies in the cathedral had robes made or produced ancient family heirlooms for the occasion. Carriages were taken out from their old coachhouses and painted and repaired. Despite the wartime gloom - perhaps because of it - Budapest set out to mark the occasion in style. Although there would be no dancing or banqueting, nothing could stop the sense of history, of pomp and majesty.

The Royal family gathered for the occasion, Charles' mother Maria Josefa and Zita's mother Maria Antonia of Bourbon-Parma among them. Crown Prince Otto was to take part in the service wearing a traditional Hungarian costume, and an ermine-trimmed robe and headress with a feather cockade. Zita's white satin coronation gown richly embroidered with royal motifs would be topped with a white veil and the Habsburg family crown, while Charles' own head would carry the ancient St

Stephen's crown, the central part of which was the domed crown which Pope Sylvester III had sent to St Stephen for his coronation in the year 1000. Stephen's wife was Gisela, sister of Henry of Bavaria who became the Emperor St Henry II. Tradition said that it was she who had embroidered the coronation cloak which would be placed around Charles' shoulders. Charles was inheriting not only the Magyar crown, but also, and especially importantly, the links with what had been the Holy Roman Empire. For Charles this ancient and sacred charge soared above the petty chauvinism of modern nationalism.

The setting for the pageantry in which Charles and Zita would play the central roles was the Matthias Corvinus Cathedral, named after the 15th century king of Hungary who died in 1490. The streets approaching it were hung with decorations and garlands, and from early in the morning a great stream of carriages carrying those who would be attending poured steadily towards the building.

The last coronation that Charles had attended had been that of George V in London's Westminster Abbey. That had, of course, been a ceremony of the Church of England, but remained in many respects indistinguishable from the Christian coronations of other countries. In the anointing with oil, crowning, and presentation of orb and sceptre, there was profound religious symbolism. The crown was linked to the crown of thorns that Christ had been forced to wear on Calvary, the sceptre to the reed which was mockingly placed in His hands. For a Christian king, educated in the Catholic faith, with an understanding of the role that Christianity had played in the formation of the civilisation he was to inherit, receiving these symbols represented an awesome and serious commitment. The orb - the round ball topped with a golden cross - which Charles was given to hold in his hands while seated on the throne after the crowning - represented the rule of Christ over the whole world, and the Emperor's rule as father of his people as a representative of Christ the King. The prayers, psalms and hymns of the coronation service all served to emphasise the great antiquity and sacred nature of the office that Charles was now accepting, temporarily putting the tragic current events surrounding Hungary into a different perspective.

Charles would always see his coronation as the time when he undertook a solemn contract with his people - and for him this meant all his people and not just those of Magyar blood. For many of the onlookers, however, the occasion served only to increase Hungarian pride and nationalist enthusiasm, focussed on the young ruler whose arrival on the scene offered new hope and encouragement. The clash between these perspectives was essentially that between an idealistic and practical ruler who saw his task in the perspective of history and eternity, and the narrower outlook of a people for whom surging nationalist feelings had become a substitute for moral and religious beliefs.

Yet it would be uncharitable to deny that the Magyar spirit also had great strengths. The ringing patriotism which was so apparent at Charles' coronation would be echoed down the years by brave Hungarians. These would include Cardinal Mindszenty, a successor of Cardinal Csernoch at Budapest, who underwent torture, a show trial, and imprisonment at the hands of Communist rulers in the 1950s. It would also include the young men and women of the city, who struggled to free it from Communist rule in the Uprising of 1956 which was so viciously crushed by the might of the Soviet army. They were also the inheritors of this long tradition of Magyar nationhood.

In 1916 these events were all part of an unknown future. The city which was celebrating a sense of its own status and identity, could not know that it would be many years before a Habsburg would once again return to this church to be acclaimed by a great crowd.

The coronation ceremony took place within the Mass and the Hungarian primate, Cardinal Archbishop Johannes Csernoch, already quoted, would later remember Charles' intense seriousness about every detail. "In the soul of the devout King there was a sense of the holiness of the crown deeply imprinted . . . . He was sincerely striving to adhere to and to accomplish the things that he was to promise on oath. And he wished that during the Coronation, in which not only the words but also every gesture and every action had its symbolic meaning, everyone would know and understand. His behaviour was open and humble, devout but dignified."[1]

For Charles a most solemn moment was the oath that he took at the altar. This pledged him, among other things, to work for peace and be a just ruler. These were themes to which he would return again and again during his reign - and afterwards. But perhaps to most of the people present the outdoor ceremony which followed had a greater drama. Here, religion gave way to folklore. Having taken a promise to defend the territory and maintain the integrity of "the boundaries of Hungary and her associated territories", Charles then rode up the ceremonial mound which was made up of earth from all the different parts of Hungary and pointed his sword to the four corners of the compass. Then church bells pealed out and gun salvoes were fired. Shouts of "Long live Charles!" rose up from all the assembled onlookers.

Crown Prince Otto would later remember sitting next to the King of Bulgaria: "He was very concerned that I should be told carefully about what was happening, but it was a long ceremony for a small boy. He kept quietly showing me the various details, explaining things, and pointing out who all the different people were."[2]

Because of the wartime sufferings of his people Charles expressly ordered that no expensive presents were to be given or received for the coronation. The only gifts presented were commemorative photographs in silver frames which were given to the bishops and dignitaries who performed the ceremonies.

For Hungarians - and more specifically for those who wielded power and owned great estates - this coronation was a celebration and affirmation of their most ancient traditions and rights. To Charles it was essentially something different: a religious event which consecrated him in service. Later he would look back on it not as a tribal ritual but as an occasion on which he had formally accepted a commission from God and asked for strength to fulfil it.

During the months to follow, Charles would recognise bitterly the gulf that separated him from Hungary's nationalists, and specifically from the narrow and pompous opinions of the great landowners.

However this was a time of hope. Charles' and Zita's attractive family life was highlighted by the coronation. This had shown them to be a team and within the faces of their children could be read the promise of a glorious future. For an Empire which for so long had had its loyalty focused on an ageing, lonely figure, these first few weeks of Charles' reign seemed full of happy omens.

These events were happening at the traditional symbolic time for fresh beginnings: a New Year. When Charles and Zita returned to Vienna after the coronation, the world was set to welcome 1917, and people throughout Europe must have wondered what it would bring to the battered and bleeding continent which was in such sore need of good news.

In Vienna Charles began the task of creating a government. Count Polzer-Hoditz, whom he had known for years, was a loyal and trusted man: Charles now appointed him head of his private office, and a *geheimrat* (privy councillor). Holders of major offices under the Crown had traditionally been members of the aristocracy: Polzer-Hoditz had been ennobled for his services to the Empire but did not belong to a great land-owning family. He would serve Charles with exemplary loyalty. The two men shared a common understanding of the Empire's role in Europe and of the great possibilities it represented, as well as the grave dangers which it faced.

Charles now hoped to achieve peace abroad and internal reform at home. The Empire needed vigorous and courageous leadership to bring it through difficult times to what could be its special destiny in the 20th century: the drawing together of mixed peoples in a common home at the heart of the continent of Europe. The Hungarian domination of other races needed to be tackled, action towards the long-term dream of some sort of federal system initiated, and above all peace achieved both on the Eastern front and with the Western allies, including Italy.

The options open to Charles were limited. There were no enthusiastic would-be statesmen waiting in the wings. Polzer-Hoditz modestly claimed his own limitations. He would prove a loyal head of the Private Office but felt himself to be essentially a civil servant lacking any political experience. Austria-Hungary's recent history had not provided a fertile training-ground for men who could combine parliamentary ability with good communication skills and a depth of vision. The Empire needed men concerned with the fate of all the peoples who were drawn together under the Imperial rule and not just with some of them, and concerned, too, about the whole of Europe and the pressing need for peace. The years of stability, and Franz Josef's own competence in handling the affairs of the Empire had left a gap which could not immediately be filled by a young inexperienced monarch, however gifted he might be. This might not have mattered, were it not for the particular combination of events and personalities which were working against the Empire.

As Foreign Minister Charles chose Count Ottokar Czernin, a member of an aristocratic family from Bohemia. Perhaps at the time something of Czernin's sense of flair and confidence communicated itself to the Emperor and made the choice seem to be the right one. However as a later biographer of Charles was to put it, Czernin was "lazy, unstable in character, unpredictable in temperament and arrogant to a fault."[4] He lacked any real political experience. He had had a series of diplomatic appointments achieved through family contacts but he had never passed the official diplomatic examinations. He had become a delegate to the Bohemian Diet and, in 1912, the Upper House.

Charles' overriding concern was to find a team who would produce practical possibilities for a peace initiative. Czernin's enthusiasm and air of competence must have been invigorating - but he was to bring the Emperor only humiliation and sorrow. From a poor selection of candidates, Charles had made his choice. As Polzer-Hoditz was to put it sadly and succinctly "Unfortunately, his choice proved not to be a happy one."[5]

As Prime Minister, Charles apointed Count Clam-Martinitz, another Bohemian nobleman, but of a different sort - gentle, courteous, and well-intentioned although ineffective. As Prime Minister of Hungary, Count Stefan Tisza was retained - a stalwart Magyar nationalist.

Charles was to spend much of his reign - as he had already spent much of the war - travelling. He set up his Army headquaters at Baden, not far from Vienna, where he used the Kaiserhaus, a small building in which the formality and officialdom were kept to a minimum. In early 1917 he and Zita made their home at Laxenburg nearby, travelling to Baden each morning.

The plight of ordinary people throughout the Empire was grim in this winter of 1916/17. Charles ordered that the carriages from the Royal palaces should be commandeered to help with the distribution of coal - a move which made him popular among many people but which was privately sneered at by some of the "old guard" at court.

The official propaganda was still speaking about "our glorious troops" and their victories. A book about the new Emperor and Empress, published for schoolchildren to mark the coronation, described the Imperial couple's youngest child, Felix, born in May 1916, as having arrived "in the sight of victory" after the successes in the South Tyrol.[6] But in reality, the potential nationalist splits, the growing misery and poverty caused by the war, the unremitting death toll from the battlefronts, and the pressure of having to fight Russia, Britain, France, and Italy, with the ever-present threat of being effectively swallowed up by Germany, made the Empire's plight a tragic one.

In attempting to grapple with the problems of his people, Charles faced entrenched opposition from those who should have been in a position to see the absolute necessity of reform. These included people in the military establishment, who failed to see the importance of uniting the whole empire, and specifically its minority races, in a common cause. Count Polzer-Hoditz recalled "At the beginning of the war Austrian patriotism, to the amazement of a great many people, was displayed by all nationalities and by all classes of the population. It should have been carefully guarded as a most precious possession. It was military justice which destroyed it. From the outset, the military authorities saw a traitor or an enemy in every Czech, every Serb, every Pole, and every Ruthenian. There began those sensless persecutions by means of which, aided by the supineness of the Government, the secession of the non-Germans in Austria was slowly but systematically effected. The Slavs whose sentiments were Austrian - and there were a large number of them - were forcibly driven into the camp of traitors and enemies . . . .

" . . . . For the overwhelming majority of the peoples of the old Danube Monarchy, the Austrian and dynastic point of view was not an 'affair of the stomach' to which level Count Czernin tried to reduce all patriotism, but an affair of the heart."[7]

Even those who have never been soldiers will be aware of the great dangers in failing to perceive the loyalty of people from minority races in a multi-racial, multi-cultural empire. Throughout the war this danger increased, and the loyalty of minority ethnic groups was questioned in a way that offended them and undermined that loyalty.

The loyalty of ordinary people to their Monarch and their Empire was strong. The Imperial anthem, although well known to Westerners in its German original, was sung in all the ethnic languages of the Empire: in Czech, Slovenian, Croatian, and Ukrainian. The fashionable intellectual currents of the age were against this staightforward and faithful loyalty. However, it was a loyalty dear to the hearts of devout people from many races, whether farmers or workers in the new industries, whose simple fidelity provides the strength on which any nation or empire depends. This had come to be despised by the destructive avant garde philosophies then in vogue.

Notes:

1. Cardinal Johannes Csernoch, May 1922, reprinted in the yearbook of the *Kaiser Karl Gebetsliga*, Lilienfeld, Austria, 1985.
2. Interview with the authors, summer 1988.
3. Gordon Brook Shepherd, *The Last Habsburg*, Weidenfeld and Nicholson, London, 1968.
4. Polzer-Hoditz, *The Emperor Charles*, Putnam, London, 1930.
5. ibid.
6. Leo Smalle, *Kaiser Karl, ein Bild seines Lebens*, Schulbuchverlag, Vienna and Prague, 1917.
7. Polzer-Hoditz, *op.cit.*

Chapter Seven

During 1917 Charles' main concern was to obtain peace, and everything that he sought to achieve in his foreign diplomacy was aimed at this end. But of course he also had work to do at home: namely the transformation of the Empire which he had always envisaged. The tragedy was that while war was being waged any reform at home - and especially the transformation of the old imperial idea into a federal union - was fraught with insuperable difficulties.

His chief ally in his attempts was Polzer-Hoditz, who saw the urgent need to draw up specific plans for immediate reform and used his position as head of the Private Office to set schemes for this before the Emperor. His idea was to give national autonomy to all the various groups within the Empire: it was an idea with which Charles readily concurred as it was wholly in line with his own thinking. Indeed he saw it to be an urgent necessity as the tensions of war had meant that people had been unable to express their needs and aspirations through the existing political framework. However, Charles was a constitutional monarch and he needed the support of his ministers. This proved much harder to obtain.

Charles was already known as a supporter of minority groups within the Empire. He recognised that many of the different groups clamoured for rights based on the history or territorial integrity of their people. Of particular importance was his relationship to the Czechs, who had long been campaigning for greater independence and status for their lands of Bohemia, and its natural capital, Prague.

The Czechs had over the years established powerful exile communities, especially in France, which were often led by people who had fled from the Empire because of their political aims and activities. Within the Empire, the chief clamour was not so much for independence as for a greater status for a full range of political freedoms. The Czechs within the borders saw in Charles a friend and ally. His liberal sympathies were known, as was his desire for peace and his concern for the rights of the poor.

The first Parliament of Charles' reign - indeed the first of the War, since Franz Josef had not seen fit to call one - met in Vienna in May 1917. It had been widely hoped that Charles' speech from the throne to this assembly would include some gesture - possibly quite a dramatic one–towards autonomy for national groups; but his speech was to prove a disappointment. Behind the scenes, Charles had presented his ideas, and the details of Polzer-Hoditz' suggestions for implementing them, to his Prime Minister Clam-Martinitz. But these ideas had fallen on stony ground. It was uncomfortably clear that no one among his government was prepared to back him by seizing this opportunity of transforming the Empire into something that could truly face the challenges of the new era. In Budapest the Magyar opposition was even more formidable. These were powerful obstacles for a monarch who had promised to rule constitutionally.

But he had far greater success with his next major domestic venture, in which he was operating in a sphere that was very definitely his alone. As sovereign, he had the ultimate authority for the dispensing of justice. For some while, he had been aware that trials of many suspected of treason against the state had been conducted unjustly, and that many were serving prison sentences which had been imposed as a result of rulings that had been blatantly politically inspired. He set Polzer-Hoditz the task of sifting through documents and checking information on the trials of various Czechs accused of treasonable offences which had been tried by military courts. The result was a wide-ranging amnesty, announced on July 2nd 1917, which freed over 2,000 people who had in effect been political prisoners. They were chiefly Czechs, who had been sentenced to varying terms for offences ranging from insulting the Royal family to disturbances of the peace. The amnesty caused a tremendous stir within the Empire - and among the Czech exile communities abroad who for the first time saw a possibility that their stance as heroes and representatives of martyrs might be challenged. Charles was, of course, criticised by hard-liners who saw in this dramatic gesture merely a weakness, and a concession to troublemakers.

For the Czechs, it might have been the beginning of a whole new era had it been followed up by some concrete proposals for political changes, but this was something Charles was unable to achieve. On 5th July he tried to establish a new committee under Dr Josef Redlich, with the aim of creating a team which would bring about the much-needed reforms. Redlich was unable to get support from his parliamentary colleagues, however, and the plan was still-born. By this time Clam-Martinitz had resigned as Austrian Prime Minister, and Dr Ernest von Seidler held the post he had taken over on 23rd June following the failure of the Clam-Martinitz government to get its budget passed because of its lack of commitment to any constitutional reform towards a federal system.

All of this formed the background against which Charles was carrying out his major work in 1917 - his work for peace.

In choosing the partner that he had - Zita of Bourbon-Parma - Charles had provided for himself, although he did not know it at the time, a remarkable and almost singular opportunity for pursuing peace initiatives with the Entente powers. For Zita's brother Prince Sixtus of Bourbon-Parma was, as we have seen, a serving officer, along with his brother Prince Xavier, in the Belgian Army. Charles grasped this opportunity with both hands. Peace was his ardent desire, so much so that after the war even his republican enemies did not deny him the title of "Friedenskaiser", Peace Emperor. No title could have pleased him more.

The initiative for what became known later as the "Sixtus Affair" began as the result of an article written by Sixtus in a French magazine. He was approached by members of the French government, and ultimately by the President, M. Poincaré himself, with a view to encouraging contact with his brother-in-law Charles, then still an Archduke, in Vienna. Even at that stage it was known that Charles was a partisan for peace and badly wanted an end to the war. When Charles became Emperor he quite independently asked Zita to contact her brother Sixtus with a view to making some representations to the Entente powers, and in particular to Britain and France.

Neither Zita nor Charles were hostile to France or Britain and personally felt more antipathy for the Prussianised militarism of the German government with whom by the accident of history, they found themselves linked as allies. Their views were commented upon by a British foreign office report marked MOST SECRET and dated June 3rd 1917. It is signed W. Gugoy and states;[1]

"From numerous conversations with the Princes of Bourbon-Parma (June 2, 3) the following points may be of interest:

1. The present Emperor and Empress are entirely pro-French and pro-English. They are strongly anti-German and hate (a) the Kaiser (b) Prince Rupprecht both on political and private grounds. The Kaiser

insulted the present Empress when she was young: Prince Rupprecht is a course [sic. must mean coarse] dissolute Prussianised atheist who bullies the Emperor and Empress for their religious and moral principles.

"The Emperor used to make an impression on the general public of being an amiable but colourless young man. In reality he is full of character and autocratic. He takes advice up to a certain point from the Empress, who is very intelligent, but is in no sense under her thumb . . . . All the recent changes have been made by the Emperor alone on his own initiative. He has become an immensely popular figure in Austria."

Thus within a few days of Franz Josef's death, peace moves were being made in both Vienna and Paris. The King of the Belgians agreed to the two Bourbon-Parma princes undertaking this mission and preliminary contact was made on 29th January 1917 in Switzerland with the Duchess of Parma, their mother. The terms included some of the points made by Sixtus himself as well as the demands of the Entente. The restoration of Alsace-Lorraine was called for, as well as the restoration of Belgium, with the Congo, the restoration of Serbia, with Albania added, and the succession of Constantinople to the Russians. None of these dismayed Charles. He sent a childhood friend, Count Erdödy, as his envoy to Switzerland, saying that he accepted all the points except for Serbia about which there was obviously sensitivity. Instead, he called for a monarchy to embrace Bosnia-Herzegovina, Montenegro, Serbia and Albania. Lorraine might well have presented problems, in the sense that it was part of the Habsburg patrimony because of the family's position as head of the House of Lorraine. But on this Charles had earlier made up his own mind, and decided that if it were neccesary to cede Lorraine for the sake of peace, then it should be done. The South Slav kingdom which he was proposing was in essence part of the federalism which Charles wanted to be the future for the whole Dual Monarchy.[2]

At this point there entered on to the stage Count Ottokar Czernin, Charles' new foreign minister. At first, he was enthusiastic, and sent a note to the Emperor on 17th February suggesting that the plan be pursued with all speed. But then, shortly afterwards, he sent a message with Count Erdödy to the princes saying that the alliance between Austria-Hungary, Turkey, Germany and Bulgaria was "indissoluble" and that the conclusion of a separate peace for Austria-Hungary was permanently barred. Czernin did not sign his memorandum - as was his usual habit he let it go forward without any signature - but it was obvious that he was its author. This action was typical of the attitude that Czernin was to display throughout the course of the Sixtus negotiations.

Charles' peace plan is worth comparing with that which had been suggested by the Pope,³ Benedict XV, a constant campaigner for peace since his accession to the papal throne. Charles' plan was similar to that put forward by the Pope, but was in fact even more generous.

The Pope had called for the return by the Entente powers of the German colonies. Charles was willing to give up Lorraine and in due course even Italy, but he made no initial call for the return of any colonies to the Central Powers. It is hard to see how Charles could have been more forthcoming, more determined for peace, and more willing to co-operate with anyone in order to achieve it. The difficulty on the Austrian side was the belief on the part of some of Charles' ministers, in the final victory of the Central Powers. They seemed to have an almost blind faith in this final victory and therefore none - with the exception, at this stage, of Count Czernin - were even prepared to consider a separate peace bid.

On 23rd March Prince Sixtus and his brother met Charles and Czernin at Laxenburg. Charles again stressed peace. Czernin on the other hand was cold and vague, questioning some aspects of the return of Alsace-Lorraine which his Emperor had already accepted. However, on the other main points, the restoration of Belgium and the setting up of the Serbian kingdom, there was no disagreement by Czernin.

At this stage there was no question of any territorial concession to Italy. Charles was prepared to say that this could follow but could not precede, in general terms, the settlement of peace with the other Entente powers, France and Britain.

Some years later, after the war had ended, Sixtus was to write about these peace negotiations: "There was considerable thought given to the principle of nationality. It was well known that the Emperor of Austria had very clear views and decided willpower on this point, that he was in accord with the cherished hopes of Poland, Bohemia, Croatia and Yugoslavia. The most bona fide representatives of those countries had expressed their entire confidence in their young sovereign. But there was no desire to go further, or to destroy further. Nobody wished to break essential and necessary bonds or to arouse interior and exterior hatreds between neighbours whose interests were naturally and solidly similar . . . . . The young Emperor was innocent of his predecessor's faults and had come to the throne with only one desire, which was to put an end to the universal slaughter. He wished to play an untramelled game, face to face with his associates and face to face with his enemies, in order to provoke a possibility and a necessity for peace. The Emperor Charles would have gone ·on further, for his duty clearly showed him that he could not uselessly sacrifice his people to the obstinacy of an ally whose pride was causing his coming destruction . . . . a separate peace with Austria would have realised the principle object of the war. It would have brought about invincibly the submission of Bulgaria and Turkey. The facts of 1918 have proved how easy it would have been after 1917 to come to an understanding with these two powers. The war would have been concentrated on the French front and brought about the results obtained eighteen months later. The lives of thousands, nay millions of men would have been saved."[4]

After the March meeting at Laxenburg, the princes extracted a promise from Czernin that he was fully behind the peace proposals, despite his constant looking towards Germany and his fear of the consequences. Charles took the step of committing himself in person. He proposed a letter in French which although addressed to Sixtus was in fact intended for President Poincaré and the Entente powers as a whole. This famous Laxenburg letter to Sixtus was a source of much recrimination and scandal when it was finally made public later in circumstances which were in total antipathy to its contents.

In the letter Charles ceded, most importantly of all, Alsace-Lorraine. He agreed to restore Serbian sovereignty and to allow it access to the Adriatic. However, he required - not unreasonably - that the kingdom of Serbia abandon all links with clandestine groups aimed at the destruction of the Empire and the monarchy. The basic desires of all Charles' enemies were therefore met except for those of Russia and of Italy, whose hold on the Entente powers, through the secret London Treaty of 1915, continued. Of course at this stage Charles was totally unaware of this treaty.

Although Alsace-Lorraine was a traditional Habsburg land, it in reality at this stage belonged to Germany, and Charles therefore lost no time in arranging a meeting with Emperor William to discuss the future of this territory. They met at the German headquarters at Homburg on 3rd April. The Chancellor and Foreign Minister of Germany were also present, and they represented, (along with the military leaders) the real power. Emperor William had already agreed to the peace moves in principle in February, but did not know about the details.

Unfortunately William was still under the thumb of his generals, and they did not look favourably on peace moves. Charles later confided to his wife that he was considering the risk of "going it alone" on peace initiatives, because he did not feel that the Germans could be brought to reason. He was prepared, meanwhile, at these negotiations at Homburg, to abandon a cherished Austro-Polish policy whereby a separate Polish kingdom under the Empire was to be established. He was now prepared to see the new Polish kingdom attached to Germany, even to the extent of giving up the Austrian province of Galicia (which was Polish-speaking and would form part of the new country). This policy of a separate Polish state was also in accord with papal policy, although it had never been intended that this Polish state would be so closely linked with Germany.

Charles, as ever, was prepared to make whatever concessions were necessary to obtain peace. This was a very considerable gesture, but the Germans neither accepted nor rejected it. It would have been considerably to their benefit, but their aim was still final victory: the dream with which the government, the military leaders and to a lesser extent the nation were so dazzled.

Charles was unwilling to conclude a separate peace without Germany at this stage. He was to do so later, but even then only because the Germans were still refusing to join in with peace talks which had already been outlined with the Entente. There was always the danger, while Germany remained powerful, that they would turn their attention to Austria - indeed German plans already existed to invade Austria and take control if it was deemed necessary.

On 6th April 1917, the USA, driven to the brink of neutrality and beyond by the German U-boat campaign against her shipping, declared war. Charles had opposed this campaign before it had even begun. He had gone to make personal representations to William saying that a submarine campaign on shipping would only escalate the progress of the war and cause the USA to join the Entente powers. But even before he had made these representations, Germany's military leaders - unknown to him and at that stage even possibly to William - had made their plans and sent the U-boats out to sea. Now the chickens were coming home to roost, and Charles had been proved absolutely right. The USA declared war against Germany, just as he had predicted - though they did not declare war, for the time being against Austria-Hungary.

The American involvement was to prove decisive. The end of 1916 had brought a stalemate on the main battlefronts of the war. It was thus a perfect moment for the peace moves which Charles was making. Unfortunately (and typically) the approach to the war of Vienna and Berlin differed considerably. William and his generals hoped to achieve their aim of victory by intensifying the war, irrespective of the feelings of their Austrian allies. Charles' own generals tended to support the Germans, mesmerised by the idea that on the high seas the mobility of the Central Powers would ensure victory. In fact Charles saw more clearly than his own military and naval advisers, despite their experience.

Repeated attempts by Charles to convince William on these matters proved fruitless. William merely parroted the cry of his generals that England would be defeated so quickly that the USA would not have time to come into the war.

The differences in outlook between Austria's "Peace Emperor" and Germany's warlord were well illustrated at a lunch-party during the official visit by Charles and Zita to William's headquarters. One of William's admirals, Holtzendorff, said to Empress Zita during lunch that she sounded as though she was against war. She replied that she was indeed against war "as every woman is who would rather see joy than suffering". Her expression angered the Admiral and he retorted grandly "Suffering? What does that matter? I work best on an empty stomach. It's a case of tightening your belt and sticking it out". Zita said "I don't like to hear talk of sticking it out when people are sitting at a fully-laden table," and cut short the discussion.[5]

Charles knew that the entry of the Americans into the war in April would lead to the disintegration of the Central Powers. Speed was of the essence if a diplomatic breakthrough was to be made. Less than ten days after Charles had left Homburg following the meeting, one of his aides appeared at the German HQ with a special despatch for the Emperor William. It was a memorandum from Czernin to Charles which in essence said that an end to the war must be made "at the latest by the summer or autumn of 1917" and that if the monarchs were not capable of concluding a peace then "their people will do it for them over their heads". Although technically signed by Czernin and addressed to Charles it was clearly the work of Charles himself. It was aimed at impressing on the Germans how desperate the situation really was. However, he received only William's standard reply, saying that England was about to give in, and that time was on their side. It seemed that Charles could not hope for anything from his German allies.

On 31st March 1917 Sixtus returned to Paris with Charles' Laxenberg letter. Previously, on 19th March, the French government had fallen and a new administration headed by Alexandre Ribot had come to power, replacing the government of Aristide Briand, who had been much more favourable to a peace settlement with Austria. Ribot was a small-minded and weak figure. After the accession to power of his government a very marked reluctance began to appear on the part of the French to pursue the Austrian peace moves.

Ribot and the British Prime Minister Lloyd George discussed the letter at Folkestone on 11th April, at a meeting specially convened for the purpose. Immediately, the problem of Italy arose. This was because of the secret agreement made two years earlier, when Britain and France had promised territorial gains to Italy (then an ally of Austria) through the Treaty of London in April 1915. This Treaty had been undertaken in order to secure the allegiance of the Italians to the Entente at a time when the combined might of the Central Powers loomed large. Arguing from a position without any real strength, the Italians were able to gain considerable territorial concessions on paper. In the treaty Italy had been promised the twelve Dodecanese islands from Turkey, some African territories, and the following from Austria: Trentino, up to the Brenner Pass (with a quarter of a million German-Austrian inhabitants), the Austro-Hungarian port of Trieste, all of Istria up to the Quarnero and some off-shore islands, half of the Austrian province of Dalmatia, and other islands along the coast. Considering that no Italian soldiers were on any of these territories, nor looked as if they would be for the foreseeable future in the spring of 1917, these demands represented aggrandisement at its worst.

Unfortunately the Italian Foreign Minister Baron Sidney Sonnino, who had been largely responsible for negotiating the Treaty on Italy's behalf, would prove to be the principal obstacle in the way of peace negotiations upon which Charles had entered with such high hopes and enthusiasm. The anti-clerical and half-English Sonnino opposed Austria at every turn.

Ostensibly, Lloyd George and Ribot could not discuss the letter outright with Sonnino in view of the oath of secrecy they had agreed with Prince Sixtus. Perhaps Sonnino would have remained intransigent even if he had known the contents of the Laxenberg letter. In any event he was opposed to a separate peace with Austria since he stood to gain so much more by sticking to the London Treaty. It seemed that Charles' generosity and open-handedness were not to be emulated by the Entente leaders. Ribot in particular and to some extent Lloyd George allowed themselves to be used and manipulated by the Italian Foreign Minister even though he was arguing from a position of military weakness.

At a meeting in the French Alps at St Jean-de-Maurienne on the 19th April the Entente ministers agreed on a negative formula stating that it would not be opportune to enter a conversation with Austria which might be dangerous for the unity of the Allies. It is hard not to feel that larger views of post-war settlement were clouding the minds of the Entente ministers as much as any real desire to end the bloody slaughter of the trenches. Whilst they may have felt honour-bound to abide by the London Treaty, in view of the weakness of Italy's position and the generosity of the Austrian offer more magnanimous leaders would surely have grasped the opportunity to save a generation being bloodied in the trenches. In view of the slaughter which followed, and the tragic events which came after the cessation of hostilities, the verdict of history must be that the allies lost a considerable opportunity for a lasting settlement in middle and eastern Europe.

The sinews which bound the Entente together were certainly stronger than those of a mere secret treaty. There can be little doubt that the political sympathies of the three ministers were joined in one aspect, if no other: they believed that the days of a strong central European monarchy were, if not over, then at least drawing to a close. This they saw as the irresistible hand of progress. While it may have been their desire to reach peace it was equally their desire to secure a post-war settlement which would build a new Europe based on this philosophy.

Without such a philosophy, and without ideological antagonism to a central European multi-national Empire, the weakness of the Italian position would have been seen for what it was and the possibility of peace would have been seized. A way to take advantage of the Austrian offer could easily have been found and the threat by Sonnino to defect from the Entente, based as it was on his desire to acquire territories which in any event were not in the gift of the Entente, could have been found.

The only man in whose gift the territories were had already shown himself willing to make concessions in order to achieve peace. If Emperor Charles had been made aware of the secret treaty and of the position of Sonnino he might well have been willing to extend the same generosity towards his Italian enemies. In the end he did this anyway.

What was the cost of the failure by the Entente ministers to take advantage of this momentous turning point? One must not forget that much slaughter in Flanders and the fierce and terrible fighting in the Alps of the Southern front were yet to come. Peace negotiations, if they had been made, would have saved Europe from this. Can there be any doubt what the peoples of the Entente powers would have wanted, if they had been given the choice? Emperor Charles, it may be fairly said, had these interests close to his heart. Can the same be said of those ministers who claimed to represent their own people better than any emperor? Ultimately it is a practical and not an ideological judgement.

As Prince Sixtus was to write after the war: "From a general point of view it was evident that breaking the united peoples grouped around Austria from their common concord through and with her meant breaking a breach in a historical bulwark whose value and necessity had long been proven against whatever hegemony threatened Europe from east or from west . . . . a separate peace with Austria would have realised the principal object of the war . . . . the general moral and economical exhaustion would not have reached the maximum level which it reached quickly after the war, all the more that Europe retained her customary life and order. Russian Bolshevism did not and could not enjoy the impunity which allowed it to organise its work of diabolical destruction. In short, the world's disease would have been checked before poisoning the human organism so deeply that it could only be cured by convalescence that was longer and often more painful than the evil itself. The result must have been too magnificent and too clear in the eyes of the negotiators for them not to have put all their energy into achieving it. Every man of mind or heart should have seconded them. Three men who were, for the moment, three irresponsible sovereigns caused its wreck: M. Ribot, Signor Sonnino, and Count Czernin. Sonnino I can understand a little, but the others?"[4]

As this was written in 1922 Prince Sixtus was then unaware of the horror that was to come which may be said to have resulted directly from the break up of Eastern and Central Europe: the Stalinist destruction of the 1930s and 40s and the rise and fall of that most terrible of all pan-German enthusiasms: National Socialism. The Austrian house-painter Adolf Hitler and his Nazi followers would claim to represent the new aspirations of the German people.

Neither can Lloyd George, whom Sixtus delicately omits to mention, be completely absolved from blame. His subsequent actions during the war and after, not least at the Treaty of Versailles, are revealing of his own views. Some of these views were most boldly stated, as for instance in the 1930s when he referred to Hitler vocally, and in glowing terms, seeing him as Germany's saviour.

On 20th April Lloyd George had another meeting with Prince Sixtus in Paris in which the British Prime Minister attempted to put the position of Italy. He said, according to Prince Sixtus, that Italy had felt that she "could not possibly make peace terms with Austria in which her own war aims were not realised".

Sixtus asked what Italy demanded and Lloyd George replied that they sought the Trentino, Dalmatia, and Trieste, although the latter might be the subject of discussion. It became clear that until Austria showed herself willing to cede these territories to her former ally the Entente would be unwilling to arrange peace terms.

Yet the weakness of Italy was amply demonstrated by concurrent events. This weakness almost made her claims too ridiculous even to discuss, were it not for the fact that Ribot and Lloyd George had given them their full backing. Incredibly, a separate peace gesture was to come from the Italian army commander, General Cadorno, and this from motives that were purely military. With low morale, and lack of any success against the might of Austria on the Southern front, Cadorno had realised that his army could go no further and that defeat was around the corner. Although acting on his own initiative he did have some political support from Sonnino's rivals such as Giolotti, Tittoni, and possibly King Victor Emmanuel himself. This gesture occurred before the meeting in St-Jean. An Italian officer arrived in Berne, Switzerland, and approached the military attaché of the German Embassy. In return for the cities of Trent and Aquila Italy desired peace and wanted the Germans to press the Austrians to agree. Two things joined to lessen the effect of this step. Firstly, it was regrettable that the first step was made to the Germans and not to the Austrians direct. Secondly, peace optimism was high in Vienna and the prospect of a separate peace being negotiated with Italy took second place to the negotiations with France and Britain. Charles still, of course, knew nothing of the secret London Treaty which was continuing to exercise its ill effects. Charles had no reason to believe that the French, and in particular Ribot were not well disposed to his peace offer.

On 7th May Sixtus and Charles met again at Laxenburg. The Emperor, on the strength of this discussion, agreed to cede certain parts of the Trentino and South Tyrol which he himself had defended in battle two years earlier. It was a gesture of considerable magnitude, and incidentally more than the Italians themselves through Cadorno were wanting. But Charles was now dealing, as he thought, directly with the Entente powers through Sixtus. He was honest enough to be direct in these dealings with the Entente, and did not undermine the negotiations by dealing with the Italian military at the same time. If he had known that his honest and earnest intentions were not reflected by the leaders of the Entente powers he may well have acted differently.

Again Count Czernin made an unhelpful contribution. He pencilled a curt note to Charles' own memo to Sixtus. While Charles noted the agreement between France, Britain and himself, Czernin spoke of absolute rejection of one-sided territorial concessions. Sixtus, returning to Paris on 20th May to talk to President Poincaré and Prime Minister Ribot, noted that while the President was "sharp, observant and incisive," Ribot on the other hand saw difficulties at every turn and appeared "aged, worn, and inactive". Subsequently on 23rd May Sixtus met Lloyd George at Downing Street, where the idea of a transfer to Austria of a German or Italian colony seems to have been ruled out. Later on at a meeting of heads of state, Ribot went so far as to show Sonnino - despite his solemn pledge that he would never show it to anyone - the entire Sixtus correspondence. One wonders why therefore he felt it necessary to retain secrecy in respect of the London Treaty, but perhaps he had other motives and foresaw, as has been mentioned, a particular kind of post-war settlement more favourable to the aims of republican France. By 5th June Prince Sixtus had still had no positive reaction from the Italians as he waited in Westminster to hear the result of the representations which Lloyd George claimed to be making to the Italian king. By 25th June he had finally given up and returned to his regiment on the Belgian front.

Charles never received a direct answer to his second Laxenburg letter. Indirectly, a rejection was to come in a statement to the French parliament by M. Ribot on 12th October 1917. The French Prime Minister apparently lacked the strength of character to give an outright "no" to the Emperor.

As for Lloyd George, the view that he continued to support the Austrian peace move by attempting to draw them out of the war or, as he was to put it, to "knock them out of the war" seems to contain an internal contradiction. The secretary to the Cabinet, Sir Maurice Hankey, paints Lloyd George in a favourable light with respect to the peace negotiations. We who live at a later date in history will know that Cabinet Secretaries, eminent though they may be, are not beyond the possibility of being economical with the truth! He was asked by Lloyd George to provide memoranda of the Sixtus affair and he produced three documents pointing to the reasons behind his master's activities.

The Hankey papers state that Lloyd George felt that Italy might have to be compelled to acquiesce, and that Sonnino should not be allowed to stand in the way of a separate peace with Austria. However, since the Cabinet decided that the acting Secretary of State for Foreign Affairs should send a telegram to Rome asking Sonnino to meet the representatives of the British and French governments, and that a committee on war policy should be set up, and nothing more, one cannot actually say that Lloyd George achieved a great deal on this matter. Neither can one really say or believe that if Lloyd George had wanted to press his Cabinet further he would not have done so if it had suited his aims. The last part of the resolutions touched upon in Hankey's memoranda shows another side altogether. Lloyd George in the second half of 1917 wanted to "knock Austria out of the war" altogether, seeing here a considerable gain for the existing grand strategy of the Entente. Yet the implication that the memoranda gives us is that he was intending to help Austria. That is one way of viewing the situation and one that we might expect from a loyal Cabinet Secretary. It seems more likely that Lloyd George was making use of the knowledge that he had of the Austrian willingness to sue for peace (with its implication of a weakening resolve to fight) to defeat them on the field of battle or in some other way. This would tend to accord with his own political aspirations which envisaged a very different post-war map of Europe.

By far the most important question to be considered by the British Cabinet's Committee on War Policy (set up on 8th June 1917) and quoted in the Hankey memorandum, was whether they should concentrate on an attack on the Western front or instead concentrate on the Italian front and attempt to knock Austria out of the war entirely. Since, as we know, Austria was quite prepared to make a separate peace and to negotiate away large sections of her territory even on the Italian front, the suggestion that the British government and Lloyd George in particular had Austria's peace motives principally at heart is stretching a point too far. Their main aim of which they never lost sight was to win the war on their own terms. Lloyd George came out with all the force he could muster for the second of the two alternatives presented: a knock -out blow against Austria. This was hardly a peace gesture and still less a handsome return to the offer made by Emperor Charles. Hankey quotes Lloyd George as saying that "there was not the smallest doubt that Austria was anxious to be out of the war. This was not a matter of conjecture but of absolute knowledge. Austria however would not be willing to pay the price demanded by the Allies, although if another blow were struck against her she might be brought to accept our terms . . . . " This in fact was false. We know Emperor Charles was indeed willing to pay the price that was being demanded at the time by the Allies, the only exception being the absurd demands of Italy which not even France and England were prepared to entertain seriously. Indeed General Cadorno who was Italy's military man on the spot was not prepared to entertain them either.   Thus it seems quite obvious that Lloyd George saw in the peace offering made by Emperor Charles a sign of weakness which he was determined to exploit. While Lloyd George's views did not prevail over those of his generals (who opted for the Flanders offensive) we can be certain of one thing: if the peace initiative offered by Charles had been agreed upon no offensive in either Italy or Flanders would have been necessary at all, and the lives of millions would have been saved.

At the end of the offensive which began with Passchendaele, the British Army in Flanders had lost 400,000 men and in the view of many military observers was in a worse position than it had been prior to the offensive. Interestingly, at the same time in August 1917 another secret Austrian dialogue had started, the so-called Armand-Revertera talks between a

French Army major and an Austrian diplomat. The initiative came from the French side with the General Staff, and not the diplomats, suggesting that if Austria withdrew from the war, and ceded Trieste and the Trentino to Italy, she might be rewarded by having the whole of pre-1772 Poland as well as Silesia and Bosnia added to the Empire. This was all handled on the Austrian side by Czernin, and the intermediaries had no knowledge about the Sixtus talks going on at the same time. It was an interesting attempt by the French military but never gained the necessary political weight to have any hopes of success. It shows, however, something of the attitude of the French military to Austria.

The situation was well summed up by the Austrian minister in Berne, Musulin, who complained in the spring of 1917; "If things go well for the Entente, they don't want to hear of peace. If things go well for us, the Germans exclaim 'Don't hurry!' "

One might be tempted to ask again why Charles did not break with Germany publicly and force an end to the war in this way. The briefest of analyses of his situation quickly disposes of this question. To begin with, it must be remembered that the young Emperor ruled over not one nation but many: a polyglot empire, which was now threatened by the fierce passions of nationalism. The Hungarians, the chief partner in the dual monarchy, were traditionally pro-German. Their tendency to chauvinistic nationalism combined with disloyalty to the crown had aroused the ire of Archduke Franz Ferdinand, the murdered heir apparent. That his fears were amply justified was demonstrated after Charles came to the throne. Finally, there is no doubt that the Germans had plans to occupy Austria should the need arise. In no time the Imperial government would have found itself completely isolated, surrounded by enemies both inside and outside the Empire. The only hope for saving the integrity of the Central European bulwark would have been a guarantee from the Entente powers. This would have demonstrated their support for any unilateral peace moves.

Much was later made by the British press and government of the role of the Empress Zita, with British voices holding aloft ancient shibboleths and appealing to latent anti-Catholic prejudices and old fears, with veiled references to "Bourbon intrigues". With hindsight such attitudes look pompous and absurd, as well as tragic. Prince Sixtus, writing after the war, put the record straight: "Legend says that my sister the Empress played a principal part in these negotiations. Too feudal to love intrigue for the pleasure of it, she was content to write me this charming letter as a woman and as a sovereign, begging me to come to Vienna: 'Do not let yourself be held by considerations which in ordinary life would be justified. Think of all the unfortunates who live in the hell of the trenches and die there every day by the hundreds, and come!'"⁶

We know now that peace guarantees were never given by the Allies despite every concievable concession on the part of the Austrian peace-emperor. It is surely an inescapable conclusion that despite the differences between the rival nations and political factions there was in fact a *de facto* agreement, among the powers, that Austria-Hungary must go, and go it did, with dire consequences for the whole continent of Europe. It cannot even be said that these consequences were unforeseen. They may have been unforeseen by the new model statesmen of Europe and America, but they were not unforeseen by the 30-year-old Austrian Emperor, whose far-sightedness many ignored.

Notes:

1. Public Record Office, file FO 371-3134.
2. The importance of Lorraine cannot be overstressed. Between the German-speaking and French-speaking peoples it had always represented either a source of contention and conflict or else provided a bridge of reconciliation, a link symbolising a common heritage and civilization. It was the middle part of Charlemagne's Empire and bequeathed to his grandson Lothar from whom it was subsequently named Lotharingia - ultimately Lorraine in French and Lothringen in German. It was then imbued with special significance by reason of its being the Duchy of Godfrey de Bouillon, Duke of Lower Lorraine, the ideal knight of medieval Christendom, the leader of the 1st Crusade, liberator of Jerusalem and elected Advocate of the Holy Sepulchre. His descendants were styled King of Jerusalem (the Latin Kingdom of Jerusalem). This title was re-acquired by the Habsburgs. When Francis, Duke of Lorraine, very wisely married Maria Theresa, the renowned successor to the Habsburg lands, he was elected Emperor at her insistence and their joint Habsburg-Lorraine inheritance was enhanced and preserved very successfully and with immense popular support.
3. Pope Benedict XV, *Letter to the Leaders of the Belligerent Nations*, May, 1917.
4. Prince Sixtus of Bourbon Parma, *Afterthoughts*, Dublin Review, 1922.
5. Gordon Brook Shepherd, *The Last Habsburg*, Weidenfeld and Nicholson, London, 1968.
6. Prince Sixtus of Bourbon-Parma, *op.cit..*

Chapter Eight

With the coming of the New Year in 1918 it seemed that any possibility of a breakthrough via the Sixtus negotiations had come to an end. If peace proposals were to come, it seemed that they would have to come from elsewhere. However, the affair did not die - far from it. In fact it rebounded back on Charles with a terrible force.

A series of events beginning with a seemingly unimportant speech by Count Czernin combined to strike the Empire with what may possibly have been its mortal blow. It seemed a cruel blow of fate that such a worthy undertaking, begun as it was with such optimism, such open-handedness and such sincerity on the part of the young emperor, should become when wielded by malicious hands an instrument not of peace but of destruction.

On 2nd April 1918 in an address replying to the Vienna Burgomeister Dr Weisskirchner, Czernin referred in the course of his comments, which were in some respects inflammatory, to the attempted Armand-Revertera peace negotiations. He blamed France for failing to grasp the opportunity to prevent the slaughter on the Western front, and in particular pointed to Clemenceau as putting Alsace - Lorraine as an obstacle in the way of peace. Clemenceau immediately fought back, calling Czernin a liar.

Clemenceau had taken over as French Prime Minister in November 1917 from Ribot. Although not aware at this stage of the Sixtus negotiations he did know about the Armand-Revertera attempt. While it was not fair to accuse him of anything in connection with the Sixtus affair it was certainly true that he had no intention of relinquishing France's desire for Alsace-Lorraine. Perhaps understandably there was frustration on the part of the Austrian negotiators who felt that they could not trust the succession of French leaders with whom they had to deal and who seemed determined at every turn to block the most generous peace initiatives. There is equally no doubt that Clemenceau, like his predecessor Ribot, was no lover of the central European Catholic Monarchy, and was indeed a republican French nationalist of the most ardent kind.

Additionally, the legacy of M. Ribot's dealings with the Sixtus affair and his lack of scruple in revealing secret negotiations now continued with a full revelation of the Sixtus affair to the new Prime Minister Clemenceau.

Both of Charles' Laxenburg letters which should not even have been in the possession of the French now lay before Clemenceau in copy form. The powers of the Quai d'Orsay prevailed over President Poincaré and the disclosures were made despite the earlier vow of silence. Here again the selective nature of the French government's attitude towards the keeping of secrets can be seen. The London Treaty with Italy was kept from Charles, but the much more explosive Laxenburg letter was revealed to the world.

It had been agreed by all involved that Prince Sixtus would show the second Laxenburg letter to the French but not allow it to be retained. However, while it was in their possession they broke their promise by making a copy.

Clemenceau's scruples ran no deeper than Ribot's and he was determined to use this new intelligence to embarrass the Emperor and his foreign minister to the full.

Clemenceau had been stung by Czernin's speech in Vienna and he began to make public reference to earlier negotiations than the Armand-Revertera dialogue. By these he meant those of Prince Sixtus. Czernin in reply stated that he "unhesitatingly affirmed" the earlier exchange but noted that this attempt proved as unsuccessful as the latter. In this he was indubitably correct.

Clemenceau now began to turn the knife. He brought Charles' name into the debate for the first time. On 9th April he rebutted Czernin's assertion that France's claim to Alsace-Lorraine had always blocked negotiations, by saying that the Austrian Emperor had given his definite support to the just claims of France in respect of this territory in March 1917. Furthermore, he referred to the second Laxenburg letter which mentioned that the Emperor was in agreement with his foreign minister on this point. He called upon Czernin to make a full admission of his error. Thus while Czernin had been foolish in some respects, it was

Clemenceau who was now treacherously going back on the word of his predecessors, on whose promises, it might have been fair to assume, he was bound to act. Here the frustration felt by the Austrian negotiators in dealing with successive French leaders can be fairly understood.

Czernin for his part seems to have allowed this frustration to overrule his judgement. Eventually, but too late, he realised his error and then instead of thinking of his loyalty to Empire and Emperor, he sought only to save his own reputation. He was particularly concerned about his note accompanying one of the Laxenburg letters which would certainly have proved his own personal involvement in the matter. In fact, his unsigned note was missing from the French files, but he had no means of knowing this.

At this point it is worth noting what agreed arrangements had been made between the secret negotiators in the event of disclosure. Charles stuck almost rigidly to what he had agreed and in this he was almost alone. It had been agreed with the French that in the event of the exposure of the negotiations a formal denial of the existence of the correspondence should be sent to the German Emperor and that this would be taken as a signal for Paris not to push the matter further. Thus Charles sent precisely such a telegram on 10th April 1918 after Clemenceau's revelation. As has been made clear, it had been agreed that no copy of the Sixtus letters were to be kept by the French. Charles himself had kept drafts of the letters in a locked desk in Empress Zita's bedroom. Czernin had a copy of the second letter. This had been a mistake, because it meant that Charles could not be sure that the French had a true copy.

On 12th April, far from abiding by the conditions which had been agreed via Prince Sixtus, Clemenceau proceeded to publish the full text of Charles' March Laxenburg letter. This included the all-important promise that Charles had made that he would support the French claims to Alsace-Lorraine by exercising his personal influence with the Germans. The perfidy of such an action on Clemenceau's part can scarcely be overstated, in view of the high hopes for peace and the generous gestures which accompanied the writing of the letter.

The behaviour of Count Czernin was scarcely better, and he became agitated to the point of pursuing his Emperor with threats. Czernin descended on the Imperial couple at their military headquarters at Baden bearing a "declaration of honour" which he had written in his own hand and which he tried to induce the Emperor to sign through various threats. It contained numerous false statements including a denial of the true version of what had been said about Alsace-Lorraine. That day, 13th

April, the Emperor had suffered a mild heart attack. His general condition had for some time been weak. Nevertheless he had to deal with the by now unbalanced Czernin. When Charles refused to sign, Czernin threatened to warn the Germans - who already had plans to invade Austria. This continued for some time and in the end Charles was persuaded to sign the false declaration in order to pacify the Foreign Minister and to prevent him from calling Berlin. There was a faint hope that Czernin would, as he said, retain the declaration for his own personal security and no more.

In fact, as soon as the paper was signed the Foreign Minister immediately got under way for Vienna. Charles, alarmed, telephoned the guards to stop him and bring him back but it was no use - Czernin escaped and, contrary to his solemn promise, published the statement that very night. Czernin was forced to resign on the following day, but the damage was done.

Charles stood discredited before the world, and his unique personal peace initiative stood irreparably damaged. The actions of the French and his own foreign minister succeeded only in driving him into the arms of his German allies. Nationalism was in the ascendancy - a monster with teeth of iron, tearing asunder the central European bulwark. Since nationalism puts nation above all else it must resolve itself into a struggle between the nations for supremacy. It was no longer a question of nations seeking peace, but of nation fighting nation in a desperate struggle to be the victor. Would Germany prevail or would France, or Britain?

It was now a fight to the finish, and the young men and women of Europe were to be the unwitting victims of the scheming politicians.

Discussing the Sixtus letter shortly after it was revealed, the British Foreign Office representative in Berne, Sir Horace Rumbold, gave full vent to his own prejudices in a memorandum back to London:[1]

"The truth is that for the authorship of the letter we must look to Rome. It is part of the great Catholic peace-offensive, which aims at pushing forward the three Catholic nations - Austria, Belgium, and France spiritually regenerated through the war - and giving them the honour and triumph of having brought peace to the earth. Nor would Rome be greatly distressed if that peace were made at the cost of schismatic Russia and Roumania, still less of Italy, the goaler [sic, presumably he means gaoler!] of the Pope. It would, at any rate, be a triumph over the two leading nations, both of whom are Protestants."

This revealing comment says more about its author than about the reality of the situation. It also shows the extent to which such prejudices passed for high diplomacy at a time when the future of Europe lay in the balance. Alongside such chauvinistic nationalism there was the destructive elixir of an older prejudice, that of religious bigotry.

Charles' peace initiatives, mirrored those of the Pope - indeed, they went further - but one can only marvel at the suspicious nature of a mind which looks upon such peace gestures and initiatives with a hostility formed from religious discrimination and which cannot bring itself to recognise a genuine love of peace. In any event where was the peace offensive being put forward by the other powers? The truth is that there was none. France, far from being sympathetic, was as we have seen the principal obstacle in the Sixtus negotiations. Germany was the most belligerent nation of all, and was indubitably the greatest threat to peace. Thus it can be seen that Rumbold's simplistic but influential analysis was worse than useless. How much did such a view, or something like it, prevail among the Ententeministers? Did such prejudices lie behind their rejection of the peace initiatives?

It may be that a similar mixture of motives guided the fevered mind of Count Czernin. In any event there can be little doubt of the result. The house of Habsburg fell, with thundering echoes and far reaching consequences. As Edward Crankshaw was to put it: "When Clemenceau published the Sixtus letter in 1918 as a retort to Czernin's blustering . . . . Austria found her last escape route closed. William II was not unnaturally indignant when he discovered that Karl had pledged himself to back France's demand for Alsace-Lorraine. Karl was summoned to the German Emperor's headquarters at Spa, there to explain, to apologise and to suffer his inheritance to be tied indissolubly to the Hohenzollern destiny: thenceforth the great Empire, already subservient to Berlin in all matters concerning the higher conduct of the war, was in every way a German satellite."[2]

The tragedy of these failed negotiations and their subsequent revelation can be gleaned from any examination of William's and Charles' different attitudes to war and peace. Michael Balfour in *The Kaiser and his Times* refers to a letter from Charles to William in 1917, in the aftermath of the Russian revolution: "We are fighting against a new enemy which is more dangerous than the Entente: international revolution, which finds its strongest ally in general starvation. I beseech you not to overlook this portentous aspect of the matter and to reflect that a quick finish to the war even at the cost of heavy sacrifice gives us a chance of confronting the coming upheaval with success". But William and his high command thought they knew better. In April 1917, while Charles was conducting the Sixtus negotiations, Emperor William's own peace ideas meant that Germany should demand Malta, the Azores, Madeira, the Cape Verdi

Islands, the Belgium Congo and Longwy-Brie; that Poland, Courland, and Lithuania should be annexed "indirectly if not directly", with Ukraine, Latvia and Estonia becoming independent. America and Britain should pay thirty billion dollars in reparations, France forty billion and Italy ten billion!

Ludendorff also wanted Liège, the Flanders coast, Luxembourg, Longwy-Brie, Courland, Lithuania and parts of Poland, and the whole of Belgium to remain under military control.

In the face of such demands on the part of Germany, it is tragic that the leading diplomats and politicians of the Entente should have been suspicious of the peace attempts proffered by the Habsburg Emperor and, for that matter, the Pope.

Further examples of the fantastic and prejudiced views that were around throughout the war may be seen by what was available at that time in England. A contemporary book notes that "A few weeks after the outbreak of the European War it was possible to buy in London from street hawkers and religious tract sellers ingenious pamphlets offering to prove that the times of distress foretold in the Apocalypse were at hand. Thus the 'Beast full of names and blasphemy' was the German emperor with his tributary states and allies while the 'woman sitting upon the beast' and 'drunken with the blood of the saints' was the papacy, partner in Germany's iniquities."[3]

The notion of a Papal and Prussian alliance against Europe and the world seemed to have gained a certain respectable currency even among apparently sane people in England. Thus Dean Inge was able to write in *The Guardian* in October 1916: "The Latin Church is one half of that imperial tyranny of which Germany aspires to reconstruct the other half" or later "We are fighting against that terrible organisation in every part of the world. The sympathy of the Vatican with German ideas and German practices is no accident."[4]

It seems scarcely credible that anyone, let alone one with scholarly pretensions, could believe such a thing. Less than fifty years previously during the *Kulturkampf* ("cultural struggle") in Germany the Catholic Church had been persecuted in what Bismark himself, who was then Chancellor, described as a "fight to the death". The German Empire was Protestant and proud of being the birthplace of Protestantism. In addition, the papacy had condemned the actions of Germany far more than it had commented on any other nation during the war.

Emperor Charles had himself had a premonition of the fate of Austria-Hungary before the outbreak of war. With his clarity of insight and his instinctive judgement he sensed the growing power of the

Prussian and Russian blocs respectively. His instincts were right, as we know with the benefit of hindsight. What is extraordinary is that this young inexperienced emperor should have been able to foresee what his elders could not.

However, it was the enemies of Charles and of peace who were to prevail. Charles had no option but to attend at the German headquarters at Spa to give reassurances to his ally. It looked like, and to some extent was, a capitulation to the pan-Germanism that existed within the Empire. A treaty was concluded which bound the two Empires closer together and which for the German part was a thinly disguised attempt at annexation. In reality Charles was able to stave off any real change by leaving room for long term discussion about the vexed Polish question. He explained his actions in the Sixtus affair quite simply. He referred William to what he said at Homburg in 1917, i.e. that he had made secret representations to the Entente and as he had said at the time, told them that Austria would be prepared to make concessions in the East if Germany would concede Alsace-Lorraine to secure peace.

On the military front a closer mingling of the two empires was unavoidable for Charles, and an exchange of officers, men, and units was made possible. The real damage, however, was in what the treaty conveyed to the Entente powers. The impression was given that the Monarchy was now simply a satellite of the German Empire. How much easier was it now for the Entente members to see the Central Powers as one conglomerate and how much easier now it was to obscure the fundamental differences that characterised the German Empire from the Dual Monarchy of Austria-Hungary.

Given the prejudices and misunderstanding that already existed it was an even greater tragedy that the differences between these two empires should have become so blurred and that they were therefore never properly exploited. As had happened before (and would happen again) the understanding, intelligence, and imagination which could have combined to secure a just and lasting peace were lacking, and the cost had to be reckoned in the blood of the innocent.

Propaganda campaigns replaced the search for truth and for peace. The Empress Zita was painted as a figure of intrigue and the Emperor as a weak ineffectual monarch and the Dual Monarchy as part of a pan-Germanic leviathan seeking to devour Europe. The fact that these notions were entirely fanciful held no weight. They were believed, and people will only act on what they believe. In a letter on May 9th 1918 Rumbold, writing to A. J. Balfour at the Foreign Office, with a round up of newspaper reports, had this to say:

"No one could blame the Emperor, that is, to say the Empress, for trying to make peace after her own fashion: she could not be expected to realise that the days are long gone by, when women and priests could sway the destinies of nations. It seems strange however, that the Entente, one of the planks of whose democratic platform is the abolition of secret diplomacy, should have availed themselves readily of her services."[5]

To a later audience, removed from the passions of the war, such sentiments are at best ironic. That only the Sixtus affair should be regarded as "secret diplomacy" when one considers it alongside the apparently sacred secret Treaty of London, not to mention a host of other secret negotiations conducted by Entente ministers, is scarcely consistent. For our own time, the prospect of women (and priests, for that matter) playing a part in the destinies of nations seems part of the future and not of the past, living as we do in days which have been marked strongly by the actions of a woman Prime Minister in Britain and a Polish Pope. It is the likes of Rumbold who truly seem to belong to a distant age.

By any judgement of history there can be few who would not applaud the attempts on the part of both the Emperor and Empress to secure peace in Europe. This makes it all the more tragic that they were to receive such an ill reward for their pains. If Louis XIV was able to say "Après moi, le déluge" then still greater was the deluge that engulfed Europe after the fall of the Austro-Hungarian Empire! The Bolshevik revolution broke out in Moscow, and there were uprisings in Berlin, Vienna and Budapest. In Russia there followed the rise of Lenin and Stalin, and in Germany National Socialism.

We must also remember the cost in human terms of the failure to grasp the young peace emperor's peace plan. In this regard one cannot but remember some words of Wilfred Owen, the war poet, which seem to point directly at this very event. Using the image of Abraham who was set to sacrifice his son until the angel called to him he wrote:

> "Then Abram bound the youth with belts and straps
> And builded parapets and trenches there
> And stretched forth the knife to slay his son.
> When, lo! An angel called him out of Heaven,
> Saying, lay not thy hand upon the lad,
> Neither do anything to him. Behold,
> A ram, caught in a thicket by its thorns;
> Offer the Ram of Pride instead of him.
> But the old man would not so, but slew his son
> And half the seed of Europe one by one."

HOUSE OF HABSBURG-LORRAINE

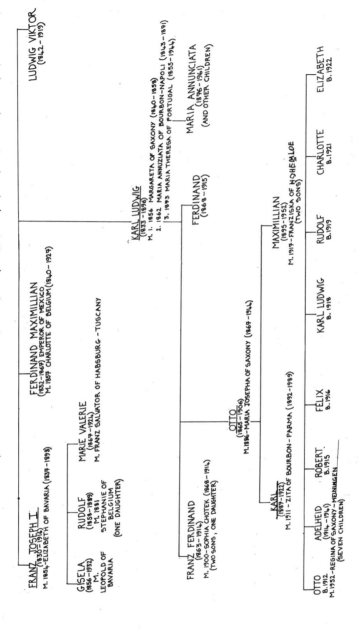

FRANZ JOSEPH I
(1830-1916)
M. 1854-ELIZABETH OF BAVARIA (1839-1898)

LUDWIG VIKTOR
(1842-1919)

FERDINAND MAXIMILIAN
(1832-1867) EMPEROR OF MEXICO
M. 1857 CHARLOTTE OF BELGIUM (1840-1927)

GISELA
(1856-1932)
M.
LEOPOLD OF
BAVARIA

RUDOLF
(1858-1889)
M. 1881
STEPHANIE OF
BELGIUM
(ONE DAUGHTER)

MARIE VALERIE
(1867-1924)
M. FRANZ SALVATOR OF HABSBURG-TUSCANY

KARL LUDWIG
(1833-1896)
M. 1. 1856 MARGARETA OF SAXONY (1840-1858)
2. 1862 MARIA ANNUZIATA OF BOURBON-NAPOLI (1843-1871)
3. 1873 MARIA THERESA OF PORTUGAL (1855-1944)

FERDINAND
(1868-1915)

MARIA ANNUNCIATA
(1876-1961)
(AND OTHER CHILDREN)

FRANZ FERDINAND
(1863-1914)
M. 1900-SOPHIA CHOTEK (1868-1914)
(TWO SONS, ONE DAUGHTER)

OTTO
(1865-1906)
M.1886-MARIA JOSEPHA OF SAXONY (1869-1944)

MAXIMILLIAN
(1895-1952)
M. 1917-FRANZISKA OF HOHENLOE
(TWO SONS)

KARL
(1887-1922)
M. 1911 - ZITA OF BOURBON-PARMA (1892-1989)

RUDOLF
B.1919

CHARLOTTE
B.1921

ELIZABETH
B.1922

OTTO
B.1912
M.1952-REGINA OF SAXONY-MEININGEN
(SEVEN CHILDREN)

ADELHEID
(1914-1971)

ROBERT
B.1915

FELIX
B.1916

KARL LUDWIG
B.1918

HOUSE OF BOURBON – PARMA

ROBERT OF BOURBON
DUKE OF PARMA (1848 – 1907)

M. 1. 1848 MARIA – PIA OF BOURBON–SICILY (1849 – 1882)
ELEVEN CHILDREN

2. 1884 MARIA ANTONIA OF BRAGANZA (1862 – 1959)

SIXTUS
(1886 – 1934)
M. HEDWIG DE LA
ROCHEFOUCAULD

XAVIER
(1889 – 1977)
M. MADELINE DE
BOURBON–BASSET

ZITA
(1892 – 1989)
M. CHARLES OF AUSTRIA
EIGHT CHILDREN

FELIX
(1893 – 1970)
M. CHARLOTTE OF
LUXEMBOURG

RÉNÉ
(1894 – 1962)
M. MARGARET OF
DENMARK

LOUIS
(1899 – 1967)
M. MARIE OF SAVOY

GAETAN
(1905 – 1952)
M. MARGUERITE OF
TOUR AND TAXIS

In exile in Switzerland: Emperor Charles and his family take part in a
Corpus Christi procession near their home at Hertenstein, 1921.
(Photo: Kaiser Karl Gebetsliga)

Empress Zita,
photographed at a family wedding
in the early 1980s.

Dr. Otto von Habsburg today. A member of the European Parliament, he has returned to both Austria and Hungary in recent years. Large crowds greeted him in Budapest in 1989 where he led mourners at a Requiem for his mother in the cathedral where she had been crowned over 60 years previously.

King and Queen of Hungary–the formal coronation picture in which
Charles is seen wearing St. Stephen's Crown.

The young Archduke Charles
in the uniform of a General
of Infantry.

Charles as a young
Archduke in his Hungarian
General's uniform with
small Prince Otto.

"God preserve and God protect our Emperor and our Country"– an official postcard sold in aid of the Red Cross for war charities in World War I.

"God Save Our Beloved Kaiser". A popular postcard of World War I: Charles and Zita look on as little Otto walks hand-in-hand with the Emperor Franz Josef: "In this charming pretty scene/Is the present and future seen".

"Three Generations": A World War I postcard showing small Otto, Archduke Charles and Emperor Franz Josef—a picture designed to show the security and safety of the throne. But after Franz Josef's death in 1916, Charles was to reign for only two years, and young Otto was to grow up in exile.

Charles (right) hearing Mass with his troops while on active service in World War I. The picture may have been designed to have a propaganda effect but was nonetheless true: Charles was a devout man who regularly attended services in the field.

The wedding, 1911. Zita's coronet, a gift from Emperor Franz Josef, was to be worn a generation later by Otto's bride, Princess Regina of Saxe-Meiningen. In this photograph, the Emperor is shown on the far right of the picture.

Archduke Franz Ferdinand, assassinated at Sarajevo in June 1914.

Emperor Franz Josef at his prayers – an angel carries to Heaven his plea for peace. This picture appeared as a postcard for popular sale during World War I.

The funeral procession of Emperor Charles in Madeira:
Empress Zita, veiled, leads, accompanied by Crown Prince Otto and followed by the other children and members of the Court.

Notes:

1. Public Record Office file FO 371-3134-1918. •
2. Edward Crankshaw, *The Fall of the House of Habsburg*, London, 1963.
3. *No Small Stir* by "Diplomaticus", Society of St. Peter and Paul, London, 1918.
4. *Ibid.*
5. Public Record Office file, *loc.sit.*.

Chapter Nine

The collapse of peace hopes and the tragedy and humiliation of the Sixtus affair heralded the beginning of the end for Austria-Hungary. From the spring of 1918 onwards, the pressure from the different minority races within the Empire and the military and political situation outside spelled doom.

Within the Empire, the first pressures came from the Czechs, and it would be their lands that were first to be prised away from the whole. In January 1918 the Czech and Moravian deputies in Parliament published a statement, the "Epiphany Declaration" which called for "a free national life and self-determination". By March these ideas were being enthusiastically fuelled by leaflets prepared by the Western Allies and used as propaganda all along the Italian front. These leaflets encouraged Czechs serving in the Empire's forces to adopt the idea that what they should truly demand was an independent territory of their own. Even at this stage, had Charles been able to implement his idea for a federalist empire with separate nations linked under the Crown, the situation could have been saved since there were more than sufficient numbers of Czechs and Slovaks whose sense of loyalty and history drew them to maintain the Habsburg bond. But since the war had prevented him from doing this the possibilities for saving this part of his inheritance melted away. The exiled Czech leaders who for years had been lobbying and working in the capitals of the various countries where they had been living quickly came into their own.

Neither France nor Britain had entered the war with the express intention of destroying the Austro-Hungarian empire, and for Britain in particular, with her world-wide chain of colonies, to denounce the idea of an empire was a matter of pure hypocrisy. For the earlier part of the war the campaigning lobbyists had found only limited scope for their activities. But now, the break-up of the Empire seemed to the Allies to be a crucial strategic step on the road to achieving victory. In June, France formally recognised the Czech exiles own chosen instrument for independence, the Czech National Council, which was based in Paris, as the legitimate government of the territory. In August Britain did the same.

Empress Zita would later recall: "After France's recognition of the Czech exiles, the Emperor knew full well that all his attempts to bring Bohemia round, or even to hold her to the idea of Empire, might well prove fruitless. Indeed, he felt that Clemenceau, in being the first to make this gesture towards the Czechs, was only trying to encourage the Monarchy's disintegration. We had a lot of Czech troops at the front and they, like the rest of the troops, were of course already war-weary and hungry. The success of the exiles made the Emperor realise the importance of reform now more than ever. But his ministers lagged behind him. Most of them, still believing in 'final victory' simply didn't grasp the significance of the Paris move. Too often one heard the scornful attitude: The Entente can *talk* about recognition, but what can they *do*? It is we who are sitting here on top of Bohemia, not they."[1]

The Czech development had been an unlikely result of what had initially seemed like a sign of peace and hope - the cessation of fighting in the East through the peace of Brest-Litovsk.

The Bolshevik revolution of 1917 had spelled the end of Russia's involvement in the war. From now on, she was to be far too busy fighting her own battles at home. The leaders of the new Soviet state would henceforth devote their energies to ruthlessly crushing all potential opponents and to the setting up of a form of governmment based on the Communist creed. In the autumn of 1917, immediately following the Bolshevik takeover, these new rulers made peace overtures to Gernmany and to Austria-Hungary. Negotiations took place at Brest-Litovsk and were to result in a strange and uncertain form of peace, which created problems for Charles and his Empire. The first formal arrangement was at least clear-cut. A peace was agreed in February 1918 with the newly-created republic of Ukraine, which had been formed when Ukrainians seized their moment following the collapse of Russia's old regime. Both Austria-Hungary and Germany hoped for much from this peace: the former desperately needed food from this territory which had been known as the "granary of Europe", and Germany was delighted by the release from the Eastern front of massive numbers of men who could now be used to launch a new offensive in the West. But the price to be paid was very high, especially for Austria-Hungary. Very little grain actually became available, despite much talk of this being a "bread peace", and meanwhile Austria-Hungary had formally recognised the boundaries of a new republic which by its very creation had angered some of the nationalists within her own territory. This new republic of Ukraine included areas which the Poles regarded as historically theirs, and which some of them had hoped to include in a new Polish republic. Charles had always been reasonably popular with the Poles within his Empire, and there had been no noticeable Polish nationalist campaigning against Habsburg rule in the territories of Galicia and around Krakow. This now changed. The Poles felt that in recognising the Ukrainian state the Crown had insulted them. There was long-standing animosity between Poles and Ukrainians, and the more chauvinist of the Poles were not slow to point to the folly of a Habsburg emperor acknowledging a Ukrainian republic which bordered on to Polish territory particularly as they believed this state included some of their territory. There were protests by agitators against Habsburg rule all over the Polish speaking parts of the Empire. A new instability and source of dissension had arisen in a territory which had hitherto caused few problems and where the people had shown no antagonism to the Empire's rule. It was a bitter time.

When the Soviets did, after a long delay, conclude an agreement with Germany and Austria-Hungary in early March, it gave Germany the signal she needed to go ahead with the massive troop withdrawals. These troops were re-grouped on the Western front ready for a fresh initiative there. This inevitably meant that any effort on Charles' part to continue peace efforts looked foolish: the thunder of battle (over a million casualties were inflicted on the Western allies during this big spring offensive of 1918) and the resounding rhetoric of war had taken over. The humiliation of the Sixtus letter disclosure, already described, took place against this tragic background.

The May 1918 meeting at Spa which had been sparked off by the Sixtus letter crisis continued to have repercussions throughout the summer, as men died in huge numbers on the battlefields and the Empire swayed and tottered under so many pressures. Charles' reputation abroad had been irrevocably damaged by the Sixtus matter, and rumours about him were now bandied about freely. In April, at the height of the crisis, Sir Horace Rumbold, the British ambassador in Switzerland, sent back a telegram to the Foreign Office in London saying: "Horodyski learns from a person who is in best position to know what is going on at Austrian court that

Emperor Charles has become a drunkard. Germans have thrown in his way wife of General Sixt von Arnim with a view to weaning him from influence of Empress."[2]

That such cruel lies could be believed seems absurd, but it appears that they were - or, at least, were assumed to have a grain of truth in them. To anyone who had even a basic knowledge of the Emperor, the notion that he was a drunkard who could be readily enticed into casual immorality by an attractive woman was one that could be quickly dismissed with a shrug. Even those within his empire who were actively working against him - such as the Czech nationalists - knew him to be a hard-working, humble and honourable man who was passionately devoted to his Empire as well as to his wife and family. A man who drew his main strength from his deep religious and moral convictions, Charles had continued, throughout the war years, to begin every day by attending Mass before the official day's work began at 7.15 a.m. Into a punishing schedule of meetings and conferences - often his working day was 18 hours long - he tried whenever possible, to cram in at least a few minutes with his children, and he was always close to Zita who spent her time with him at Laxenburg or Baden.

Throughout the summer the plight of the Empire grew worse and worse. In May Charles and Zita were forced to make a visit to Bulgaria, to bolster their alliance which was visibly floundering. They also visited neighbouring Turkey. There were cheers, smiles, welcomes and parades - but beneath the surface the vital commitment was lacking. For all the superficial enthusiasm attending the five-day trip, there was an underlying sense of the continuing futility of the war and the impossibility of ultimate victory. The ceremonies in Sofia and Constantinople could not alter this. Just four months later, in mid-September, Bulgaria's King Ferdinand would abandon his country and flee, leaving the alliance in tatters behind him.

At home, the passionate longing for peace was still blended with much personal loyalty to the monarch. Nationalist feelings were also to some extent confused by commitment to the community of peoples which made up the Empire. While Czech nationalists were demanding independence, the Slovaks could still turn out in their hundreds and thousands to cheer the Emperor. In July Charles and Zita made an official visit to Pressburg (now Bratislava) in the heart of the Slovak lands, to take part in the annual harvest celebrations. They travelled down the Danube accompanied by six-year-old Otto and four-year-old Adelheid and were greeted with great enthusiasm. Zita, wearing a straw hat trimmed with flowers, held the hands of the two small children who were dressed in white, while beside them Charles, dressed in uniform, acknowledged the salutes of a guard of honour. It could so easily have been a scene from a nation at peace. But Emperor and Empress both knew that they should not draw any reassuring conclusions from what they were seeing: the steady death toll on the battlefronts and the rising nationalist fervour were combining to make the future an unpredictable one.

Pressburg had seen much history. Its citizens included German, Hungarian and Slovak-speakers, and in its 11th century cathedral many Hungarian kings had been crowned. To the Hungarians the city was called Pozsony, to the Slovaks it was Bratislava, the name by which it was to be known on all maps after the creation of Czechoslovakia following the abolition of the Empire. Down the centuries it had seen fighting against the Turks and also battles in religious wars, and it was the place where Napoleon and Francis I signed peace after the battle of Austerlitz. In 1848 its parliament building had seen the great debates on reform. Now this city was seeing the passing of an era, as its last Habsburg ruler was acclaimed in its streets by an enthusiastic populace.

While this visit was taking place the scene on the Western Front was being set for the final counter-offensive of the Western Allies. This offensive after yet more slaughter was eventually to bring the Allies victory. It was a response to the German offensive of the early summer, and began on August 8th. By August 14th, when Charles was due to meet Emperor William at Spa, the implications of its success were all too obvious. The Allies had forced their way through the German-held territories of France with ruthless speed and the war was all too obviously approaching its final stages. The Germans now tentatively agreed to what Charles had been urging since he first inherited his responsibilities - a serious attempt to sue for peace. Yet even now they attempted to delay. Although Charles' military advisers made it clear that Austria-Hungary could only hold out, at the very latest, until the end of the year, the Germans were slow to respond to specific ideas for peace action. They were cool towards Charles' suggestion of a meeting between all the belligerent powers on neutral territory, and hinted instead at finding some fresh neutral European leader who could be introduced as a referee. Although recognising the grim realities of the situation, they appeared to cling to the hope that the Allied advance might eventually be slowed and further time gained to propose peace on terms that would be more satisfactory to them.

It was in this atmosphere that Charles marked his birthday three days later. He was 31. Within three months, William would be in exile in the

Netherlands, (whose queen he was now suggesting as an intermediary in potential peace negotiations) and Charles would be contemplating a future of confusion and doubt. Charles spent his birthday at Reichenau. It was an ordinary working day. In the morning there was a small informal parade at which he presented medals for bravery to various soldiers. Zita and the children watched the ceremony. The medals were the Maria Theresa Order, the Empire's highest decoration for valour.

September brought news of the Bulgarian capitulation, which came hard on the heels of what was now a decisive German defeat in the West. As the Germans had failed, throughout the past month, to agree to any concrete plans for achieving peace, Charles was now working on his own again. Baron Burian, the Foreign Minister who had replaced Czernin, had been instructed to send a message to the Allied governments calling for an end to speech-making on all sides and an immediate meeting on neutral soil to discuss a settlement. It had been ignored and had merely irritated Emperor William. The equally urgent need to introduce reform at home to appease the nationalist activists throughout the Empire, especially the Czechs, occupied his attention just at the time when he needed all his energies to be devoted to the search for a workable peace. A Crown Council meeting on 27th September paved the way for creating the new system of a group of federal states which Charles had always wanted.

Charles was at the epicentre of all the pressures that had been building up in the Empire for months if not years. Things had now reached a stage where one by one the people who might have been there to help him were melting away, just when the tension mounted to an almost unbearable pitch. He was alone at the centre of it all, unable to act effectively and all too well aware that had his advice been taken at a much earlier stage, his initiatives followed and his attempts at peacemaking and reform allowed opportunities to flourish, then his Empire would not be in the plight that it then was.

Baron von Hussarek, the new Prime Minister, who had succeeded Seidler after his resignation in July, read aloud a constitutional declaration to Parliament in Vienna on October 1. It was vague and did not give any real details on how a new system could be created, concentrating instead on generalities about the desirability of "internal reconstruction".

The Hungarians continued to be incensed over any suggestion that the lands they ruled might be handed over to other national groups who shared the territory. In any case, events were moving far too swiftly for a delicate set of negotiations to begin. The very next day saw the German high command bowing to the inevitable and demanding from its own government that peace negotiations be started. On October 4th both Germany and Austria-Hungary sent formal notes to President Wilson asking for an armistice. Austria's note referred to her efforts for peace and justice - an oblique hint that reform was being promised at home. Would America listen and allow time for some such reform to get under way, so that the framework of Empire might yet be salvaged?

Everything was held in abeyance until America replied to Germany, acknowledging receipt of the peace note and demanding the evacuation of France and Belgium. No one knew what response there was now going to be to Austria-Hungary's note. On October 10 Charles, without waiting any longer, proclaimed his "People's Manifesto", announcing that the Empire was to become a federal state "in which each racial component shall form its own state organisation in its territory of settlement". He was at last doing what his heart had wanted from the moment he had first become ruler - but the verdict of America was that it was all too late, and that he had been overtaken by events.

In fact his "People's Manifesto" would have been extremely difficult to implement, since it included a let-out clause referring to the Magyar lands, which could have lent itself to almost indefinite wrangling on the part of chauvinistic Hungarians who were not prepared to give up even an inch of their soil. Nevertheless, the basic concept was not the product of any panic measure, but an idea which had been fostered and discussed for a long time. The American refusal to have anything to do with it really spelt its doom. The Americans were by now fully committed to recognising the Czechs as independent rulers in their own territory, and refused to accept that the Empire should any longer have any say in their affairs.

Charles no longer had any room for manoeuvre. His Hungarian and Austrian governments both resigned. The American dismissal of his "People's Manifesto" was followed within days by a new military offensive begun on his Italian front with the British and French pressing hard on his armies in the territory he himself had held for the Empire but two years before. In Hungary confusion erupted following the publication of the Manifesto. The Empire was beginning to disintegrate in just the way Charles had feared. His priority, now as always, was to seek peace and to salvage whatever was possible of an ordered framework of government for his people. With the situation of the Czechs more or less resolved - it was clear that they were going to be an independent nation, forged out of the support being given to them by the French, British, and Americans - and the rest of the Empire in a state of confusion, he took the final and irrevocable decision to make peace with or without the German allies who on every previous occasion had held him back or frustrated his efforts.

On October 27th he sent a telegram to Emperor William informing him of "my unalterable resolve to sue within the next twenty four hours for a separate peace and an immediate armistice" adding "I cannot do otherwise; my conscience as a sovereign commands me to act in this way."

The Czech nationalists seized their moment and declared the country formally independent on October 28th, the Czech National Council taking over the Corn Distribution Office in Prague and the office of the Imperial Governor. The National Council knew that it could rest comfortably on the security of its American backers: recognising this too, the Empire's army could only accept what had taken place, and the local commander accordingly announced that he would co-operate with the new authority. In what almost seemed like a mood of anti-climax, the new Czech leaders found that no struggle was necessary: their new status had in any case been proclaimed in the Emperor's own "People's Manifesto" and in place of an heroic struggle came an orderly handover of power. The National Council however, now stated finally that it would be severing all links with the Habsburg crown; it announced officially on the evening of October 28th: "The independent Czechoslo-vak state is herewith founded".

What the Czech nationalists were doing with warm support from abroad, other nationalities were now to do also. Following the message of the Manifesto, the Croats and Slovenes immediately announced inde-pendence for their countries as did the Polish and Ukrainian nationalists. While Charles struggled to deal with peace negotiations abroad and to assert some authority in Vienna and Budapest, new independent states were springing up in what had been the outlying regions of his Empire.

Revolutions and declarations overthrowing the constitutional and established order rarely occur after a great and bloody struggle between classes.[3] In fact, as in this case, the result is usually achieved by a handful of skilled politicians or military men who use their positions of trust to manipulate events at an appropriate moment. External war, not civil war, provided the moment in both Russia and Austria-Hungary. The Armed Forces of the legitimate governments were directed to defending the integrity of the realm. This was therefore an opportunity for dissent to show its face. The skilled agitator and revolutionary encouraged by an antagonistic foreign power could then attempt to seize the reins of power without fear of having to put up a fight.

It cannot be said that the new governments were supported in their nationalist aspirations by all the peoples of each nation, many of whom remained loyally devoted to the Empire. However, it can be said with certainty that almost all were agreed in wanting an end to war as soon as possible.

The Austro-Hungarian Empire was now approaching its final days. On October 22, while the Czechoslovak crisis and the peace negotiations were at their height, Charles was not at Vienna but working from his train on the way to Hungary. He was still fulfilling public duties while holding the ropes of the ship of state in his hands, and he and Zita were on their way to Debrecen where they would open the university, before going on to Gödöllö just outside Budapest. At Debrecen the huge enthusiasm that greeted them wherever they went on public occasions was in evidence again, and cheering crowds gathered. But it was an emotional display, without substance or political power. Charles had just come from a meeting with Czech leaders who were about to take their territory out of the Empire. Ahead of him lay a major crisis in Budapest, where the radical left wing and the nationalists had renewed their demands in the wake of the confusion that had followed the publication of the Manifesto and the rumours of impending peace.

The next days in the royal castle at Gödöllö were to be the last that Charles would have in Hungary as undisputed King - and even now his position was becoming an uncertain one. The children joined their parents there in these last days of October while Charles strove to form a government that would be acceptable to nationalists and to the growing radical mob element. Revolution was simmering just below the surface. The only faint hope was that of a genuine federation of independent states, linked under the Crown. This had been Charles' dream from when he had first begun to take an interest in the Empire's politics years before. In the heated atmosphere with the political and military situation changing almost every hour, it was impossible to create the conditions for discussion of a new Hungarian state along these lines. Barely sleeping - the Empress was later to recall that he snatched two or three hours of rest a night despite the warnings of his doctors - Charles struggled in meetings with first one faction and then another in a vain attempt to get some one who would accept the responsibility of forming this new kind of government. Meanwhile out on the streets the people fed on rumours. They were hungry and bitter and facing yet another grim winter. Their sons and husbands had died in huge numbers on battlefields far away to the West and East and every week new sacrifices had been demanded of them. The supply of food and of all other basic commodities had dwindled to the point where the framework for normal living had disappeared. Now rumours were spreading that the different parts of the Empire would secede or that the Empire itself would disintegrate. Old hatreds surged forth anew. Political agitators found they had almost limitless scope for creating instant support for extreme ideas. The actual physical safety of the Royal family became uncertain.

The name on everyone's lips was that of Count Karolyi, leader of the left-wing faction in the country and in parliament, and street riots began with demands that he be appointed to rule the country. Charles finally left for Vienna with Karolyi accompanying him. The royal children were left behind at Gödöllö, as a public gesture of reassurance that Habsburg rule still existed in Hungary and as a pretence at normality.

But the tide of chaos was too strong. Charles had nominated Count Johann Hadik as Prime Minister but no government under his direction was ever formed. Instead, as the news spread that the various national groups were seizing power in their different territories, Budapest exploded. Street mobs took over, the Royal Insignia was ripped down from public monuments, Hadik resigned and Karolyi hastened to take his place, and Hungary plunged into complete confusion. Waiting in the wings was a man from Moscow - dedicated Communist Bela Kun who, three months later in the middle of a hungry and bitter winter, would grab his chance of power and subject the country to a rule of savage Communism.

Charles was now back in Vienna. The Empress received the initial telephone call from the garrison commander in Budapest which reported that mobs on the street were now out of control: Charles had just fallen asleep after another exhausting 20-hour day. She woke him and he at once took command: but the orders that he gave to hold the city were never fulfilled. Meanwhile in Austria itself the tide of confusion and revolution was increasing, lapping at the palace gates and gathering pace with every hour.

It was the collapse on the Italian front which had brought about an immediate crisis in Austria. On October 24th the Allied armies - British, French, American, and Italian - attacked fiercely here in the mountains, where Charles' army had been holding out, defending territory which he himself had been instrumental in helping to hold, earlier in the war. The Empire's troops were cold, hungry, and short of all vital supplies but during the initial three days of the attack they fought back with great bravery. Czechs, Austrians, Poles, Magyars and Slovaks, united in their loyalty, battled against the Allies in the grim mountain territory as if this were still the optimistic period of 1915 and the hope of final victory had not faded. For weeks, basic supplies had not been reaching them: they had barely any food, their uniforms were in tatters, and they were unable to sustain any prolonged campaign. Above all, they were aware of the news from home. The Magyars among them, in particular, were fearful of the dangers of an invasion of Hungary by Rumania. They wanted to fight not for Austrian territory in the South Tyrol but for their own homeland, now threatened by all sorts of dangers. It was this, and no essential loss of loyalty to the Empire, that caused the troops on the Italian front to crack. Exhausted and hungry, aware that they were fighting an enemy which was their superior both in supplies and numbers, the Empire's soldiers were nevertheless prepared to battle on - until they realised that the real battles were going on nearer home, and that even as they risked their own lives in the mountains, their families were facing confusion and chaos behind them.

Over in the enemy camp, *The Times* in London revealed something of the battle the Austro-Hungarian troops had put up by referring obliquely to a difficult start to the campaign - the nearest it could get, under its wartime censorship, to admitting that Charles' troops had put up a better fight than expected. Then it went on (Oct 30th 1918): "The operations on the Italian front, which began rather quietly last Thursday in the mountain sectors between the Astico and the Piave, have rapidly developed and extended. If they continue to meet with the success which has attended their enlargement during the last three days they will unquestionably have a considerable effect upon the critical internal situation in Austria.... an excellent start has been made with the liberation of the occupied territories of Italy, and there is every reason for thinking that the process will now be rapid.... We are reaching a stage of the war when it is necessary to bear constantly in mind the effect of political developments upon the enemy's forces in the field. The effect on their subject Slav nationalities has long been obvious enough. But are the Magyars likely to fight stubbornly now, when their chief desire is to return home in order to conserve their separate interests? And will German divisions be willing to sell their lives dearly on Italian soil for an Austrian cause at the moment when Austria has announced her intention of seeking peace with or without her German confederates?"

As this report was appearing, confusion was indeed breaking out all along the Empire's lines on the Italian front. Hungarian units were begging for transport back to Hungary in order to defend their homeland - and receiving no answer, as Hungary by this time had no government and mob rule was taking over in the streets of Budapest. Soon almost half the divisions in the front line against the Italians were effectively refusing to fight. There was nothing anyone could do except sue for an armistice. On 29th October, while that report for *The Times* was being written by the paper's correspondent in Zurich, the armistice negotiations began. The terms of these negotiations were broken by Italian abuse of Austrian good faith. The Italians insisted on rigid terms: complete demobilisation of the Austro-Hungarian army, and withdrawal of its troops right back to the Brenner Pass, and freedom for Italian troops to move within the Empire's territory. They were determined to claim all the lands that had been mapped out for them and agreed secretly at the illicit Treaty of London negotiations with the British two years before.

To achieve this, they had to practise duplicity with regard to the timing of the cease-fire: by being vague about when exactly it should come into effect, and unforthcoming in response to urgent Austro-Hungarian requests for specific information, they were able to spring a final forward march which gave them all the territory they wanted. Effectively, they negotiated a one-sided ceasefire in which Austro-Hungarian troops were committed to laying down their arms while, in a picture of general confusion, the Italians were able to continue to advance. As Gordon Brook-Shepherd writes: "In those twenty-four hours, the Italians thrust specially-organised flying columns of cavalry and motorised infantry through the soggy, unresisting, disorganised mass of the Austrian armies. Many Austrian units, believing it was all over, were just sitting, with rifles stacked, on their kitbags. The Italians thus rode unopposed into all that Austrian territory which, in twelve previous campaigns since 1915, they had failed to conquer by force. When they duly stopped, at 3 pm on 4th November, they had reached a general line running from Male and Val Sugano, across to Pontebba and the Adriatic town of Grado in the East. The Italians were sitting on their long-coveted *fino al Brennero* at last."[4]

Charles was at Schönbrunn for what were to prove the final days and hours of his reign. He had to deal with armistice negotiations with the Italians while at the same time trying to create some sort of government for Austria itself - now cut off from the rest of the disintegrating Empire. It proved an impossible task.

As news of the Italian defeat spread, crowds gathered on Vienna's streets. The collapse on the Italian front had been precisely what Charles had feared and predicted: a hard-hitting blow from the Allies at a time when there was confusion at home and a lack of supplies on the battleground. The failure to grapple with badly-needed reforms within the Empire had caused splits and divisions within the Army as soldiers inevitably feared for the safety of their own families and homelands as the chaos spread. Now all Charles' predictions were coming true. There was no point in saying "I told you so!" to those of his ministers who had earlier been belligerent and optimistic but were now hurrying to run away from their responsibility for the war.

On the streets, rumour fed rumour. The Allied armies had for some while been bombarding the troops in Italy with propaganda, including a leaflet which told them that the "Italian-born" Empress was giving away their positions and military secrets. This, of course, was nonsense: Zita's family had been deposed from their throne in Italy by precisely the same Italian rulers who were now fighting Austria-Hungary, but ill-informed Czech, Hungarian or Slovene soldiers were unlikely to know that, or to be aware of the details of the finer points of Italian history generally. Other rumours picked up the story of the Emperor's drunkeness - equally untrue and equally fed from enemy sources.

Creating some form of government for Austria while the streets seethed with angry people, aware of their humiliating defeat and of the destruction of the Empire which was the only form of government they had ever known, had an air of unreality about it. The territory of German-speaking Austria, cut off from all the other lands the Habsburgs had ruled, had never been considered viable as a nation in its own right. It did not even have a name, since "Austria" was usually taken to mean the whole Empire. Vienna was nothing if not an Imperial capital. Charles was an Emperor, and was also King of Hungary - but in Austria itself he was technically only an archduke. Trying to find a name for this new territory, most people settled for "German-Austria", attempting to define it by the language spoken there.

Into this seething confusion came the American pressures, which took for granted the establishment of a small, independent, and probably republican Austria, sitting alongside other republics clustered together in what had been the Empire's lands, along the Danube.

On October 30th *The Times* in London reported gleefully: "The appointment of Professor Lammasch as Austrian Premier opens up the whole question of the liquidation of that Empire. The Vienna newspapers are aghast at the magnitude of the task. They appear to agree only on one point, namely, that the old Austria must be maintained until the new States have completed their administrative organisation."

The socialists in the emerging Austrian power struggle were all for a republic, while other groups were uncertain or divided. The hungry mobs on the street were angry about the Italian defeat, desperate for food, fearful of the coming winter, and only too well aware that the ordered world in which the monarchy had had an assured place was vanishing before their eyes. To many of them the collapse of the Empire must have seemed sudden and dramatic: to Charles it was not so, as he had long foreseen what would happen if his peace manoeuvres and attempts to achieve a just frame-work for ruling his Empire failed.

As the chaos mounted, for the first time there was talk of his abdication, and of abolition of the monarchy. Already, millions of people who had been his subjects only a month before, were now citizens of independent countries. Hungary was in ferment. How could Vienna retain a monarch when no proper government could be formed?

As Charles attempted to gather his ministers together for audiences or conferences, it became rapidly clear that not one among them was prepared to take ultimate responsibility for attempting to form a government under his rule. It seemed as though the days of the Habsburgs were drawing to an inevitable close.

In the middle of all this, his name-day was celebrated. It had traditionally been honoured by a special Mass in the cathedral. Charles' patron saint was St Charles Borromeo, bishop and cardinal of the 16th century who played a major part in reforming the life of the Church after the Council of Trent: his feast day is November 4th. But this year of 1918 was not a time for all the normal trimmings associated with a family name-day celebration - gifts and special food and festivities - or of the formal public ceremonial of a king's special day with parades and music. Instead, people who gathered in the cathedral did so in a tense atmosphere of fear and mutual sharing of agonised worries. Significantly, many were not wearing their uniforms or anything which would formally link them with the Habsburg dynasty. At the end of Mass when the National Anthem "Gott erhalte..." was sung, many among the congregation wept.

The people who came and went around the Royal family during these last days in Vienna all brought their own story of doom. Lammasch, Austria's nominal Prime Minister, was trying to bring together people who might form some kind of coherent government, Admiral Horthy from Hungary was on his way to Croatia to supervise the handing over of part of what had been the Austro-Hungarian fleet, and politicians came and went with ideas while military men brought news of the collapse from the Italian border.

Abroad, the disintegration of the Empire was watched with either exhausted lack of interest - all of Europe was simply dragging out the last days of a savage war with little understanding or comprehension of the long-term effects - or else with some satisfaction by those who had hoped all along for its downfall. This latter view had been enthusiastically adopted by certain factions in America who had decided that the creation of new republics in the old heart of Europe would somehow prove better for the common lot of mankind than the old Empire - a belief in which they were to be proved sadly wrong.

The end came on November 11th, with the arrival of a paper for Charles to sign from a group of politicians who had finally agreed on a form of words which would allow for the creation of a new state of Austria. It was brought by Lammasch and by Gayer, the Minister of the Interior, both of them in a hurry, and urged Charles to sign the document at once. It was the latest in a series of comings and goings. Charles had by now had very little sleep for a long period. Outside crowds were milling in the streets, their mood angry.

At first glance, the paper seemed to be an abdication document, but a second reading revealed that it was technically a withdrawal from power. Charles would not sign until all other avenues of hope had been explored. It was clear that the people on the streets could not be held down by force. Already in neighbouring Germany Emperor William had been deposed and was fleeing the country. All the politicians had already decided to abandon the Crown - including those who had pledged their loyalty to it many times. There could be no question of summoning his army to fire on his own people or imprison members of his parliament. Charles had no choice. He signed, and with the short word "Karl", written with his own metal pencil produced from his pocket, ended the centuries of his family's rule over a Central European empire.

The Emperor's statement was immediately made public, being printed and distributed in the streets:

> "Ever since my accession I have tried ceaselessly to lead my peoples out of the horrors of a war for whose inception I bear no trace of blame. I have not hesitated to restore constitutional life and I have opened up for the peoples the path of their development as independent states. Filled, now as ever, with unwavering devotion to all my peoples, I do not wish to oppose their free growth with my own person. I recognise in advance whatever decision that German-Austria may make about its future political form. The people, through its representatives, has taken over the government. I renounce all participation in the affairs of state. At the same time, I relieve my Austrian Government from office. May the people of German-Austria, in unity and tolerance, create and strengthen the new order! The happiness of my peoples has, from the beginning,

been the object of my most ardent wishes. Only an inner peace can heal the wounds of this war."

At the time it was hoped that the door remained open, and that once saner times arrived the Monarch would be able to resume his place at the head of his people. There was no suggestion in the document that he was renouncing all claims to rule in the future. The hope among many was that this could be a tactical move to deal with the immediate situation.

However, for all practical purposes, it still meant an end to Charles' reign. All that was needed was for him to say farewell. It was decided that he would go to Eckartsau, a family hunting-lodge some way north-east of Vienna. The children, who had been brought back from Hungary amid considerable adventures a few days before, would go there too. Both Charles and Zita were adamantly opposed to any suggestion of exile. They both wanted to stay on in their own homeland. Charles had not relinquished his sense of duty to his people and wanted to be at hand to do whatever was needed to bring about a return of order to the lands he had inherited.

The removal to Eckartsau was not a simple matter: alternative wild suggestions were made at first by people convinced that the Royal family would be murdered by mobs if they remained for a moment longer on Austrian soil. But Charles stood firm. One by one the members of his last government came to say goodbye. Then the family gathered for a final prayer together in the palace chapel. Finally, it being now night, they were dispersed into various cars and these left the palace grounds by an unobserved route. The journey out to Eckartsau was uneventful. A long dark winter of waiting had begun.

Virtually every faction in what had been Austria-Hungary now had its own ideas about what form of government it wanted for the future. Some of the pan-German enthusiasts in Austria were convinced that the future lay wide in a full union with Germany. At one point amid scenes of enthusiasm the frontier stones marking the boundary between Austria and Germany were removed. But on November 12th *The Times* in London was reporting: "A Vienna telegram states that the German-Austrian National Assembly will decide on Tuesday the question of the union of German-Austria with Germany. The form of state will remain open until this question has also been settled in Germany by the Constituent Assembly. The German-Austrian Assembly will take its decisions on the principle of the right to self-determination of every people. According to Vienna telegram received on Saturday the German

Consulate-General has given notice that the frontier between German-Austria and Germany has been absolutely closed to traffic from today." The pan-Germans were to be thwarted at least temporarily in their plans to suck Austria into a Greater Germany - and perhaps they felt checked in any case by the revolutionary fervour which was now gripping much of Germany including Bavaria.

Meanwhile all over Europe commentators were pointing to the end of the Habsburg dynasty's rule over Austria-Hungary. Britain's Catholic *Tablet* magazine, which had been such an enthusiastic supporter of the dynasty before the war, and had praised Franz Ferdinand as "a prince upon whom Catholic Europe had learned to build her highest hopes" now seemed to be smacking its lips gleefully over the dynasty's fall from power. Undoubtedly, the tragic casualty lists which it had been carrying week after week in the months of slaughter, bearing the names of so many of England's Catholic young men, were the reason for this. The war had robbed all the belligerent nations of the best of their young men, and had left behind thousands of bitterly mourning families - a scapegoat was needed. It was unthinkable that so much sacrifice should have been in vain and that a better world was not to emerge from what had happened. "In Austria things keep steadily moving" the magazine reported. "The Provisional Government of German-Austria has published its Bill for the elections to the Constituent Assembly, which are to take place on the last Sunday in January or the first in February, so that the new Assembly may be ready to meet on March 1st. Meanwhile an important manifesto has been issued by the Christian Socialists, who, with the Socialists, are the best-organised parties in the new Republic. In this document the Christian Socialists declare their unanimous recognition and support of the Republican form of Government decided upon by the Provisional National Assembly and promised to collaborate to the best of their ability in the development of German-Austria on the basis of free democratic principles. This is regarded, says a Berne correspondent, as the *coup de grace* to the Hapsburg dynasty, and the decision is undoubtedly based on the knowledge that it is fully approved by the population."

This was certainly not the case. Almost alone among the Kings and Emperors leaving their former lands, Charles and Zita enjoyed the support, affection and loyalty of the majority of their peoples. The small percentage of agitators and revolutionaries were only able to gain the upper hand because of the support of foreign governments, foreign republican movements and the united opposition of those outside Austria-Hungary who were implacably opposed, at any cost, to the existence of a central European monarchy.

A couple of weeks earlier, *The Tablet* had informed its readers that Empress Zita was already in Switzerland, while Charles was at Eckartsau; but this was wholly inaccurate. Neither Charles nor Zita had any intention of leaving home. Extremely unwell, with a bad attack of 'flu coming after several heart attacks following on the period of extreme overwork and worry, Charles was to spend the Christmas of 1918 in the uncertainty and discomfort that was also the lot of most of his fellow-countrymen. At Eckartsau, the Royal family and their court - about fifty people, members of staff, visitors, etc - were not actually starving, as it was possible to shoot game for food, but they were not well fed and were lacking many basic essentials such as soap and matches. The children became ill and the youngest, Karl Ludwig, very nearly died. The 'flu was the ferocious Spanish Influenza which was to encircle the world during the winter of 1918/1919 causing many deaths.

The realities of their plight were evidently unknown to those who persisted in seeing the family as being at the focus of a network of schemes for power. Britain's Sir H. Rumbold in Berlin sent a telegram back to the Foreign Office in Whitehall from Berne in Switzerland[5] on December 2nd:

> "An agent of the Military Attache's department has had an interview with Prince Hohenlohe Waldenburg, who told him that the Empress Zita and her court have resumed intrigues in favour of the reconstruction of a small Austro-Hungarian Empire.
>
> This movement is supported by many members of the Hungarian aristocracy who hope to overthrow Karolyi. The Emperor has informed his Magyar supporters that he had not definitely renounced his rights to the Habsburg crown. It is hoped that support will come from the Belgian court, and it is intended to put the question of the Austrian crown before the Peace Conference. The Emperor Charles has also endeavoured to gain Bavarian support for the creation of a new Austrian monarchy comprising South Germany and German Austria. This attempt has failed and the Emperor now bases his hopes on the support of the Pope with whom he is in constant contact of the aforesaid Magyars and of a group of German-Bohemian aristocrats who promise to start a monarchial movement in Bohemia."

Meanwhile the court at Eckartsau was actually effectively powerless. The Emperor and Empress who had put so much work and dedication into the search for peace were now, along with so many others, victims of the war, their future uncertain.

In the New Year the position of the Royal family became even worse. Elections were planned to create a new government for the rump of Austria which had been left following the dismemberment of the Empire. When these eventually took place in February a confused picture emerged, with the extreme left clearly defeated but with the monarchist group without a majority. The concept of Austria as a Republic was formalised, and the role of the court at Eckartsau suddenly looked even less clear than it had before.

In the Europe of 1919 the position of ex-monarchs was not a happy one. The example of the slaughtered Russian Romanovs was before their eyes. Empress Zita's family now moved to offer her the help and protection they could see she needed. The Princes Sixtus and Xavier, whose efforts during the abortive peace negotiations of 1917 had brought them into contact with the British Royal family, now renewed the links they had established at that time. They travelled to Britain and contacted King George V at Buckingham Palace. The result of their negotiations there was immediate: an officer was despatched, with all the authority of a representative of the victorious British Army and the very considerable status that this represented in defeated Austria at that time, to offer protection and support to Charles and Zita. Initially, a Colonel Summerhayes was despatched, on the recommendation of Colonel Sir Thomas Cunninghame, British Military Representative in Vienna. This appointment was quickly rescinded however and Colonel Edward Strutt was appointed in his stead.[6] He was to prove a loyal and devoted friend of the Emperor and Empress: acting indeed in an almost Rudolf Rassendyll fashion in support of their well-being and, later, their legitimate claim to their throne in Hungary.

Colonel Strutt found a sad group at Eckartsau, and one of his first tasks was to arrange for a British army lorry to deliver food. A longer-term problem was that of the Royal family's future. Charles and Zita flatly refused to flee from their homeland as if in panic. Any attempts to persuade them to cross the borders in disguise or travel to Switzerland under some sort of subterfuge were doomed to failure. As their position became more and more untenable, however, it became clear that they would have to leave. Through Colonel Strutt they were able to do so in a manner that at least made it clear that Charles still considered himself ruler, and would return as soon as it became possible.

There was never at any stage a suggestion that the Royal pair were personally unpopular among their subjects. Sadly, the Royalist groups among those bidding for power in Vienna were unable to organise themselves sufficiently to gain the control at government level. Among the ordinary people Charles was still widely regarded as the "peace Emperor", the embodiment of popular sentiment and a man who had suffered and struggled along with his people during the miserable years that had followed the outbreak of war. It was known that he had worked against all possible odds for peace, and that he represented a gentler tradition and view of life than did those who now currently wielded power in Europe. The difficulty was to see how he could be fitted in to the new order of things, and to the desperate power-games that were being played out in the aftermath of war.

It was clear to everyone who recognised the legal realities of his position that Charles had not abdicated. Colonel Strutt put it to the Emperor and Empress that in order to safeguard this position it would be better to go abroad. To remain at home might force the abdication issue or even provoke bloodshed. Budapest remained in a state of revolutionary chaos, and the borders of the new post-Empire states were still disputed. Within Austria itself there were unpredictable movements. While the ordinary people still loved their Emperor, plenty of minority factions did not, and any one of these might carry out an assassination attempt or successfully provoke an abdication crisis.

Eventually, Charles and Zita agreed to leave - but only on the understanding that the departure was not viewed as an abdication of their duties and responsibilities.

Meanwhile they had been given an ultimatum by the new republican government that had emerged from the elections. Immense pressure was put on Charles to abdicate, and he was told that if he refused to do so and remained in the country, he would be interned. If he did abdicate, he could remain in the country with his family, living as private citizens. It seemed at least to offer the promise of a quiet and even comfortable life, providing of course he was prepared to accept the status quo. This however was not acceptable to Charles. Hoping that it would not be for long, he decided to opt for exile as the only logical course. The British (who deemed themselves to be in charge of the whole operation) had already selected Switzerland as the most appropriate home for the the Emperor and his still young family. It was Colonel Strutt's own personal commitment to the Habsburg cause, however, that proved the most important factor in enabling Charles and Zita to leave their homeland with dignity. He also provided for them to send a clear message to their countrymen that they took with them a conviction that their duties and responsibilities had not ended and that they intended to return.

Strutt arranged for a special Royal train to take them from Vienna across the borders to Switzerland. He provided for a British armed guard, and he ensured that their departure took place in a proper style and in the full public gaze. He did this so that there could be no question of a legend emerging that the Royal family had departed in a 'blind panic'.

Dr Otto von Habsburg later recalled (1989) the departure from Eckartsau. It began with a packed Mass in the house chapel, at which he acted as altar server: "It was a gesture in keeping with my father's mentality" and it was a profoundly emotional service, which no one who shared in was ever likely to forget. The date was March 23rd 1919. That afternoon local people, including the Mayors of the surrounding villages, and many people who lived in the surrounding countryside, gathered to make their farewells as Charles and Zita came down the staircase together and into the main hall at Eckartsau. All fell to their knees as the Imperial couple came slowly down. Outside the dusk was gathering, and a convoy of four cars was waiting together with a contingent of British soldiers. As the last Habsburg Emperor and Empress made their way into exile, darkness fell and rain began to slash down. It was a fitting epitaph to a sad and fateful evening. In Vienna a huge crowd had gathered at the railway station. Silently they watched their Emperor enter the train that would take him away. At five minutes past seven the steam hissed and the journey began. A journey that was taking the last ruler of the Austro-Hungarian Empire, the direct historical descendant of the Holy Roman Empire, out of his ancestral land and into exile.

Notes:

1. Gordon Brook-Shepherd, *The Last Habsburg*, Weidenfeld and Nicholson, London 1968.
2. Public Record Office FO 371/3134.
3. The Marxist notion of a great struggle between social classes leading to a new and higher plan of civilisation, while possibly of some interest as an academic theory for armchair radicals has no bearing on historical reality which is much more complex, varied and unpredictable.
4. Gordon Brook Shepherd, *op.cit.*
5. Public Record Office FO 371 3134, from Sir H. Rumbold in Berne, April 24th, 1918.
6. Lieutenant Colonel Edward Lisle Strutt was a grandson of the 1st Lord Belper and also the famous 19th century convert to the Catholic faith, Ambrose March Phillips de Lisle. He was himself a catholic, an excellent linguist who had learned German at Innsbruck University. He was an extraordinarily highly decorated officer who had been educated at Oxford and had served in the Boer War before getting a DSO and Croix de Guerre while serving in the Great War as an officer of the Royal Scots Regiment. He could not have been a better person for the job now before him.

Chapter Ten

Although Charles and Zita were going into exile, they were also going to a home that belonged to their extended family. Wartegg castle in Switzerland was owned by the Bourbon-Parmas: Zita's father had bought it in the 1860's, and it was one of several properties which he owned in different parts of Europe. Sixtus, Zita's brother, had even been born there. The ancient castle contained numerous family members. Zita's mother had gathered a party to welcome her and make her feel at home. Princes Felix, René, Louis and Gaetan were there, along with three of her sisters. They were shortly afterwards joined by Sixtus.

The first few weeks of exile were thus spent in an atmosphere of good cheer. A visitor to the castle found Charles and Zita playing with the children in the grounds, helping to make a snow-man. Wartegg could only be a temporary refuge: it lay close to the Austrian border and the Swiss authorities had specified that Charles must settle further away from his own homeland, and choose somewhere in the west of the country. The next month therefore found them moving to the Villa Prangins on the shores of Lake Geneva. A substantial residence with its own grounds and enough space for a comfortable household.

Here their fifth child, Rudolf, was born, and a family routine established. This was perhaps the most peaceful and contented time that Charles had enjoyed since the early days of his marriage at Hetzendorff. There was of course always the pain of exile; the knowledge of what had been lost and of the chaos and misery in the lands which he still considered his responsibility. During 1919 he and Zita watched the unfolding of events in Austria and Hungary. In the former the

121

consolidation of republican rule included the arbitrary acquisition of all Habsburg family property and the banning of family members from the country. In the latter the grim Communist rule of Bela Kun, his eventual overthrow following a Rumanian invasion, and the establishment of a formal regency under Admiral Hothy.

The inherent instability of the Bela Kun regime, and the continuing economic and other problems of Hungary and the neighbouring territories made it seem very unlikely that the new system of fragmented states could continue for very long. In any case, Charles was still King of Hungary - while Austria had formally declared itself a republic, this other half of the Empire had taken a very different course. When Horthy finally marched into Budapest to restore order at the end of the Bela Kun confusion, it was in the name of the Monarch and at the head of an army committed to the return of the monarchy.

Admiral Nicholas Horthy had been a much-decorated officer and he seemed to many people to be a man who was genuinely committed to the old ideals of loyalty to monarch and nation. The Bela Kun regime gave Hungarians a taste of what Communism really meant. It had been a period of bloodshed and terror, of arbitrary shootings and imprisonment, and the fear of sudden arrest and death. The daily misery of poverty and hunger had climaxed in the humiliating occupation of Budapest by the army of Rumania, Hungary's long-time rival and enemy. The whole country was therefore ready for a strong initiative and a forthright challenge to any notion of Socialist ideas. Horthy seemed both a gallant fighter and a reassuring link with the past. He certainly would not have been able to take control as he did if he had not appeared as a representative of the faction which was wholly committed to restoring the lawful government under the still-popular King.

In January 1920 a coalition government was formed in Hungary. This established that the country was to be governed by an elected Regent who would hold provisional power until the return of the Monarch.

It seemed a sensible arrangement. Hungarians desperately needed a period of stability, having undergone misery and death under the previous brutal regime. The dismemberment of their territory meant that the country was now only a fraction of its former size. Under the post-war Treaty of Trianon, which was finally signed in June 1920, large areas of Hungary had been given to Czechoslovakia, Rumania, and Yugoslavia.

This Treaty was in fact to lay the foundations of many years of problems. Indeed even today the Hungarians living in Rumania have suffered because of their "minority" status in an alien culture. In 1919 and 1920, in the aftermath of a tragic war, the loss of so much land and so many people represented a massive blow to national confidence.

Horthy was to show himself to be a very different figure from the selfless patriot he claimed to be. He extended his powers from the merely "provisional" to the long-term, and was in fact to rule for over twenty years, aligning his country with Hitler's Germany before being forced to flee in the wake of the Red Army from the USSR. He had supreme confidence and believed that he was the right answer to the nation's needs. This extended even to his choice of successor. (He had appointed his son to rule after him but this son was killed fighting in the German army on the Eastern Front, and Horthy was swept aside when the country was taken by the Communists.)

Charles' plans for a restoration were not motivated merely by a ruler's obvious desire to regain his properties and title, but by a shrewd analysis of Hungary's recent and present rulers. In the summer of 1919 it seemed as if there was a real chance of Charles returning to Hungary to regain his throne. In fact it seemed to be the one logical answer to the area's many problems. At Prangins there were daily meetings with people who had recently come from Hungary. Through them Charles received regular news bulletins and was therefore fully *au fait* with events within Hungary.

However despite the time and attention which they still devoted to what they saw as their continuing duties, Charles and Zita were still able to make a life for themselves in exile. This was not easy as politics and the pressures of their unique position constantly intervened. Father Maurus Carnot, of the Benedictine monastery in the small town of Disentis, would later recall meeting the Emperor when plans were being discussed to send the children to that town for a little holiday. There had been fog by the lake at Wartegg and as a consequence they had all been unwell. Charles asked what the town was like and the priest told him that both the place itself and the surrounding countryside were more beautiful than anywhere else in the world, waxing lyrical about the snow and the fresh air: "Smiling, Emperor Charles listened to my hymn of praise. Then he stopped me with a question that I didn't understand at all. 'But can you reassure me that in Disentis my Otto would not be stolen?'" He told the Emperor that he didn't know what he meant, and Charles went on to tell him that there were plans in Hungary to make Otto, who was of course still only a small boy, King, and use him as a political football. Father Carnot assured him that the people of Disentis were extremely loyal and would certainly stop any would-be robbers who came into the area, and that they had, as he put it, "true hearts and ready fists". So the children went to Disentis, not only for that first winter, but also again the following year.

Father Carnot was one of a number of priests who played an important part in the life of the Royal family. Charles usually attended Mass every morning in exile, as he had always done back in Austria. Every special occasion or anniversary in his life was invariably marked with an appropriate religious service. Father Carnot presided, for instance, at a special Mass in the crypt of the Marienkirche in Disentis on December 30th, 1919, to commemorate the anniversary of Charles' and Zita's coronation. The next year, Charles and the children travelled to the village for the New Year. On the train he had caught a bad chill and later began to run a high temperature. Despite this he was still anxious to get to Mass on New Year's Day. Since it was obvious that he could not manage the journey to the church, Father Carnot arranged for Mass to be said in his hotel room.

However well they adapted to exile, Charles and Zita continued to see their stay in Switzerland as temporary. Always, Charles put his duties and responsibilities first. He had never considered that he had laid down the burden of what he had inherited: he felt that he had carried it all with him into exile, and he must work to ensure a just solution in the territories he had been called to rule.

As Horthy consolidated his rule in Hungary, the situation became more worrying. Initially, he had sent his monarch loyal messages of support, requests for permission to act, and assurances that all government was being carried out in his name and in the prospect of his return, but gradually things changed. Horthy established a new oath of allegiance for officers in the armed forces, which bound men to the service not of their monarch but to Horthy personally. Charles found that the messages and proclamations which he sent into Hungary were not published as he had intended. His questions on vital matters were not answered. His regent moved from being evasive to being more remote and inaccessible. It was time for the King to return and establish his right to rule.

There was considerable French support for a restoration bid, although this was not given publicly. Britain remained neutral throughout 1920, but she was later to show considerable hostility. Charles was eventually smuggled back into his homeland in March 1921, for what became known as the "Easter bid" to regain his throne.

Among his main helpers was Colonel Strutt, the British officer who had been such a support to the family at Eckartsau. Acting purely privately, and with no authority whatever, he helped to arrange for

Charles to leave Switzerland for France, and after this a network of contacts took over, with travel documents under various names being used as the King travelled by train across France to Austria. He arrived in Vienna late at night on March 25th - Good Friday. Once here, he was in the hands of his many and varied supporters: a Count who could put him up for the night, loyal drivers who could take him in relays to Budapest.

It was characteristic of Charles that, when his journey took him through a town where the traditional Holy Saturday procession was being held the next morning, he stopped the car and got out to kneel down as it passed, an example which was followed by his companions. After a hurried meal at a local inn, they continued their journey. Later they were forced to abandon the car when it broke down, and change to a horse and cart for the remainder of the journey.

They were aiming to make contact with the local Bishop at Szombathely, as it was thought that once this had been achieved a link could be established with the Prime Minister, Count Teleki. However in attempting this they encountered the first indication of how difficult it was going to be to wrest power from the Regent's hands. Teleki was formally correct but unenthusiastic about the arrival of the King. He announced that he would go on ahead to Budapest to report events to the Regent, but when Charles himself arrived the next day, Easter Sunday, at the Royal palace (where Horthy now lived) he found that Teleki was nowhere to be found and that the promised negotiations on his behalf had not been opened.

Finally, Charles met his regent face to face in the palace. Charles was alone. Teleki had urged him not to take any soldiers with him - even though there had been plenty of loyalist troops at Szombathely who would have supported him. He had left behind his only companions at the palace gates. Although the interview began with the King formally announcing his return, thanking the Admiral, and taking up again the burden of government, this could not be sustained. Horthy knew his power. He told the King that his return was premature, that a new government could not be formed, that neighbouring countries would see the arrival of the Monarch as a threat, and that the Army might revolt. The two men argued for more than two hours. Finally Charles played his only trump card and told Horthy, in complete confidence, that he had support from France. This meant not only diplomatic recognition but economic help for any new government. When Horthy then switched his own arguments, urging Charles to collect troops and march on Vienna to reunite the whole Empire, things had reached stalemate. It was eventually agreed that Charles would return to Szombathely and that Horthy should either join him there to follow up the Vienna plan, or expect to see him again in Budapest.

Charles was exhausted and ill - the secret journeying from Switzerland had meant that he had gone for two nights without sleep. When he returned to Szombathely it was in an open car in freezing weather. He remained at the Bishop's house in Szombathely while negotiations proceeded, and telegrams went to and fro. The tense battle of wills continued while Charles simultaneously sought to gather together supporters and shrug off what was turning into a severe bout of influenza and bronchitis.

Although he had plenty of supporters in western Hungary, in the area around Szombathely, these would be wholly insufficient if Horthy succeeded in uniting the rest of the Army against him. An even more tragic scenario than this was also possible. Neighbouring Serbia and Czechoslovakia were showing signs of alarm as the news of a Habsburg return spread, and if both these nations chose to flex their muscles then a divided Hungarian army might well find itself roundly defeated by invaders. Meanwhile Horthy had contacted the French to check that they were indeed offering the King their support. This was despite his promise to Charles that the information concerning France be treated as completely secret.

Naturally the French officials continued to state that their government's public policy was neutrality. Charles seemed to be increasingly isolated. For over a week, he battled on. The Regent was reminded of his own oath of loyalty to the King - an oath he had sworn twice, once as an officer and once in his civilian peacetime role in government.

But Horthy not only had control of the major part of the armed forces, but was also in charge of the communications network. He set up control posts along the roads leading to Szombathely and gradually isolated the area from the rest of the country. He issued orders to the Army reminding officers that their newest oath had been sworn personally to him.

In the first few days of April Charles was seriously ill. Although he remained determined to uphold his rights as monarch, it became obvious that his position was daily becoming more untenable. Finally, he agreed to withdraw temporarily to Switzerland provided certain conditions were met. He drafted a public message to his people to be distributed widely; he asked for full assurances that all those who had supported him should be given complete immunity from arrest or harassment; and he sought re-entry to Switzerland and continued temporary residence there on exactly the same terms as his previous stay. To all of this Horthy agreed.

The Hungarian nation may have been confused and uncertain as to exactly what was being done in their name, but there was absolutely no doubt that once people were given the opportunity of affirming their support for their king, they made their reactions clear. Perhaps it was mere romantic attachment, with no real intellectual support, but the message from the crowds that now greeted the King as he appeared in public following his illness was one of love and loyalty.

Preparations were made for his journey back to Switzerland, and on April 4th he was well enough to go. He had already made it clear that he regarded this trip as only a temporary retreat while certain matters were sorted out: he would be back. He appeared on the balcony of the Bishop's house to resounding cheers, with crowds packing the square below, waving and singing the national anthem. As he stood at the salute, joining in the singing and seeing below a wildly enthusiastic crowd, he must have felt a surge of hope for the future. All along the route to the station the mood was the same, with people rushing to show their support and to call out the traditional greetings of loyalty. The train itself had been specially hired and the journey turned into a royal tour, with stops at every village and town for special greetings to be passed on and for Charles to take the salute at parades, view dancing or singing in his honour, and accept the cheers of the crowds.

This "Till we meet again" theme echoed and re-echoed so strongly that some of those who had been dividing their loyalties between Charles and Horthy must have found themselves embarrassed. It certainly made Charles more determined than ever to ensure that the battle of wills continued and his seemingly immovable regent finally ousted.

Horthy's own protestations of loyalty also continued right up to the end. He continued to affirm that everything was being done for the ultimate good of the Crown as well as for the unity of the government.

He even begged Charles to give him various Royal favours and decorations before he left Hungarian territory. Nevertheless, he had got what he wanted. Charles was leaving and once back on neutral soil again would be much less of a threat to the Regent's own power.

Zita had been in touch with Charles by telegram while he was in Hungary. Now, on hearing of his return, she hurried from Prangins to meet him at the Swiss border. News of the restoration bid had of course been carried by all of Europe's newspapers for the past several days, and there was now much speculation about Charles' next move. The Swiss authorities were worried, and immediately started to impose many new restrictions on Charles' future behaviour. These were quite different in tone from the regulations which had hitherto governed Charles' life as an ex-monarch on their soil.

These restrictions had been cabled to Charles in Budapest when news of his impending return was announced. For reasons which have never become clear however Charles had never been informed of them. The Swiss authorities not unnaturally assumed that by crossing the frontier he had shown himself to accept these conditions.

However by the time he was learned of them he was already on Swiss territory and it was therefore too late. He was told that he could no longer remain at Prangins, but must remove himself and his family away from border areas. Furthermore it was necessary that he from now on inform the Swiss government in advance of any move to another place of exile. This was a crucial point. It was discussed and negotiated over the next few weeks, without anything being set down in writing. Finally at a meeting with an official to sort the matter out Charles set out his position as clearly as he could. He was rightful King of Hungary and could not recognise that he must inform Switzerland when he needed to return to his native land. Discretion and secrecy might be necessary in order to ensure that he return to Hungary safely - these would be impossible to achieve if his departure was heralded in the Swiss newspapers or surrounded by a whirl of diplomatic activity. He announced clearly that he understood the Swiss government's desire to be that he inform them of any removal to any new place of exile. He repeated the final phrase to ensure that he had not been misunderstood, and wanted to ensure that he was being seen to be choosing his words carefully. Hungary - or any other part of his Empire - could never for him be a "place of exile". He was willing to show his Swiss hosts all the courtesy he could, and he was not prepared to lie to them, but he was deliberately finding a form of words that was both morally acceptable and allowed him some possibility of action.

From now on, however, he was more closely watched. All foreign embassies in Switzerland took note of what he was doing, and sought to keep an eye on any link between him and his homeland. Attitudes were changing for the worse. Where previously Horthy had been seen as an upstart, he was now recognised as being an authoritative figure with an army at his command. A desire to maintain the status quo at any cost replaced a wish to see the return of legitimate government to Hungary

The British attitude certainly showed this approach. From the British representative in Vienna a letter sent to the Foreign Office in London on June 17th 1921 reported "I have always made it quite clear to the various partizans [sic] of the Habsburgs with whom I keep in touch that His Majesty's Government is absolutely opposed to any return of the ex-Emperor to either Austria or Hungary". From W. Athelstan-Johnson at the British High Commission in Budapest came a detailed report of June 22nd: "I have the honour to report that Count Banffy at his weekly diplomatic reception yesterday himself brought up the whole question of the return of Karl to Hungary, and the extraordinary number of intrigues and counter-intrigues that were attending these manoeuvres. He told me that those who really desired the ex-King's welfare were anxious to procure him a residence in Sweden, but that all the members of the Hungarian Andrassy group, and the Hungarian Karlist magnates, who fluctuated between Switzerland, Vienna and Budapest, were desirous of keeping him in Switzerland, where he was handy for their intrigues."[1]

This report went on to show the inherent instability of the Horthy government, and their panicky approach towards any hint of a return of the King, noting that Banffy had reported that "the Hungarian Government had recently become so alarmed at the success of certain Karlist plots in the Hungarian Army that they had had to deprive some of the higher grade officers of their command and were carefully considering a further removal of undesirable junior officers . . . . " This seems to show the complete contempt which Horthy regime's held for Charles' request that those who had shown support for him should not suffer any consequences. Further, the letter shows that the government was not above asking for foreign intervention in its attempts to block a restoration of Hungary's rightful King. Banffy, according to Athelstan-Johnson "requested me to urge on His Majesty's government the necessity of having some British control at Vienna, and up the Danube, to prevent the ex-Emperor from slipping down the river to Budapest. He had no faith in the Austrian control, and would be glad to put at the disposal of any British Control a Hungarian official to assist him." Athelstan-Johnson concluded this particular letter with the plea that Charles be found a home in Sweden "from which country it may be hoped he could no longer trouble the peace of the Hungarian Government."[2]

Meanwhile Charles had settled his family at Schloss Hertenstein, a pleasant building which for a time had functioned as an hotel. Money was now beginning to be a problem for the exiles, and this new base was considerably cheaper than Prangins. Although a great deal of his time was necessarily taken up with politics, Charles continued to enjoy the company of his children. The local Swiss became used to seeing the family on outings and at church events. In the winter months they had been enjoying the snow in the mountains, and they were also visitors to local monasteries and shrines.

There were now seven children: the youngest, Charlotte, had been born on March 1st, shortly before her father's bid to reclaim his throne. The Almanack de Gotha of 1920 listed them all as Archdukes and Archduchesses and described their father as having "renonce temporairement a l'excercise du gouvernement en Autriche par manifeste du 11 Nov. 1918 et en Hongrie par manifeste du 13 Nov. 1918" and said that he was "declaré dechu de ses droits souverains at autres prerogatives en Autriche et expulse du pays 3 Avril 1919". It said nothing of his exact status with regard to resuming power in Hungary. As far as Charles personally was concerned, his coronation oath had bound him to his people, and a return to serve them was a moral obligation.

There were rumours and counter-rumours about his activities throughout the summer of 1921. He himself remained calm at the centre of the storm. A visitor to Hertenstein that summer later described him with warmth: "The Emperor was standing in the middle of the room and held out his hand. He was of medium height, slim but sturdy and upright, wore a dark tweed suit and dark purple tie. I was chiefly impressed by the kindly expression of his big blue eyes and full Habsburg lips.

"He motioned me to a chair opposite him and began to talk in perfect French, one of the seven languages he commanded like a native, and he at once put me at my ease. As I had just come from Austria he encouraged me to describe conditions there under 'the so-called Republic' 'la soi-disante republique'. . . . He gave me a very lucid summary of the evil effects of cutting up the Empire, with details of the various regions which could no longer support themselves or obtain raw materials. He marshalled all his facts and figures so convincingly that there was never room for doubt or hesitation, and he possessed the rare gift of making every topic interesting. . . . "[3]

On 13th June Charles and Zita commemorated the tenth anniversary of their engagement with a special Mass celebrated by Father Maurus Carnot at Disentis. This was in fact to be their last visit to the little village where they had made so many family trips during these years of exile. Already, there were more schemes being discussed involving their return to their homeland. Time was running out. Failure to grasp the opportunities presented could mean that history would simply pass them by.

Rumours continued to fly round Hungary about Charles' plans. Athelstan-Johnson wrote - in cypher - to the Foreign Office from Budapest on 21st July: "I have been informed of an extraordinary story which my French colleague considers sufficiently substantial for him to have telegraphed it to his Government, to the effect that Karl is about to proceed to Denmark to visit his brother-in-law Réné de Parma. He will take with him aide-de-camp who has striking resemblance to him on the journey to Copenhagen.

"He will go to a Cistercian monastery near Szombathely where everything has been prepared for him by Count Batthyany Strattman and from there endeavour to make another attempt to regain the Crown on St Stephen's day. I give the story under all reserve."[4]

This Copenhagen story seems to have been a sudden development, for the previous day the idea of Charles re-entering his kingdom by slipping unnoticed up the Danube was still regarded as likely. Athelstan-Johnson had written back to London on 20th July "Count Banffy called on me this morning. He was so agitated that he rushed into the room with his hat and stick and at once informed me that the Hungarian Government had just received word from their Agents in Switzerland that all was arranged. . . . ." The details on this occasion were for a river attempt on 24th July, but the evidence for it seems to have been about as substantial as for the Denmark venture.

The Entente powers remained convinced that the long-term future for Charles and his family must lie much further away. Negotiations were proceeding with Spain - which had of course long links with the Habsburg family - and with Sweden. King Alfonso of Spain was known to be sympathetic to the family's plight, but the details of any specific arrangement were proving tricky. For Charles, it would of course have meant a further blow to his hope of an eventual return to his homeland, because Spain belonged to a wholly different part of Europe and geography would ensure that any return attempt would be much harder, and also because these physical facts would also spell out a psychological message for all his supporters and lower morale very substantially.

Finally at the end of July Count Alfonso Merry del Val, the Ambassador, was writing to Lord Curzon from the Spanish Embassy in London: "Your Lordship was kind enough to call my attention to the service which Spain would render to the cause of peace in Europe by giving asylum to the Emperor Karl.

"In reply to your proposal and its confirmation in writing, I am now authorised to inform Your Lordship that in order to comply with the wishes expressed by the British, French, and Italian governments, and in the interests of the peace of Europe, His Majesty's Government consents to receive the Emperor Karl in Spain.

"At the same time, however, I have to make it clear, as the Marquis de Lema has already stated direct to the British Chargé d'Affairs and the French Ambassador at Madrid, that the Spanish Government accepts no responsibility whatever for the Emperor's movements after his arrival in

Spain. On the other hand it is necessary that the Government should receive guarantees in advance that the Emperor possess means to live in Spain with the dignity befitting his rank . . . "[5]

Perhaps the statement referring to the Emperor's "movements after his arrival" caused some jitters - at all events Charles did not go to Spain, although knowledge of King Alfonso's friendship was to remain in his mind and emerge at a crucial stage later on. Meanwhile there were other plans, and a new dramatic chain of events was about to unfold.

It was clear that if there was to be any chance of wresting back power from Horthy, then action had to be taken as soon as possible. Every month that passed the Admiral established himself more firmly in the minds of foreign governments as the legitimate ruler of Hungary. In the minds of Hungarians the image of their king was becoming that of a shadowy figure, miles away, who had no tangible link with their land.

Although the Danube route seemed one obvious way of getting into Hungary, a far more efficient means of travel was now at hand and one which would minimise the need for elaborate subterfuge, forged passports, and the like. Charles could fly into his kingdom. His supporters went into action and through a discreet network of contacts a small private light aeroplane was obtained, and plans laid for a great venture. The King would be flown into Hungary, muster support among loyalist troops and seize power at the palace in Budapest, putting Horthy's supporters under arrest.

The troops that were to be a central part of this campaign were those under the command of a Major Ostenburg. They had been based in western Hungary but had been sent by Horthy to the Austrian border as a result of tension that summer over disputed territory, as the Austrian republic and the Hungarian regency tussled over which government could claim certain specific areas of land. Now that the dispute had been settled by a diplomatic agreement, Ostenburg's soldiers were being recalled to Budapest. Horthy doubtless planned to break up what was all too obviously a cohesive royalist unit and disperse its members among other units. The plan was that Charles should make contact with the train which was bringing the men back to Hungary's capital, assume command of the troops and travel with them to regain power.

Charles had never flown before. Perhaps as he and Zita made plans for the trip their minds went back to their first-ever joint visit to an airfield, which had been at Wiener Neustadt with Princess Cicca. This was during their engagement, in those halcyon days before the War. Now this newest form of transport was to take them back to their homeland to fulfil their continued sense of duty to their people.

They would be making the trip together as King and Queen. A great deal was at stake - if the enterprise failed, then the Habsburg cause would have received a possibly irretrievable setback. If it succeeded, then the most exciting but also the most serious period of their lives lay ahead - the reconstructing of a peaceful and united nation in the remnant of the ancient Empire which had been bequeathed to them by history.

Zita was now expecting their eighth child. Despite her pregnancy, she was determined to be with Charles on this great venture and to see it through to the end. The Easter bid had shown the need for an all-out effort and a strong presence. Every possibility that might strengthen the cause must be brought into play. The presence of Hungary's queen might help to show that the stakes were serious, and that what was intended was a full restoration of the Royal couple at the head of the nation.

The great venture was finally timed to start on October 21st. By pure coincidence, this happened to be a most significant date for Charles and Zita - their tenth wedding anniversary. The whole map of Europe had changed since that sunny day at Schwarzau back in 1911, but the unity of purpose that had been established between them at their wedding was the one thing which had remained constant and strong throughout the years of war, heavy responsibility, sorrow, and exile.

The children were, of course, to be left behind in Switzerland. Only Otto, as the oldest, was given some inkling of what was being undertaken; it was right that he have some idea of what was happening, because he was old enough to recognise what his father's position meant. The others were too young to understand.

Detailed arrangements were made for the flight, and for the couple's arrival on an estate in rural Hungary. Messages went back and forth between Hertenstein and the campaigners within Hungary itself. Eventually, on October 20th, Charles and Zita were boarding a light aircraft in Switzerland that had been hired privately to take them - they had been given a false name for the occasion but no passports or official papers of any kind - across the borders and into their homeland.

Years later the Empress was to be quoted as saying after a jet flight to Rome, "I've never liked flying". On this Autumn day in 1921 when she faced the flight to Hungary she was still a young woman. Moreover she was pregnant with her eighth child. She faced an uncertain future that depended upon her husband's ability to make contact with a troop train and assert control in his capital city. It was a risky venture indeed.

The couple landed safely and were taken to meet Colonel Lehar who was the senior loyalist officer responsible for bringing together the Ostenburg group of soldiers and arranging for the surprise arrival in Budapest.

When the world's press caught up with the story, the details brought out the flavour of adventure that accompanied it. "On Wednesday, four tickets were taken at Dubendorf, at the Ad Astra company, for a flight to Geneva and back", reported *The Times*. "The Junker aeroplane, CH59, was detailed for the journey, and on Thursday at noon five passengers arrived in two automobiles. They were muffled up, so that their faces were hid. The pilot, whose name is Zimmermann, is a German who was in the employment of a German enterprise and, was engaged to stay at Dubendorf, till the Ad Astra Company should take over the aeroplane. He neglected to announce his arrival at Geneva, as he was told to do. The flight seemed to take a western course, but nothing was seen or known of it at Geneva as there was no news of the whereabouts of the aeroplane. The Ad Astra Company announced the facts on Saturday to the Swiss Aviation Office."

Their wedding anniversary was a day of triumph. There was an open-air Mass which Charles attended at the head of his troops, and the thrilling ceremonial of men swearing allegiance to him before boarding the train which would roll through the night to the capital. Crowds gathered as the troops paraded and the Royal couple were hailed with cheers as they took their place in one of the front trucks, which had been roughly converted for their use. It had a table and two bunks with army blankets, but for the next dramatic hours it would be in effect a court train and the centre of Charles' strategic planning.

News of the whole bid was of course now public, and Horthy knew that battle was joined. The message was sent down the line from him in Budapest to stop the king's advance, but as the train rolled inexorably forward, town after town declared allegiance to Charles, and soldiers, instead of stopping him, joined his forces. It seemed as though the tragic muddles and problems that had beset the Easter bid were not to be repeated and that finally all was going to be well and the great opportunity seized. Events were also moving rapidly in Budapest. One major problem for Charles was that although many people were declaring themselves in his favour, not all did so whole-heartedly. A few key senior figures were divided in their loyalties. In addition the position of Britain was being made extremely clear by the British High Commissioner in Budapest, and Horthy was encouraged and strengthened by this.

The British were unequivocally opposed to any idea of a Habsburg restoration. The British line was that Charles' action was provoking civil war and that Horthy must be encouraged to stand firm at all costs and prevent him reclaiming power.

Among Charles' senior officers confusion and doubt began to be evident as the train stopped outside Budapest. During critical hours of planning and negotiations, while battle-lines were drawn up around the city and the army prepared to fight, Charles found that in the final analysis only Lehar and Ostenburg and those in their immediate circle were fully reliable. Horthy had gathered together troops under his own officers, and given out his own version of what was happening and the threat that it posed, as he saw it, to the nation. A key figure was his long-time supporter, Captain Gömbös. College students were brought forward to swell the ranks of soldiers ready to fight their King. As Herbert Vivian relates: "The Technical students had proved very useful patriots, resisting Communist attacks after the withdrawl of the Rumanians. They might serve again. Gömbös had the town plastered with posters during the night, announcing that hordes of Czechs and Communists were at the gates, that it was the duty of every able-bodied man to shoulder a musket and save the population from pillage, ravage and destruction such as had been known in the days of Bela Kun. He called the students together and addressed them as follows: "Our poor, well-beloved King has been led astray by Czechs and bands of Communists and is now advancing at their head against the capital. It is our duty to deliver the King out of their hands and save our country from a foreign occupation".[6]

Many factors played their part in frustrating Charles' plan. Confusion was rife amongst both his supporters and the general populace at large and this coupled with the muddled loyalties of many of the country's elite meant that Charles' room for manoeuvre was always limited. The problems that he faced are amply illustrated by the actions of General Hegedus. Hegedus, having first come out as a supporter of the restoration of the monarchy, reverted to Horthy's faction at a crucial point in the struggle. After the wholesale carnage that he had witnessed during the war, Charles was not prepared to countenance the further slaughter of Hungary's young. Finally, after two sleepless nights at their positions during which emissaries went to and fro, the royalist soldiers were finally overrun by the superior forces of Horthy's army. Charles was rendered helpless. In the last minutes, his faithful Lehar and Ostenburg leapt from the train - which during the two days of the struggle had been the royalist stronghold - prepared to lay down their lives in his defence. It was now quite useless however, and Charles called out to them not to get themselves killed pointlessly. The train drew out of Budapest, and with it went the hopes of the royalist cause.

In London, *The Times*, in a remarkably biased leader, asserted that Charles had broken his word to the Swiss authorities at the beginning of the whole venture, by failing to tell them what he was planning. It quoted Charles as having said, back in the spring, that he was bound to Hungary by an "indissoluble and sacred oath". It went on: "He was sure to endeavour to vindicate his claim whenever he supposed that 'The Day' had come. The only surprise is that he should suppose it to have come now, and that the Swiss government and the Entente Powers, knowing his intentions, should have placed implicit reliance on his word. Had it been 'an indissoluble and sacred oath' he would doubtless have respected it". In fact, Charles had taken care all along to be as open and honourable as he could. When he gave assurances to the Swiss he pointedly stated that he recognised an obligation to inform them if he were to leave for a "place of exile". Since Hungary was his home, this obligation could not apply.

In both London and Paris the official line was one of smug satisfaction that what *The Times* had referred to as "Karl's new putsch," had so completely failed. There was warm praise for Horthy, who was hailed as a firm and dedicated leader of a nation which had decided to take a sensible course in abandoning a troublesome king. In fact, the nation was by no means united behind Horthy, and the division and uncertainty which as Regent he gave to the country was to reach its climax twenty years later when the Nazis were able to exploit it during World War II. It was a pity that *The Times* leader writers were not as prescient as the Emperor they chose to mock.

Just as the earlier Easter bid had seen loyalty and affection on the part of ordinary Hungarians who rallied to their monarch, so this second and more vital venture was to end with manifestations of support from large numbers of people. They rallied to him as the train pulled in at a station near the country estate of the loyalist Esterhazy family, and cheered him to the echo as the Esterhazy carriages took him to a safe refuge for a night's rest. However they could not be a solace in what was to follow. Charles and Zita were handed over to the Allied authorities on the orders of the victorious Horthy. A chilling journey into an unknown future of exile had begun.

On 25th October, Charles and Zita were moved to an abbey at Tihany, a remote spot where they were effectively held captive while the Horthy government and the Allies decided on their fate. It was agreed that he would be taken away to board a British warship which would then ferry him to whatever place of exile was deemed most suitable. Both Malta and the Canary Islands were mentioned as possibilities. The mysterious coalition of hidden forces which opposed the ancient Habsburg dynasty was now exercising its malign influence to the maximum.

While in Tihany, Charles had a visit from Hungary's primate, Cardinal

Csernoch. "I went to his room with anxiety" he said later. "I had expected to find a broken, fearful, suffering king, for whom one could find no words of consolation . . . . I had been deceived. The storm had passed over the King. His hair had gone white, his face was lined by anxiety. His appearance was solemn and serious, that of a man who has taken a full consciousness of his suffering. He was fully and clearly in charge of his position, and required neither explanation nor consolation. He accepted the final consequences yet still kept his trust and his hope."

Recalling Charles' words to him on that occasion he remembered that the king said: "I have done my duty, as I came here to do. As crowned King, I not only have a right, I also have a duty. I must uphold the right, and the dignity of the Crown." He said that he considered himself to be under a debt of honour to the nation. "For me, this is not something light. With the last breath of my life I must take the path of duty. Whatever I regret, Our Lord and Saviour had led me."

Later the Cardinal commented "For such a soul, no comfort was necessary. He evoked admiration for his wonderful strength."[7]

On October 30th Charles and Zita went by rail from Tihany to Baja, where a British ship *The Glow Worm* was waiting for them. A British correspondent described the scene: "The train conveying the two exiles left Tihany, where they had been interned since their surrender at Tata, last night, and did not arrive at Baja until this morning, when the sun was well above the horizon, shining on woods and meadows glittering with hoar frost on either side of the Danube.

"Looking up from the quay where the two British monitors, Glow Worm and Ladybird, were lying at anchor, to the high railway viaduct, one saw a long train slowly coming to a standstill. Immediately, four figures, Lt. Col Selby, Commander Johnson and Cols Hinaux and Cuzzoni representing the Entente were seen coming to the steps and along the quay . . . . a strong military escort lined the way from the train to the vessels. Then came the ex-King in Field Marshall's uniform, and Queen Zita in a blue costume . . . . as he went on board the ex-King showed a cheerful countenance and was extremely gracious to everybody . . . . . He set his face from the beginning against receiving any representative of the Hungarian government on the grounds that the government was in rebellion against him.

"The Papal Nuncio - the ex-King is a devout Catholic - was the last possible instrument of negotiation, but all attempts to shake Charles' obstinate refusal to abdicate have as yet proved futile".[8]

Notes:

1. Public Record Office, file FO 371; 180; 11790.
2. ibid.
3. Herbert Vivian, *The Life of Emperor Charles of Austria,* Grayson and Grayson, London 1932.
4. Public Record Office, file FO 371; 180; 15431.
5. ibid.
6. Herbert Vivian. *op. cit.*
7. Cardinal Csernoch's memories, published in the *Kaiser Karl Gebetsliga* yearbook, Lilienfeld, Austria, 1985.
8. *The Times,* Oct 31st, 1921.

Chapter 11

The plight of the Royal couple from the moment they were handed over to the care of the British navy was later summed up dramatically but accurately by an Austrian author: "They journeyed down the Danube into exile, to a destination still unknown to them, separated from their children, their country, without any means, completely destitute."[1]

They were not told where they were going, and they could not get in touch with their children in Switzerland. They had no goods with them, and not even an adequate change of clothes. As the journey down the river continued, people heard what was happening and when the Royal couple were taken off by car to meet a British warship which would take them to their final place of exile, crowds gathered. In many places they knelt as the couple passed, in others people wept openly and called out "We kiss your hands". At one point the crowds were driven back by soldiers using their rifle-butts.

At Sulina Charles and Zita were taken on board the British warship HMS *Cardiff*. They still did not know what their final destination would be. In order that Charles would not have to be treated as a prisoner, the ship's captain asked him to give his word of honour that he would not try to escape during the voyage. This he gave readily, using this opportunity to set the record straight about the rumours which had been circulating - and which were being published in the British press - that he was not a man of his word. It was being said that he had not been honest with Horthy about his planned return to Hungary, and that he had not informed the Swiss authorities of the trip either. The Empress, in her diary notes, later published, described on 8th November how the

Emperor cleared this matter with Captain Lionel Maitland-Kirwan of the *Cardiff* before the latter went to report to his admiral when the ship arrived at Constantinople: "The Emperor managed to get hold of the captain before he left the ship to make it clear to him that both allegations were untrue. He had promised to let Horthy know and he *had* let him know. As for the second case (of not informing the Swiss authorities of his departure in October) the Swiss had only expressed 'a desire' to be told and the Emperor had told them they would be informed forty-eight hours 'before he left for *a new place of asylum*'. This, however, did not describe Hungary. The captain was quite relieved but said even without these assurances he would not have believed the newspaper stories."[2]

The next day Charles and Zita were told that their final destination was probably to be Madeira. Two days later this was confirmed, and Charles was informed that he would be formally handed over to the Portugese authorities who ruled the island. In the meantime they had to endure the acute discomfort of seasickness, and the anguish about their children - although this was relieved when Zita was finally allowed to send them a letter and a telegram from the ever-faithful Colonel Strutt arrived saying that they were well and in good care.

As always Charles and Zita were keen to attend Mass and receive Communion: they asked for this and it finally became possible two days before the end of the long journey, on November 17th. Then as the ship steamed away from Europe the sea became rougher and after forty-eight hours of constant seasickness they drew towards Madeira and were arriving in Funchal harbour.

A crowd had gathered here to watch their arrival, and there was comfort in the welcome given to them by the local church dignitaries, who did their best to show concern and support. It was 19th November, the feast of St Elizabeth. As the ship came into harbour, Charles saw the two flat towers of a mountain church rising above the other features on the island and pointed them out, saying that it must indicate a shrine of the Virgin Mary. "It reminds me of our churches at home. We'll visit it as soon as we can!" His words were strangely prophetic, for it was here, in the church of Nossa Senhora do Monte, that he would be buried a short time later.

For the first few weeks of their exile, they were based at the Villa Victoria, part of a local hotel. Their overriding concern apart from their worries about the fate of those who remained loyal to the monarchy back in their homeland, was for their children. It was by no means certain that they would ever be allowed to be reunited with them. It was a sad and lonely Christmas. They were allowed to send letters and receive news, and Charles sent the children a message reminding them that "At Midnight Mass, before the Eucharist, nothing can separate us" and exhorted them to courage and hope. Finally, after many weeks, it was announced that the children would be on their way, but there was a delay: one of the youngest, Robert, was very ill with appendicitis and needed an operation. Empress Zita was allowed, under very stringent conditions, to leave Madeira to be with him.

No concessions were made to allow for her pregnancy, and she and the people with whom she stayed were subjected to humiliating searches, long waits, and questioning. A later biographer Herbert Vivian, described the trip: "Being in a delicate condition, she shrank from the long journey and asked leave to rest a night in Paris on her way. Even that was curtly refused. Indeed, worse conditions were imposed. For some incomprehensible reason, the journey must be made via Geneva and Bordeaux, which, owing to bad connections, meant 36 hours *en route*, no sleeping-cars, frequent changes and long waits at stations during the nights, not to mention extortionate Swiss charges between Zurich and Bellegarde." The charges were a highly relevant factor in making the journey difficult: the Royal pair were now extremely short of money. There would be long wrangles over just who was responsible for their upkeep, and while these continued no actual cash was sent to them for ordinary expenses. All the Habsburg property in the old Empire had been confiscated by the new governments. There were disputes over certain private properties which promised to continue for a long time and in the meantime they produced no actual income for the exiles on Madeira. The only possible source of funds were the family jewels, and even these were now found to be of less use than had been hoped. Some had mysteriously disappeared and could not be traced. While Zita was away looking after Robert, Charles had to face the prospect of supporting a large family and small attendant group of helpers on virtually no money at all. He had never had to deal with financial matters, had no advisers, and no access to international bankers or possible sources of practical help.

Once the operation was over, Robert was still too ill to travel, and it was arranged that Zita would return with the other children to Madeira and that he would be brought on later. Charles was waiting at the quayside in Funchal when his family arrived. Onlookers saw tears on his face as he ran up to greet them and sweep the smallest children up in his arms. He looked much older now: although he was not yet 35, his hair had turned grey and his face was lined.

Along with the children had come various items of luggage and household goods, and plans were now made to establish a proper home in exile. It would be a very impoverished establishment. All the items which might have linked the family with the past or been a source of solace or personal comfort had been left behind in Switzerland, and there was no money to buy new luxuries. Indeed, there was no money even to maintain their stay at the Villa Victoria. It looked as though the family might become homeless.

Perhaps a man of more bravado and a less tender conscience might have remained at the hotel, running up bills and confidently asserting that the responsible governments would eventually pay them. But Charles thought in a different way, and simply wanted to find somewhere that would offer shelter and not incur debts that he could not honour. He and Zita were for all practical purposes alone and he had no guarantee that anyone would ever come to their aid or that the governments who were nominally responsible for them would produce money to pay day-to-day bills in the immediate future. Thus when he was offered the chance of a house completely free he accepted at once and made plans for moving the family there as soon as possible.

Various other people had offered accommodation - but at a price, because it was not unnaturally thought that an ex-emperor must have considerable means at his disposal. The only offer of any practical use came from a local landowner who had a holiday house, the Quinta do Monte, which as its name suggests was up on the hill, overlooking Funchal and the harbour. Charles now arranged for the family to move there, personally packing their goods into carts which would take them up the hill.

The house had been built as a summer holiday retreat. It was unsuitable for use during other months of the year as it was damp and chilly. When the sun was shining down by the coast, the hillside was still misty and cold. Fires were necessary in all the rooms but they could not disperse the lingering chill or help to remove the huge growths of fungus on the walls. Basic household necessities were lacking. It was hard to get washing clean and dry and there was not enough money for decent meals. Charles and Zita refused to complain and tried to make the best of everything, although the future looked grim. There was no nurse or midwife to help the Empress with the baby who was due in May, and they were still cut off from all sources of help or information from their homeland.

Charles continued to remain cheerful, encouraging the family to retain faith and hope, emphasising that they still had one another and were in many ways "undeservedly happy". A priest, Father Zsamboki, had now joined the household, and on their first day on the Monte Charles had him bless each room and gather everyone together to pray.

Years later Archduke Otto would recall how, over the next few weeks, he and his sister Adelheid spent long hours on walks with their father while he talked to them about a whole range of things. He answered their questions and tried to help them understand the particular position of their family and the duties of a Christian ruler under God. This was their last time of family togetherness. When little Robert arrived in early February (brought by a loyal friend of the family) Charles had only two months more to live. Perhaps he somehow had some inkling of this, in his anxiety to communicate something of his ideas and life's work to his children while he had the opportunity. Always, he had found a special joy and support in his children's company - now they seemed closer to him than ever.

During March he caught a bad chill on a visit to Funchal with two of the children to buy toys. It was sunny and warm by the sea but the cold damp air hit them again as they returned up the mountain. A few days later he had to admit that he was ill and was confined to bed. Pneumonia set in. His condition rapidly worsened: doctors were summoned although he at first pleaded against this because funds were so low. A tormenting cough meant that he got very little sleep, and the various efforts of the doctors - including turpentine injections in the leg which were meant to "draw down the infection" and hot cupping of his back which raised terrible blisters - brought him more agony. He remained courageous and uncomplaining. An altar was set up in his room, where Mass was celebrated every day. He was anxious about the children, two of whom were also ill, and he wanted to know what the newspapers were saying about his homeland and about events in Europe. He prayed a great deal of the time: for the future of his people, and for peace and better times for them all.

He refused to complain even when he was all too evidently in severe pain. He was heard to say "I must suffer like this so my people will come together again."

By now he desperately needed oxygen. This could be obtained in Funchal only in small old-fashioned containers which allowed about seven minutes' relief each. Uncomplainingly, he fought for breath.

He became delirious, thinking that there were visitors from his homeland and trying to sit up to greet them. Most of the time however , he was in perfect control of himself, still remembering to address the doctors in French and trying to show gratitude to everyone around him.

When it became obvious that he was dying, he was given the Sacrament of the Sick. He asked that Otto be brought into the room to take part in the ceremony. The next day he was anxious about the little boy. "I would have liked to have spared him all that yesterday. But I had to call him to show him the example. He has to know how one conducts oneself at times like this - as a Catholic and as an Emperor."

At one point he turned to his wife and said in a heartrending voice: "Oh, why do they not let us go home? I want so much to go home with you." He seemed to be aware however , that a different path had been prepared for him. He publicly forgave his enemies, and all who wished him harm.

Later he suddenly told the Empress, very seriously and calmly, that she must go to the King Alfonso of Spain for help and protection. He was clearly looking ahead to a time when Zita and the children would be left without him. "He is chivalrous . . . . he has promised me," he told her. Zita was puzzled: neither she nor Charles had seen Alfonso in years, but a short while later she was to recall these words.

Charles' concern in his final hours was not only for his people - to whom he still felt bound by his coronation anointing and his solemn obligations - but also for his children. He listed each one lovingly by name, and then mentioned the littlest one of all, as yet unborn: "Protect their bodies and their souls . . . .". He was holding a cross in his hands.

It was Saturday, April 1st. He had not slept properly now for many days and nights. His exhaustion was complete, and his body with its sores and racking cough seemed only a light frame for his spirit. Now he seemed to have no breath left. He had called out for Otto to come into the room again, and the child had slipped in and was kneeling , crying, by the bed. Charles had a final message for his wife: "I love you so much," he said.

His heart beat faster and his face grew completely pale. He had no strength even to kiss the cross which his wife held before him. After some while he panted "I can't go on much longer". He murmured: "Thy will be done . . . . Yes . . . . Yes . . . . . As you will it . . . . Jesus! . . . . " and saying this he died.

News of the death was swiftly reported around Europe, producing a flurry of political and diplomatic activity as well as newspaper commentary. In both Vienna and Budapest there was a period of official mourning, with flags flown at half-mast and requiems held. *The Times* on April 4th published a report from its correspondent in the Hungarian capital: "The Regent, Admiral Horthy, and the Prime Minister, have sent heartfelt condolences to the Queen. The Government has ordered all public buildings to fly a flag at half-mast. Theatre performances and music are all forbidden. The wedding of the Regent's daughter has been postponed. Church bells are tolling. The Cardinal Primate will personally celebrate the Requiem Mass. It is, at any rate, agreed that Hungary must by united expressions of mourning fulfil its chivalrous duties towards the Monarch banished by foreign decree. An imposing manifestation of mourning is expected. . . . . "

There was no question of Charles' body being allowed back to any part of his former Empire for burial, and those who remained loyal to him could only attend requiem services and organise parades and rallies in his honour. Hungary's official Requiem was held on August 4th at the church in which Charles had been crowned less than six years earlier. The church was packed but the only foreign representatives were the Papal Nuncio and Ministers from the American and German embassies. The private report from the British Legation back to the Foreign Office in London commented rather sourly: "The death of the ex-king in exile - following upon reports of the alleged hardships undergone by himself and his family in Madeira - has keenly affected Hungarian public opinion. To popular imagination his misfortunes seemed, perhaps, to typify those of his unhappy country, and it is characteristic of the romantic strain in the temperament of the Magyars that many of them should now regard as a popular hero - if not as a martyr - a ruler whom they esteemed but little until he had ceased to rule . . . . "[4]

From Vienna on April 7th *The Times* correspondent noted that the Requiem Mass at St Stephen's Cathedral on the 6th "gave the Monarchists their first opportunity since the establishment of the Republic to express their long-repressed Monarchial feelings". They mustered in what he described as "unexpected strength", many in the old Imperial Army or Navy uniforms, and joined Habsburg family members, former Prime Ministers, and some of the current Members of Parliament in a packed cathedral. "After the service many of the younger members of the congregation, led by the Archduke Rainier Charles, and Leopold Salvator, his father, formed an imposing column with cries of 'Down with the Republic' which mixed with the strains of the Imperial Hymn as they made their way to the Houses of Parliament. Here a deputation waited upon the President of the House and demanded that appropriate honours in the shape of flags at half-mast be rendered to the Emperor Charles as a former sovereign. With this demand the President complied."

In Budapest Horthy made an ostentatious display of himself at the ceremonies, leaving an immense floral tribute. His overriding concern with the security of his own rule was shared by the British authorities present, who seemed only too happy to give him the fullest possible support. "Mourning is being observed here for the ex-Emperor", a telegram from the British representative in Budapest reported back to London. "Legitimists already declare that Otto is now the lawful king and that the ex-Empress should be proclaimed Regent. Situation is perfectly calm but Hungarian government apprehend disturbances would occur if the funeral were permitted to take place in Hungary. Presume arrangements will be made for his burial elsewhere, and ex-Empress and children will not be allowed to leave Madeira."[5]

The unknown official who sent this message need not have worried. Charles was to be buried in Funchal, where his widow and children (their sad plight still not alleviated by any hope of practical assistance on the part of those who had control over their fate) acted with a dignity that was touching all local hearts. An Austrian lady in Madeira wrote home to a friend about it: "I went up to Monte on Wednesday morning to pay my last tribute to the Emperor. It was all so sad and miserable. He lay on a plain coffin on the floor and no priest was present, only one gentleman who must have been the children's tutor. The Emperor wore the ordinary field uniform and the Order of the Golden Fleece. Beside his head was the wreath of the Austrian colony with black and yellow ribbon, and there were masses of flowers, the only relief to the piteous impression."[6]

In his hands Charles held a golden rosary, the gift of Pope Pius X. The Catholic Church, which had been a source of consolation and hope for him all his life accorded him what support it still could. So too did many ordinary people who recognised in him a tragic figure overwhelmed by events.

The funeral took place on April 6th. Thousands watched the procession, in which the local Portugese public authorities together with Madeira's various organisations were represented. Charles had been a familiar figure on the island at church events. Now the place he had once described as his "ever-faithful Funchal" was paying him all the honour it could muster . Formal representatives also came from the Consuls of the various European nations which had offices on the island.

All attention naturally focused on the young widow, dressed in black and heavily veiled, who walked with her children behind the coffin. Also impressive was the sight of Count Karolyi, carrying the dead Emperor's decorations on a cushion. The Austrian lady's letter brought out the poignancy of the occasion: "The body was laid to rest in the old pilgrimage church of Monte. It was brought thither in a low, two-wheeled cart, drawn by one of our gentlemen and the Emperor's Austrian servants. Carriage horses are not to be found here. The whole society of

Funchal followed, and an enormous crowd had gathered round the church. The Empress was there with her three eldest children. All the children are the most charming you can imagine, especially the two eldest boys. After the funeral, one of the Austrian gentlemen kept vigil till nightfall. Then the Empress came again with the heir to the throne. She is indeed a wonderful woman. Not for a moment did she lose her composure, nor did the children give way. I did not see one of them shed a tear. They were merely very pale and very sad. As they left the church, they bowed on all sides. Then the Empress spoke with those who had helped with the funeral. All were impressed by her charm. The coffin was covered with the old Austro-Hungarian flag, displayed perhaps for the last time. What is to happen now to the unfortunate family?"

This last question was also vexing the minds of many British officials, not out of concern for a pregnant woman stranded penniless with her young children, but because they believed she represented a challenge to their own view of what was right for the territories her husband had ruled.

The question of the Empress' future, and that of her children, was an urgent one and needed to be settled. They were without funds and her pregnancy was now far advanced. Obeying Charles' expressed wish, she contacted King Alfonso of Spain. He was to prove a chivalrous protector. He sent a telegram to the Pope, which was made public, asking that help be given to the Empress and, alluding in delicate terms to her "present condition", suggested that it should call forth the most generous and helpful response on the part of those who had control over her position.

The telegram said:

> "In the conviction that His Holiness the Pope, as doyen of the Sovereigns, is sincerely affected by the circumstances of the death of the ex-Emperor Karl, I beg your Holiness to add your venerated plea to mine to the end that his widow and children may be provided with the necessary means of livelihood, especially in view of the Empress's present condition, for which the most elementary principles of humanity demand respect and protection. I am convinced that the Sovereigns and heads of State of the nations which were victorious over the former Austro-Hungarian Empire will join us with their proverbial generosity."

The official British reaction, in the first few days following the funeral, was unsympathetic to the point of callousness. One British member of Parliament who took up the cause of the Austrian royals, Colonel F.B.

Mildmay, was given a rather dismissive reply when he wrote to Lord Harmsworth about what was happening.

"I am not out to sympathise with the fallen rulers of enemy countries", Mildmay wrote "but I am anxious to know whether, directly or by implication, the British government, in common with those of our Allies, made itself responsible at Versailles for receipt by the family of the late Austrian Emperor of the bare means to live. I am told, on authority which to me is unquestionable, that if any responsibility does lie with us, and with the powers who signed at Versailles, we are open to a charge of culpably ignoring it.

"We, and those who acted with us, banished the Emperor and his family to the island of Madeira, which is by reputation a health resort - but it must be remembered that only certain positions in the island are healthy. When he arrived at Funchal, the Emperor lived in the Villa Victoria, a very healthy position. But he had to give it up in February as, in view of his condition of penury, he could not pay the rent. He removed his family to a villa in the hills - Quinta del Monte, then damp, cold and unhealthy - as it was placed at his disposal gratis. He could not heat the house, he had no money to pay for fuel, and the consequence was that he contracted his fatal illness and died. His lack of any means at all had alone forced him to dwell in the unhealthy part of the island.

"I suggest, but I may be quite wrong, that the powers banished the Emperor to this far island and then washed their hands of him, not troubling as to how he was to live . . . . The Austrian Government then seized their private fortune and property, and ever since 1918 the family has been living on the proceeds of the Habsburg family jewellry which is not very valuable. When they got to Madeira, little was left, so that real want and distress compelled their acceptance of the free house, which brought the Emperor to his death, at which moment his wife and six or seven children [in fact there were seven children already, with an eighth on the way] had nothing but starvation to contemplate.

" . . . . Since then it would seem that charitable assistance has been provided in order that they may be enabled to transfer themselves to Spain, but I am under the impression that they are still left without means of any kind, and that the widow and the many orphan children, are all but destitute".

The colonel ended with a gentle reminder that Charles had not, after all, been the major villain figure of the recent War: "Although neither you nor I can be expected to sympathise with those who have ruled Austria in the past, it is to be remembered that this Emperor, from the moment he succeeded to his most unenviable Crown, did his utmost to break away from the tight hold of the German Emperor...."[7]

The reply which he received not only repeated what was to be a standard British line on the subject - that Charles had "dishonoured his solemnly pledged word" in attempting to regain his kingdom, but went on to deny even the basic facts relating to the cause of his death. Cecil Harmsworth wrote: "I cannot accept what you say in relation to the climate of Madeira, and all my information goes to show that probably no spot on the island can seriously be called 'damp, cold and unhealthy'. With regard to fuel, I am told that the only houses on the island which have any fireplaces at all are the few built by English residents, who occasionally burn a few pine cones on a hearth, for sentimental reasons rather than for purposes of warmth." He said that the problems over money followed disputes with the new republics carved out of the old Empire: "The difficulty is to fix the actual amount and to secure payment. But I have no doubt that a settlement will not be long delayed." Then he went on to add a particularly acid note: "In the meantime the Emperor's private funds may no doubt have become exhausted. If much of the money spent by him on propaganda in Switzerland came from his private pocket, their early exhaustion is not very surprising."

The Spanish King's intervention had, however, evidently stirred some other Royal consciences. On 20th April Sir W.G. Tyrrell at the Foreign Office received a letter from Buckingham Palace. It was signed by George V's equerry, Lord Stamfordham, and consisted of just one sentence: "The King asks whether any progress has been made in Paris about the arrangements for the ex-Empress Zita?"[8]

The reference to Paris was to the Conference of Ambassadors of the victorious Allied nations then taking place in the French capital. It raised a rather touchy subject. The French were being rather more conciliatory about the plight of the Empress than the British seemed inclined to be. The official British line was one of complete support for the governments of the newly-created post-Empire States, especially Czechoslovakia. Tyrrell replied to Stamfordham with a copy of a report of the Ambassadors' meeting, commenting:

"Our proposal had been that a pledge should be obtained from [Empress Zita] that she should refrain from any intrigue in favour of a Habsburg restoration, and that if she gave such a pledge she should be free to return to Europe. Both the King of Spain and the Pope had evinced great interest in her fate and to the former we have suggested that His Majesty should grant her asylum in Spanish territory, provided she gives the desired assurances, and to the latter we have suggested that if

His Holiness himself could extract a pledge from her, that would afford additional security, as she would doubtless regard this as a solemn undertaking of a binding nature . . . . You will recall that on the occasion of the ex-Emperor's second attempt last year we only restrained the neighbouring states from overrunning Hungary by presenting to the Hungarian government the demands of those States for the definite exclusion from the throne of all members of the Habsburg family. It was to the principal Allied Powers that Hungary gave the pledges in this sense that averted her own national disaster, and we feel it would be unwise, after the difficulty we had in overcoming that crisis, to leave undone anything that might prevent a similar situation from arising. If it did arise, we could have no confidence that we should be able to avert hostilities, which would almost certainly break out before we could have time to intervene.

"May I add that President Masaryk told a friend of mine not long ago that, if a fresh attempt were made by the Habsburgs, nothing would prevent the Czechs from marching on Budapest . . . . ". This was in fact pure bluff on the part of Masaryk who was in no position to march on Hungary's capital.

On May 8th, a Foreign Office memo, referring to the French and Italians "yielding to sickly sentiment" and to the British demand for "drastic and logical action", was still trying to urge that the Empress "be kept in Madeira unless she gave a pledge that she behave herself." However the British soon accepted the inevitable and a telegram to Lord Hardinge, the British representative in Paris, from London on May 16th, said that "His Majesty's government, while adhering to their opinion that it would be most desirable to induce the ex-Empress to give pledge before her departure from Madeira, does not wish to prevent her leaving on the 18th for which, we understand, she is making arrangements." It went on "The action of the French government, against which you have been instructed to protest, will no doubt now make it more difficult to obtain the pledge and practically ties our hands" and concluded sulkily "in any case we remain of the opinion that pledge ought eventually to be obtained, and that at least grant of allowance should be made conditional on this."⁹

So Zita and the children went to Spain, where they were made welcome by the Spanish Royal family. When they arrived at the Royal palace, according to one account, Alfonso told Zita of a strange experience he had had when he learned that Charles was lying fatally ill: "King Alfonso related to her, how in the night before the death of the Emperor Charles, he was overcome with a feeling that, in the event of the Emperor's death, if he, the King, would not take his widow and the children under his protection, his own wife and his own children would suffer one day the same fate. He only found peace, after he had firmly resolved to give the bereaved family a home in Spain, as the death of the Emperor seemed to be certain. King Alfonso was not less overcome than the Empress Zita, when she then told him what the Emperor Charles had said before his death."[10]

Zita's baby was now nearly due. The child was born on 31st May, eight weeks after Charles' death, and was baptised Elisabeth, the name that Charles and Zita had agreed on some while before, in memory of their arrival in Madeira on St Elisabeth's day.

The family now faded from the public scene. After staying for a while with the Royal family at the Prado palace in Madrid, they moved to Lequeitio on the Basque coast. In 1929 they moved to Steenokerzeel, a moated castle owned by the Marquis de Cröy in Belgium, not far from Brussels. Otto went to school at Clervaux and then to the University of Louvain. Zita was occasionally seen at Lourdes and other places of pilgrimage. From the day of Charles' death she wore nothing but black - and she was to maintain this throughout her 67 long years of widowhood. As one later writer was to describe it, "shunning a life of comfortable exile in the fashionable watering-places of the world, she lived by the strict principles of her belief. Staunchly devout, immoveable in her faith, she became the matriarch of a vast family which would reach into the fourth generation . . . . "[11]

Notes:

1. Katharina Rasinger, in a privately-published pamphlet "The Emperor Charles I of Austria - a Great Christian Monarch, a short history of his life and death", based on the biography by Hans-Karl Zessner-Spitzenberg, who died in Dachau in 1938.
2. Gordon Brook-Shepherd, *The Last Habsburg*, London, 1968.
3. Herbert Vivian *The Life of Emperor Charles of Austria*, Grayson and Grayson, 1932.
4. Public Record Office file FO 371; 7618.
5. *Ibid.*
6. Herbert Vivian, *op.cit.*
7. Public Record Office, file number FO 371, 250; 7621.
8. Public Record Office FO371; 7618.
9. *Ibid.*
10. Katherina Rasinger, *op cit.*
11. *Imperial Gazette*, a memorial magazine published in Austria in 1989.

Chapter Twelve

We have seen how the determination of the Entente powers to effect the break-up of the Austro-Hungarian Empire, led them to assist the nationalist leaders in each of the countries that had been part of the Empire in the realisation of their plans.

The old system that formerly had held central Europe together had come apart. Progressive thinkers believed that this would herald a new dawn of peace and prosperity. With the benefit of hindsight we know that this was not to be the case.

Even at the time there were some who could see that this new dawn was in reality a false one. The disintegrated firmament of Europe provided no bulwark against any future threat to the security and peace of the continent. The reparations required by the Treaty of Versailles (negotiated by Lloyd George, Clemenceau, President Wilson and the Entente ministers) only added to the bitterness induced by the political and moral vacuum that now existed after the fall of the Empires. A wave of dissatisfaction and disillusion swept over the peoples of these territories. Within a few months the Spartacists had risen in Berlin and the whole sorry history of the Weimar Republic begun.

This dissatisfaction expressed itself first in support for the insurrectionary uprisings in the capital cities. These were never really popular however and were essentially the work of feverish fanatics. More popular was the reaction against such movements. These conflicting ideologies mixed together to form a potent brew, which a skilful and manipulative politician could work to his advantage. Gestures of fraternal solidarity towards the defeated powers were conspicuous by their absence from the

Entente side. Perhaps the human and social costs of the war had simply proved too high for these to have been easily forthcoming. Revenge was rather the order of the day, and it brought forth its usual fruits. The French were particularly anxious to repair the damage done to their national pride that had resulted from their disastrous defeat in the Franco-Prussian war some fifty years before.

It need hardly be said that this was no basis for the future peace of Europe. Within the governments of the victorious powers some had come to believe that hatred of the old order was a sufficient foundation for the creation of the new. Of course, it was not.

Years later Adolf Hitler with his cunning skill was able to promote himself as the personification of the ordinary German soldier who had been "stabbed in the back" by the politicians. In addition, he claimed to be standing for the rebuilding and revivification of Germany. With memories of the Spartakusbund in Berlin, of Bela Kun in Hungary and the Communist uprising in Vienna, Hitler's claim to be anti-Communist was also immensely useful to him. The Nazi party were able to manipulate cleverly the worst instincts of the pan-Germanists, both within Germany and the German speaking areas of the new republics. In such places as the Sudetenland, Silesia, Pomerania, and certain parts of Austria they would find ardent supporters for the idea of a 'Greater Germany'. This in part explains a mystery which has long seemed inexplicable to modern British minds: namely why so few raised their voices in dissent against the German troops marching into the Sudetenland and against the Anschluss (annexation) of Austria. In all of these territories the population was predominantly German-speaking, and only by accident of history had these people found themselves isolated. Such a situation was perhaps the inevitable result of the Entente powers (and in particular the United States, whose leaders were not well qualified to decide on the future of nation states in Europe) attempting to draw boundaries along arbitrary lines in the hope that a peaceful future would ensue. In the midst of such confusion extremist forces had been able to gain a foothold; first the Communists, such as Bela Kun, and then the Nazis. Fleeing from one terror, the peoples of this part of Europe now found themselves running headlong into another. The hopes of a new dawn for liberty which had come with the demise of the Habsburg central European empire quickly foundered. Its demise led not to the peace and prosperity for which so many had ardently hoped, but instead to the black hell of National Socialism and to the frigid darkness of Communism.

The Nazis were as implacably opposed to the old order, and as determined to root it out and replace it with their own ideology, as were their official enemies the Communists. To begin with, they were careful to disguise their motives, but once they had gained control their plans became clearer. Weaving their way into the institutions that had once been an integral part of the old order, they quickly subverted them. In this, they more than emulated the tactics of Lenin, whom they officially repudiated. In stark contradistinction to the Imperial policy of encouraging ethnic minorities within the polyglot Empire, the Nazis sought to exterminate them and replace them with ethnic Germans. In this, Nazism fulfilled all the worst aspirations of the old pan-Germanism. References to the Slavic races and to the Jews as being in some way biologically and culturally inferior exist in pan-Germanist literature stretching back to the 19th century. Indeed alleged anti-semitism can be found in the writings of Martin Luther, a fact which was cited in his own defense by a prominent Nazi at his trial in Nuremburg. It was precisely this kind of pan-Germanism that both Emperor Charles and Empress Zita so ardently detested. They also detested Bolshevism and it was by a cruel irony that while Charles himself opposed with all his strength the sending of Lenin in a sealed train through his lands to start the Bolshevik revolution in Russia, his Prussian allies were nonetheless determined to bring it about. At that time there began the peculiar mixture of co-operation and hatred that characterised the relationship between Prussian-dominated, and later Nazi, Germany and the Soviet Union.

These two powers were now unleashed upon Europe, and there was no protection against them since the House of Habsburg and its associated central European empire had fallen with the connivance of the Entente Powers. However good his motives may have been, President Wilson had attempted to redraw the map of Europe according to his own political pre-conceptions. Sadly he was in no way qualified to do this. He simply had no idea or understanding of the undercurrents and complexities, the rivalries and the strengths, of Europe. Even with the best will in the world Europe could not be reorganised along the same lines as the United States of America. In the smaller countries of Europe, that had once been part of the Empire, there was now nothing to prevent the growth of extremist groups and indeed it almost seemed that the momentum of progress was with them. Thus in Rumania there arose the Iron Guard, and in Hungary the Arrow Cross Party. Elsewhere there were various other extreme nationalist groups. Events were moving inexorably towards another war.

In 1932, ten years after his father's death, Archduke Otto von Habsburg was studying at the Berlin University of Agricultural and

Social Sciences. He was approached by Prince August Wilhelm of Prussia, a son of Emperor William and a member of Hitler's Nazi party in the Reichstag. He wanted Otto to agree to a meeting with Goering. Through this meeting Hitler hoped to begin the process of using the Habsburgs to open the way for the Nazis in Austria. Otto refused; but the Nazis had others who were more amenable to their plans. On March 14th Hitler annexed Austria, and entered the country with German troops. The old dream - or nightmare - of pan-Germanism had finally been achieved. It was to have devastating consequences.

The Habsburgs were living in Belgium when war broke out and fled, along with so many other refugees, as the Nazis invaded. They spent the rest of the war in America, where Otto led Austrian exiles in an anti-Nazi campaign. His brothers organised similar groups in Spain and Britain. In the Autumn of 1943 he had a meeting with Winston Churchill in Quebec. Churchill had been impressed with his outline plans for organising an overthrow of the Horthy government in Hungary (Horthy was by this time co-operating with the Germans) and his warnings about a planned Soviet takeover of Austria.

Otto's plan was that at a given signal from the Allies, Nazi sympathisers in the Horthy government would be arrested and the Regent would resign. The country's official status, proclaimed by its Parliament, would be one of neutrality, which would mean that German troops could not cross Hungarian territory or use her airfields. Hungary would thus pass to the side of the Allies as German troops would use force to continue to cross the country, and the Hungarians would resist. Reliable contacts within the country affirmed that the plan was ready to be implemented.

The government was already unwilling to continue its support of Germany, and Horthy might even step down. In the separate case of Austria, Otto was in touch with anti-Nazi groups who were ready to spring into action as soon as the Western allies approached the border.

Churchill was sympathetic to Otto's efforts, with their implications for a possible Habsburg return in Hungary and perhaps possibly also Austria and he wrote to Anthony Eden, the British Foreign Secretary: "One of the greatest mistakes made after the last war was the destruction by ignorant hands of the Austro-Hungarian Empire. Considering the ruin into which they have been plunged it may well be that these disillusioned peoples may see a way out of their troubles through some symbolic chief. Pray think this over on large lines . . . . " The plans came to nothing however, because Eden and others opposed any possibility of a Habsburg restoration and in any case were inclined to dismiss Otto's warnings about Soviet greed and aspirations.[1]

Eden, as subsequent historians have shown, was personally mesmerized by Stalin and believed that the Soviet dictator and mass-murderer was amenable to political negotiations which would ensure peaceful prosperity for post-war Europe.

Events took another path. The Soviets seized Hungary and, initially, Austria, and the war ended with them, and not the Western allies, as the dominant power in the territories of Europe that had been Charles' empire. Churchill's later hopes for a new Habsburg kingdom which might have brought together Austria and Bavaria came to nothing as he was not supported by others in Britain or the USA. The post-war years were to show a very different and more tragic Europe than the one which might have emerged had Eden and others not been so easily duped by the Soviet leader.

The conclusion of the War saw the division of Europe into two sides, one the Soviet and the other the Western. Although technically allies, the two met in the centre of Europe facing each other uneasily. There was much fraternisation and embracing among the troops on the ground when the meetings first took place in a conquered Germany - but their leaders, both military and political, knew that they were really allies no longer. Indeed, some astute members of the leadership of each side knew that they had never in a real sense been allies at all, but mutually supporting players in a game which had as its goal the continent of Europe, either for Western capitalist democracy or Soviet-style Communism. Despite the increasing tensions over territory which had developed towards the end of the war and which continued, there was at least a measure of tacit agreement between the powers that ruled out a return to the Central European system of 1914.

Thus at the conclusion of the Second World War the political map of Europe had changed utterly. Instead of the old, stable and ordered Austro-Hungarian Empire there lay the embattled forces of fragmented states caught in a gigantic pincer movement between the advancing Soviet forces and the Western allies. Some of these forces (from lands that had once lain within the boundaries of the Empire) looked to the West, and in particular to Britain and the United States, for help. This was only logical as some of them had been allied to the Western powers at an earlier stage of the War. Units of the Royal Yugoslav Army, of the Slovenian Home Guard, and of ex-patriate anti-Bolshevik Russian forces found themselves in an increasingly narrow triangle centred upon Austria. In addition to the Soviet forces, the Yugoslavs were pursued by the partisans of Marshal Tito, the communist Croat leader who now enjoyed the favour of the Western allies. The Allies had adopted him in place of the Royalist

Yugoslav forces to whom they had earlier given their support.

The fate of these people is a peculiarly shameful episode which has only recently come to light. While some political leaders recognised the new reality which was to divide Europe, East and West, Soviet and non-Soviet, others still clung to the vain hope that common ground remained between the intentions of the Soviet bloc and those of the Western political leaders. Perhaps for these reasons, if no other, it was agreed between the leaders of the forces on the ground, both Soviet and Western (British and American) that the embarrassing presence of these people, who seemed like an echo from a distant, more ordered and perhaps more attractive world, should be terminated. Tricked by cowardly and deceitful measures, they were sent by the Western allies over to their Soviet enemies, by whom they were brutally massacred. The remnants of the old world had been ruthlessly extinguished. The new world was about to begin. Was it to see the dawn of a new era upon which the sun of prosperity, peace and equality would never set? The history of Eastern Europe in the ensuing years tells a different story.

Austria, although occupied by the Soviet army in one part and by the Western allies in the other half, managed by good fortune and perhaps the hand of Providence , to end up in the Western camp. The Hungarians, for so long a thorn in the side of the Empire, with their nationalist aspirations, now found their desire for independence realised - but in name only.

Hungary found itself yoked to a ruthless totalitarian power. Similarly the minority nations of the old empire found themselves ensnared in a new, and repressive, empire. Bohemia, Moravia, Slovakia, Galicia, Hungary, Bosnia, Herzegovina, Dalmatia, Slovenia, Croatia - all former countries of the Habsburg Empire - now found themselves trapped in Soviet-style tyranny.

In 1945 Empress Zita celebrated her birthday on the first day of peace, May 9th. She was to spend the next two years touring America and Canada to raise funds for war-ravaged Austria and Hungary. Parcels of food and clothing began to cross the Atlantic as part of the massive relief operation through which Americans brought new hope to a hungry Europe. The continent was now being divided into the pattern in which it would remain for the next forty years. Hungary under Stalin was to experience continued repression and misery. Austria was divided between the victorious Allied armies, and its fate hung in the balance.

In 1949 the lonely grave in Madeira, so far removed from the tense events of post-war mainland Europe, came once more briefly into prominence. It was announced that the cause for the canonisation of

Emperor Charles had been opened: the start of a process which could result in his being formally declared a saint by the Catholic Church.

Meanwhile, Austria was eventually declared an independent republic. The Russian threat had receded and the status of the country was proclaimed as officially neutral. Otto was banned from the new republic. Much later (1966) he would be allowed in as a private citizen. From 1953 he had his home in Bavaria, having married Princess Regina of Saxe-Meiningen in 1951 in Nancy in Lorraine.[2]

In 1956 a massive uprising in Hungary brought thousands of young people out into the streets, in an heroic attempt to gain freedom. They ripped the communist symbol from their national flag, to show that they wanted a country free of this new tyranny, and with home-made weapons they prepared to fight for an independent nation. Setting up street barricades and preparing for battle they begged the world to help them win their country back from Soviet rule. The rising was eventually crushed by Soviet tanks, leaving many thousands dead. In its savage aftermath there were executions and show-trials to crush any remnants of hope and to re-establish Communist power with savage ferocity.

The division of Europe into East and West, the boundary marked by an Iron Curtain which was a literal fact of barbed wire and guard-towers as well as a barrier between Communism and free nations, had been fully consolidated by the end of the 1950s.

In 1961 Otto's first son was born and given the name Charles. The empire over which the child's grandfather had ruled had vanished beneath tanks, barbed wire and ideology.

Czechoslovakia made a bid for freedom in 1968 when its government under Alexander Dubcek attempted to map out a new approach for the country: "Socialism with a human face". There was a brief period of greater freedom of speech, open discussion of what had gone on under Stalin and during the consolidation of Communist rule, and a suggestion that a greater pluralism of views and ideas might be allowed to influence the country's future. Soviet tanks then rolled in during August 1968 to crush all this, too, and Prague's status as the capital of a Soviet satellite state was rigidly confirmed. The nationalist dreams of politicians like Masaryk and Benes had ploughed into the sand of Soviet tyranny. Bohemia, once (like Hungary), a source of dissension in the days of the Habsburg empire was now silenced by the iron fist of Communism.

The Habsburg name no longer had any tangible link with Eastern Europe. The family was spread across various Western European countries. After the years in America, Empress Zita went to live in quiet retirement at a convent in Switzerland. Still always dressed in dignified mourning, she was a figure almost unnoticed on the public scene, although occasionally photographed at the weddings of her children, and, later, her grandchildren.

In 1977 Dr Otto von Habsburg - the title by which he prefers to be known - became a member of the European Parliament. He had already achieved prominence in his own right as a writer and lecturer in many languages.

Through the "Pan European Union" he sought to keep alive the idea of freedom for all the countries of Eastern and Central Europe, and he saw his family obligations as essentially a commitment to upholding the basic rights and dignities of the people of the lands with which the Habsburgs had been associated for so many centuries.

The 1980s were to see dramatic changes in these countries. Communism, victorious where Nazism had failed, was on the rack.

Changes often come from unexpected sources and in unexpected places. The election of a Polish Pope turned on its head the dictum of Stalin "How many divisions has the Pope got?" It became rapidly clear that he had a great many. A triumphant tour of his native land in 1979 was directly responsible for the new surge of hope and optimism which resulted in the formation of the Solidarity movement and the long road towards a peeling away from Communist domination in Poland. Ten years later, in 1989, Poland achieved its first non-Communist government in 40 years, following elections which allowed for a limited number of parliamentary seats to be available to members of other groups.

The Pope had himself been born in that part of Poland which had been ruled by Austria-Hungary, and his father had served in the Imperial Army. Poles in that region had memories of good government from Vienna with considerable local autonomy and no attempt to crush their language, culture, customs or identity. In contrast, Poles under the Russians and Prussians had suffered the reverse; total suppression and subjugation of their Polish identity. Then, after a brief period of national independence, had come Nazism and Soviet Communism.

The arrival of the Gorbachev era in the USSR with its promises of "openess" and "reconstruction" sparked off a whole series of events. The map of Europe, which had seemed fixed on its 1945 boundaries, was effectively being re-drawn.

The Soviets formally apologised to Czechoslovakia for the invasion of 1968 which had crushed the "Prague spring". Within the USSR, nations were in ferment, struggling to achieve freedoms which at one stage seemed to have vanished for ever.

Hungary had liberalised its economy and now faced the inevitable pressure to make dramatic changes in its methods of government. The ruthless suppression of all opposition to Communism melted away. Free elections were held and there was an acceptance of the idea that the era of Communism was fading into the past: a past that will always be described as a black period.

In 1989 the heroes of the 1956 uprising, denounced for three decades, were publicly honoured in official approval at a massive symbolic ceremony. In June 1989 in Budapest during the commemoration the Hungarian flag with the communist symbol ripped out, fluttered again from every street as it had done in the Uprising. Discussion arose about whether the Red Star's place should be once again taken by the Crown of Stephen on the national flag. In the Autumn of 1989, on the anniversary of the 1956 Uprising, Hungary formally shed its official Communist title. No longer would it be known as the "People's Republic" of Hungary but simply as a republic.

The year 1989 had earlier seen another milestone, but this time a little sad. The Empress Zita died aged 97. In 1982 she had returned to Austria - finally allowed in to the land of which she had once been Empress. She was greeted by cheering crowds, songs and posies. Many groups had come to see her dressed in their own local costumes. Thousands turned out in Vienna to see her attend a special church service, and commemorative books published page after page of photographs showing her accepting the greetings of officials and the flowers of children.

In March 1989 newspapers headlined her death. She had been the last tangible link with the vanished Europe that had existed two world wars before. The photo-portrait taken of her as a young princess of Bourbon-Parma on her engagement to the heir of the Austro-Hungarian Empire gazed out from magazines and newspapers across Europe and America.

She had been a widow for sixty seven years, matriarch to over thirty grandchildren and sixty great-grandchildren. Her rare newspaper or magazine interviews - only to small-circulation publications - had revealed her continuing sense of purpose, wide command of languages, and serene faith. The obituaries recalled her husband's role in World War I, the hopes and sorrow of the Sixtus affair, the events of 1918 and the years of exile. There was considerable speculation about where she would be buried. Had she died even a few years earlier, it seems unlikely that a funeral in Vienna would have been allowed, but by 1989 the mood in Austria was one peculiarly open to the significance of the event. It was announced that the Empress' body would be laid in the crypt of the

Capuchin church, alongside those of generations of Habsburg rulers.

Her death was on March 14th, the anniversary of the Anschluss. The funeral was arranged for April 1st, anniversary of Charles' death. Crowds lined the Vienna streets to watch the magnificent carriage hearse - last used for Franz Josef's funeral in 1916 - make its way slowly in procession to the Cathedral. The event was televised. People who had never lived under the old Empire felt drawn to take part in this commemoration. Traditional groups arrived to march in their official costumes, and bells tolled. In a scene reminiscent of the heyday of the old Empire the congregation in a packed cathedral rose to its feet and sang the old Imperial anthem "Gott erhalte . . . . "

The Habsburg family led the mourners, walking behind the coffin from St Stephen's Cathedral to the Capuchin church after the Requiem Mass, for the final burial ceremonies. Here the ritual last used for Franz Josef was observed right down to the last detail - the knocking on the door, the repetition of the Empress' full titles, the denial of entry, and then the final admission after she had been described as simply a " mortal, sinful soul".

Perhaps more outstanding even than the funeral in Vienna was the requiem in Hungary, where once again Dr Otto von Habsburg led the mourners. Only a short while before, the arrival of a Habsburg in Budapest would have been impossible and his presence at such an event in the city's main church unthinkable.

Dr von Habsburg himself described his reception there as "absolutely overwhelming".[3] Trying to explain the enormous enthusiasm of the crowds he said, writing in September 1989: "The first messenger from a free world is always well received by those who are under an oppressive regime . . . . I am also the only member of the European Parliament - and Europe is the great hope of the Hungarians, be they of the Right, Left, or Centre - who speaks their language and who therefore can be relied on to do his best to help them". He was touched by the way in which his father's memory had been honoured in Hungary: "Most people vividly remember my father or have heard from their parents and grandparents about him. The sense of tradition is very strong in the country.

"Faith in Communism has completely collapsed, even among the leaders of the regime. They still consider Communism as the defence of their wealth and privileges, but they know perfectly well that the doctrine is false."

In the Autumn of 1989 Czechoslovakia erupted into street demonstrations and toppled its Communist rulers. A new era began. Former dissident Vaclav Havel became President, and spoke of his country's historic destiny at the "Spiritual crossroads of Europe". The move towards freedom and a free enterprise economy had begun. All Communist symbols were removed.

The changes in these countries and in Poland may mean that the territories of Europe which have had so much suffering and have been the "poor relations" of the Western Europeans for so long, will come into their own again, and will start to make a significant impact on European life and culture.

The rebirth of political freedom in lands once ruled under the black-yellow emblem of the Habsburgs represents a kind of return from exile for the nations of central Europe. These nations are emerging from the aftermath of the fall of a great empire. This empire, having as its roots the Holy Roman Empire, may be said to have begun, at least symbolically, with the crowning of Charlemagne on Christmas Day 800 and of St. Stephen, King of Hungary, in the year 1000. Its later manifestation as the Austro-Hungarian Empire, although representing an attenuated form of its mighty predecessor, continued to act as a central sheet-anchor to the political structure of Europe as a whole. It was at the heart of Europe and was also in a sense its foundation. Built up more by marriage alliances than by war and conquest, its position was all the more secure. However, as the certainties of the old order began to be replaced by the doubts and querulousness of the new, the foundation became less solid. Other empires began to threaten, seeking to achieve their purpose more by conquest and aggression than by the arts of peace. Then came the heyday of nationalism, and later of totalitarian ideologies. While all these aspirations fought with each other, they mutually conspired to destroy the heart of Europe.

That this Empire might have been able to adapt to changing conditions is evident from Charles' own vision of the future. Returning to more ancient constitutional structures he was at the same time immensely forward-looking. His conception of a federal empire with local government and autonomy nurturing the language, culture and identity of each ethnic grouping was as much in advance of its time as it was an attempt to look back to a time before national chauvinism had worked its ill effects on the Empire as a whole.

It has been said that this Empire was too old, too unwieldy, and too unchanging ever to survive - in view of the vision of the young Emperor such an opinion is open to question. Given a chance of survival, there may never have been a collapse, and without the collapse perhaps the inroads of Nazism and Communism might have been avoided altogether. Sadly however, the Empire was given no such chance.

The peoples of the Danube basin, once united under the Habsburg Crown, are today seeking again a basis for their own security which makes sense of their geography and history. The experience of having their borders drawn by other nations has not been a happy one. Watchers from other lands would do well to reflect that the heritage that binds together these people is one rooted in a Christian, royal, and imperial past which has been improperly understood by outsiders. The future is not secured by ignoring this past - stable, ordered, long-lasting. Rather they should learn from it whatever lessons are necessary and appropriate for the future safety and security of Europe and the world as a whole.

Notes:
1. Richard Lamb, *The Ghosts of Peace*, Michael Russell, London, 1987.
2. The choice of Lorraine for the marriage was replete with significance because, as has been stated elsewhere, it was the meeting point between German-speakers and French-speakers, a former Habsburg land since the time of Francis, Duke of Louraine, (who married Empress Maria-Theresa) until it was wrested away from the Habsburgs and became disputed territory between Germany (or Prussia) and France. Some would say that, given its later history, peace would have been easier to preserve had it remained in Habsburg hands.
3. Letter to the authors, September 1989.

Conclusion

There can be no denying that until recently the figure of Emperor Charles has been somewhat marginalised by history. It is a matter of speculation as to why this should be so. Perhaps it was due to the fallout from the polemical and unfactual reporting of the time. Perhaps it was due to the continued existence of strong negative feelings held by the generation who had participated in the events of the First World War. Whatever the reasons, today as we stand on the threshold of yet another realignment of Central and Eastern Europe after the division of two world wars and the disintegration of the Warsaw Pact, it maybe possible for disinterested and objective historians to look at these events with impartiality. Sufficient time has now elapsed to make this task easier.

The present generation of writers did not lose their sons or close relations in either of the two wars, and the events of the period are sufficiently remote for us to take a less prejudiced view. From such an objective viewpoint, it seems fair to say that the evidence appears to indicate that a significant opportunity to prevent the tragedy of the First World War was missed by the Allies. In failing to grasp this opportunity they facilitated the slaughter of a whole generation of young men.

By any reasonable criteria the young Emperor was one of the more remarkable rulers of his age. His intelligence and foresight enabled him to see what could be done and his strong and practical conscience told him what should be done. For various reasons, as we have seen, it was the enemies of peace who were to prevail and the desperate campaign waged by the young Emperor to end the slaughter ended in defeat. His failure provides a useful lesson for those who imagine that the power of kings and emperors to sway the fate of men and nations is irresistible and despotic. It shows that false ideology when combined with the narrow vision of self-seeking and time-serving statesmen, can wreak devastation if permitted by a complacent and compliant public opinion. It is fashionable to view the rise of the dictators which followed the fall of the monarchs as a unique isolated aberration. In fact, the conditions that led to the rise of extreme ideologies and which encouraged the adoption of demagogic figures by the general populace, were the direct result of the weakening of the social and cultural framework which accompanied the fall of the monarchies in Austria-Hungary, Russia, and perhaps even Germany.

There remains the scarcely escapable conclusion that the Allied governments, in conjunction with the newly emergent nationalist groups bidding for power in eastern Europe, were determined at whatever cost to see the end not only of the power of the traditional monarchies but more particularly of the Habsburg dynasty. This determination seems to have taken precedence over the small matter of the slaughter of a whole generation of young lives. The struggle for victory was carried out by generals who worked far behind the lines and politicians in comfortable armchairs. No sacrifice of other people's lives seems to have been considered too great. It is a peculiar perversity that sees Charles' humane endeavours as part of a sinister plot, begotten of Bourbon intrigue by Habsburg ambition. It is easier now to see these unfortunate prejudices for what they really were. In doing this we are not simply writing a panegyric of Bourbon or Habsburg policy down the ages, but merely avoiding the reverse, which is to say being unable to see any good in those policies at all.

After the Great War the loss of the central European power which had drawn together disparate nations, cultures and languages, created an immense vacuum. This must have been obvious at the time and with the benefit of hindsight it becomes obtusely plain. The dream of a series of loosely connected nationalistic republics which emerged from the violent overthrow of a centuries-old Austro-Hungarian Empire proved to be incompatible with the harsh realities of European geo-politics as they emerged in the post-war period. Sadly for Europe it was largely statesmen who held this dream who were to determine the continent's fate at the conclusion of the First World War. The way was left open for Hitler and, after his fall, for the Cold War era with two spheres of influence, the one Soviet and the other Western.

Following the defeat of Nazi Germany at the end of the Second World War, there was no attempt to go back to the Europe of 1914. Instead a new Europe emerged. The countries of Eastern Europe were divided between the former allies. After much argument and a genuine threat of further war Austria was placed in the western sphere of influence (albeit with severe conditions on the forces that could be raised or stationed in its territory.) Poland, Hungary and Czechoslovakia and Bulgaria were effectively given to Russia, as was the Eastern portion of Germany - broadly speaking the old Kingdom of Prussia. In some ways this arrangement of Eastern Europe cruelly mirrored the old Austria-Hungarian empire. The fledgling democracies were once more placed into a geo-political system, but this time it was one which attempted to suppress their national identities and cultures, as well as their basic human rights.

This European dispensation has now crumbled in its turn. It is not therefore surprising that many of those living in the lands of the former Habsburg Empire, look back to the days of stability and prosperity which it brought to the majority of its citizens for the majority of its history. Their memories for these days contrast starkly with the instability and oppression of more recent years. It cannot even be said that this represents mere nostalgia for a past golden age. All of us have witnessed the success of the Spanish Royal family in ensuring the peaceful transition from the dictatorship of Franco to stable democratic government. This has shown us very powerfully that monarchy can hold together a state, even when extremist forces from both left and right attempt to pull it apart. Why then is it so unrealistic to suppose that a restored monarchy in say, Hungary, could not help that country in its transition from Communism to democracy?

One curious irony of the European situation in 1918 cannot fail to strike the impartial observer of today. President Woodrow Wilson, who purported to be such a great believer in the principle of self-determination for all nations, was in reality an eminent practitioner of the less morally sound business of imposing one's political prejudices on others.

Today self-determination for the nations of central Europe seems to have more likelihood of success than in the 1920s.

In this climate the idea of a loose federation of states linked for mutual development, progress and defence around the Danube basin becomes one natural possible option. Such an organisation would in many ways be a modern version of the Austro-Hungarian Empire. It is difficult to say whether such a federation has a future. What is clear however is that the very real wish on the part of nations to join the European Community shows that they feel that they need to be part of a larger socio-economic political grouping in order to prosper and survive (It does not mean they want a United States of Europe).

Artificial boundaries which take no account of geographical and cultural differences cannot be imposed against the wishes of the people except through tyranny. When such tyranny subsides the natural boundaries resurface. That these natural boundaries may well date back to ancient times, is a distressing thought for those who like to see political issues in an ahistorical vacuum. Others may be ideologically predisposed or prejudiced against such boundaries - but we have seen all to often where such prejudices lead.

Perhaps these prejudices are now fading into history. *The Times* - the very newspaper which proclaimed so vehemently against the fallen Habsburg monarch in the 1920s - favourably considered the possibility of the restoration of the monarchy, in 1989, under the engaging headline "Ruritanian Restoration?".

To a generation which has seen the restoration of a Bourbon monarchy in Spain, the possibility of revived monarchies seems less unlikely now than it did in the 1940s, 50s, and 60s. The monarchial principle, based as it is upon the family as the focus of loyalty and to some degree of government, may prove a more attractive alternative to the apparent choice between a crumbling Soviet-style collectivism and Western capitalist individualism.

The assumption that these aspirations represent a return to a kind of absolute monarchy need not of course be seriously entertained. As has been shown, Emperor Charles himself had already envisaged the need for constitutionalism and federalism. His ideas provide fertile soil for the development of similar ideas today.

The question of sovereignty is a key issue in the Europe of the 1990s. It is by no means universally accepted that the locus of such sovereignty should reside in the somewhat artificial bureaucracy which exists in the modern tower blocks of Brussels.

At the end of 1989 while newspapers, television and radio in Britain were reporting the destruction of the Berlin Wall and of the Iron Curtain dividing East from West, domestic news was briefly dominated by revelations about the repatriations which occurred at the end of World War II.

In 1945 after the fall of the axis powers, central Europe became a power vacuum - the place of interface between the Communist East and the Allied West.

This vacuum was quickly filled, and those unfortunate enough to be in the area were crushed between the forces of the former allies. Amongst those groups who suffered this fate were the unfortunate victims of repatriation - including Serbs, Slovenes, Cossacks and Yugoslav royalists, as has been mentioned elsewhere.

Recently the emergence of new evidence on these repatriations has led to the reassessment of the post World War II policies of the British and Allied governments. There has been a considerable shift in the attitudes of commentators and general public alike. The discovery that Allied politicians had been willing to order their

armies, often against the better judgement of their officers, to send
back hundreds of thousands of innocent men, women and children
of Eastern European origin, in the full knowledge that they could
expect only death or imprisonment, naturally sickened many people.
We have seen the results of such "pragmatic" decision making; the
expediency of such actions has been exposed. We are perhaps in a
better position to reassess the similar "pragmatic" decisions which
were taken by the victors at the end of the First World War.

The common factor has been an almost ideological compulsion to
be allied with the apparently most "progressive" force. Were it not
for the fact that such considerations are matters of high state, it
would seem that the allied nations attached an almost pathological
importance to the task of always being on the "winning side". In the
long run such an expedient policy is not in fact expedient at all. It
is usually an efficient means of gaining a reputation for perfidy.

After World War 1 the "progressive" forces were thought to be
those who were anti-Habsburg, anti-monarchical, nationalist, free-
thinking republicans. They were supported by the foreign policy of
the United States which was predicated on the belief that such an
ideological stance was self-evidently true. Self-determination or no
self-determination, President Woodrow Wilson was determined for
his part to support them. In time the British came to support these
"progressive forces" too.

In the Second World War Britain (and in particular Anthony
Eden, the Foreign Secretary) adopted a similar outlook and the
Communist forces were supported against their more traditionally
minded rivals. The Americans, choosing to back those most like
themselves and less committed now to backing only "winners," became
less willing to support the Communists.

Whilst the Emperor Charles' work can be said to have ended in
failure, his humanity and principles stand in stark contrast to the
treachery and expediency of many of the statesmen of his period.
However in a sense it is still too early for his legacy to be assessed.
In the long run it may well be that many of his ideas will be
incorporated into the fabric of the new Central Europe. What
we can say without equivocation is that the Communism which
sprouted in the old countries of the Habsburg empire after the
cessation of the Second World War had no roots and is destined for
oblivion.

One episode in which Charles' character was clearly shown was
his opposition to the attacks on neutral shipping made by German
U-boats. He opposed these attacks as both inhumane and strategically foolish. By contrast the German military rulers saw in it
short-term gain. In the end they were proved wrong: it brought the

Americans into the war. Equally, his views on aerial bombardment were stangely prophetic: he opposed civilian bombing. The argument will continue to rage over whether the Allies' "carpet bombing" of civilians at the end of the Second World War was essential for victory. Indeed many believe that such bombing was monstrous, and motivated purely by rage. What is clear is that the diversion of resources and the serious miscalculation about its effects upon morale, manpower, and production almost certainly lengthened the war and could have jeopardised victory.[1] The whole discussion has now been transformed by the development of sophisticated nuclear weapons and even the most energetic prophets of expediency are loathe to look upon the indiscriminate nuclear bombing of cities as an acceptable means of waging war.

Emperor Charles was by any criteria a remarkable ruler. Though slight in build and of by no means strong constitution, a reluctant warrior, and a lover of peace, he managed to preserve a workable vision for the future, to work for it with his whole might and to adapt it as best he could whilst being bitterly opposed by forces beyond his control. He cannot be blamed for failing; indeed he was never given a chance to succeed. Surely, however, he should be given credit for the way in which he persevered in the search for justice and peace. It is a tragedy that others did not have sufficient moral qualities to do likewise.

It should be no surprise that the Church to which he was so fully devoted should now be considering his relative merits and demerits and that the cause for his canonisation should have been opened by the appropriate authorities. Whether or not this remarkable young Emperor will be thus recognized remains to be seen. However the fact that he showed a heroic devotion to duty throughout his life cannot be in dispute.

For some Christians in today's world heroism appears to be inextricably linked to the image of the armed revolutionary determined at any cost to overthrow and destroy those set in authority. The idea that those set in authority should seek peace and justice is not a fashionable one among such people. Throughout the ages, however, Christianity has embraced as its heroes men and women of all classes and backgrounds. It has not usually promoted the cause of belligerence, but has preferred to choose as its heroes those who dedicate themselves to the more arduous and exacting task of preserving peace and restraining the will to destroy. Thus good kings and rulers are as much fit candidates for exemplary status as anyone else.

It is an interesting coincidence that shortly after the death of the Empress Zita on March 14th 1989 (the anniversary of the Anschluss of Austria by Nazi troops) Eastern Europe began to open up. Those ancient lands of the Habsburg empire, which latterly had been held in a kind of Babylonian captivity under the heel of Communism, started to throw off their chains and in the process to rediscover their common heritage. Older tensions may threaten to resurface and it is difficult to predict the future direction of these lands. No doubt the rulers, philosophers and idealists, of the new regimes will look to history and to the times before their captivity to help them secure a just solution for the peace and strength of their nations in the future. They would be well advised to spend some time at least in reviewing the plans and aspirations as well as the trials and tribulations of the young Habsburg Emperor whose life was dedicated to finding just such solutions.

Notes:

1. See the 1960 Godkin Lectures given at Harvard University in 1960 by Lord Snow printed with an appendix as: C. P. Snow, *Science and Government,* Harvard University Press, Massachusetts, 1960. In the Appendix, Snow quotes from Professor P. M. S. Blackett (scientific advisor to the Admiralty for the D-Day Landings in 1944), "Tizard and the Science of War", *Nature*, No. 185, 1960, pp. 647-653 and *Scientific American* April, 1961. He also quotes Sir Charles Webster and Dr Noble Frankland, *The Strategic Air Offensive Against Germany 1939-45*, HM Stationery Office, London, 1961, vol 1. Finally, the Official Naval Historian is also quoted: S. W. Roskill, *The War at Sea 1939-45*, HM Stationery Office, London, 1954-61, vol 2 pp. 83-85.

Bibliography

Michael Balfour, *The Kaiser and his Times,* Cresset Press, 1964.

Gordon Brook Shepherd, *The Last Habsburg,* Weidenfeld and Nicholson, London, 1968.

Burkes Royal Families of the World London, 1977.

Erich Feigl, *Kaiser Karl, personliche, Aufzeichnungen, Zeugnisse und Dokumente,* Amalthea, 1984.

Erich Feigl, *Kaiserin Zita von Österreich nach Österreich,* Amalthea, 1982.

Dorothy Gies McGuigan, *The Habsburgs,* W. H. Allen, 1966.

Prof. Dr. Ernst Görlich, *Der letzte Kaiser – ein Heiliger?* Christiana – Verlag Stein am Rhein, Switzerland, 1988.

Dr Hans Karl, Zessner-Spitzenberg, *Kaiser Karl,* Baron von Salzburger Verlag fur Wirtschaft und Kultur, 1953.

Richard Lamb, *The Ghosts of Peace 1939-1945,* Michael Russell, 1987

Montgomery of Alamein, *A History of Warfare,* Collins 1968

Arthur Polzer-Hoditz, *The Emperor Charles,* Putnam, 1930.

Leo Smolle, *Kaiser Karl I, Ein Bild Seines Lebens,* Schulbucherverlag Wien und Prag, 1917.

C. P. Snow, *Science and Government,* Harvard, USA, 1980

C. L. Sulzberger, *The Fall of Eagles,* Hodder and Stoughton, 1977.

Herbert Vivian, *The Life of the Emperor Charles of Austria,* Grayson and Grayson, 1932.

Index

172